The Unity of Movement

Linguistik Aktuell/Linguistics Today (LA)

ISSN 0166-0829

Linguistik Aktuell/Linguistics Today (LA) provides a platform for original monograph studies into synchronic and diachronic linguistics. Studies in LA confront empirical and theoretical problems as these are currently discussed in syntax, semantics, morphology, phonology, and systematic pragmatics with the aim to establish robust empirical generalizations within a universalistic perspective.

For an overview of all books published in this series, please see
benjamins.com/catalog/la

General Editor

Elly van Gelderen
Arizona State University

Founding Editor

Werner Abraham
University of Vienna / University of Munich

Advisory Editorial Board

Josef Bayer
University of Konstanz

Cedric Boeckx
ICREA/UB

Guglielmo Cinque
University of Venice

Amy Rose Deal
University of California, Berkeley

Susann Fischer
University of Hamburg

Liliane Haegeman
Ghent University

Heejeong Ko
Seoul National University

William Kruger
Arizona State University

Terje Lohndal
Norwegian University of Science and Technology

Will Oxford
University of Manitoba

Ian Roberts
Cambridge University

Florian Schäfer
Humboldt University

Carola Trips
University of Mannheim

C. Jan-Wouter Zwart
University of Groningen

Volume 283

The Unity of Movement. Evidence from verb movement in Cantonese
by Tommy Tsz-Ming Lee

The Unity of Movement

Evidence from verb movement in Cantonese

Tommy Tsz-Ming Lee
City University of Hong Kong

John Benjamins Publishing Company
Amsterdam / Philadelphia

The paper used in this publication meets the minimum requirements of the American National Standard for Information Sciences – Permanence of Paper for Printed Library Materials, ANSI Z39.48-1984.

DOI 10.1075/la.283

Cataloging-in-Publication Data available from Library of Congress:
LCCN 2023059683 (PRINT) / 2023059684 (E-BOOK)

ISBN 978 90 272 1458 4 (HB)
ISBN 978 90 272 4708 7 (E-BOOK)

© 2024 – John Benjamins B.V.
No part of this book may be reproduced in any form, by print, photoprint, microfilm, or any other means, without written permission from the publisher.

John Benjamins Publishing Company · https://benjamins.com

Dedicated to my wife Ellie, my parents, Kathy and Jimmy, and my late Grandma.

Table of contents

Acknowledgments	**XIII**
List of tables	**XV**
Abbreviations	**XVII**
Abstract	**XIX**
Preface	**XXI**

CHAPTER 1. Introduction	1
1.1 The theoretical goals and empirical domains of the volume 1	
1.2 A unity approach to movement 3	
1.3 The outline of this volume 5	

CHAPTER 2. Approaching head movement	7
2.1 Introduction 7	
2.2 The origin of head movement 7	
2.2.1 From independent transformation rules to Move-*n* 7	
2.2.2 Constraints on head movement 9	
2.3 The debates surrounding head movement 11	
2.3.1 Theoretical concerns of the adjunction approach to head movement 11	
2.3.1.1 The Extension Condition 12	
2.3.1.2 The Empty Category Principle/Proper Binding Principle 13	
2.3.1.3 The non-successive cyclic nature 14	
2.3.1.4 Locality constraints 15	
2.3.1.5 The Chain Uniformity Condition 15	
2.3.2 Empirical differences with phrasal movement? 16	
2.3.2.1 The locality constraints on head movement 16	
2.3.2.2 The interpretive effects of head movement 17	
2.3.2.3 The morpho-phonological realization of head movement 18	
2.4 Non-unity approaches to head and phrasal movement 19	
2.4.1 Eliminating head movement from the syntax 19	
2.4.1.1 Post-syntactic movement/operations 19	
2.4.1.2 Remnant phrasal movement 20	

VIII   The Unity of Movement

2.4.2   Reformulating head movement in the syntax   20
2.4.3   Interim summary   21
2.5   Recent pursuits of a unified theory of movement   21
2.5.1   Head movement to the specifier position   22
2.5.2   No head-specific locality constraint   23
2.5.3   The interpretation of head movement   23
2.6   Summary   24

CHAPTER 3.   Intervention effects: Verb movement to peripheral positions   **25**
3.1   Introduction   25
3.2   Intervention effects and head movement   29
3.2.1   Intervention due to identical structural types   29
3.2.2   The particular nature of the HMC and exceptions to the HMC   32
3.2.3   Base generation and remnant movement and as alternatives   35
3.2.4   Interim summary   37
3.3   Verb doubling constructions and discourse effects   37
3.3.1   Types of verbs   38
3.3.2   Morpho-syntactic properties and variants   42
3.3.2.1 Topic constructions of verbs   42
3.3.2.2 'Even'-focus constructions of verbs   44
3.3.2.3 Copula focus constructions of verbs   45
3.3.2.4 Dislocation copying of verbs   46
3.3.2.5 Interim summary   47
3.3.3   Discourse effects   48
3.3.3.1 Contrastive verbal topics   48
3.3.3.2 Additive verbal foci   49
3.3.3.3 Exhaustive verbal foci   51
3.3.3.4 Defocused verbs   52
3.3.3.5 Interim summary   54
3.4   Evidence for verb movement   55
3.4.1   Lexical identity effects   55
3.4.2   Island effects   59
3.4.2.1 Island sensitivity   59
3.4.2.2 Long-distance/Cross-clausal dependencies   61
3.4.2.3 Interim summary   61
3.4.3   Idiomatic expressions   62
3.5   Focus Intervention Effects   63
3.5.1   No intervention by heads   64
3.5.2   Intervention by focused elements   65
3.5.3   No intervention by quantificational elements   70
3.5.4   Interim summary   72

3.6   Proposal: Head movement to the specifier position   72
   3.6.1   Details of the proposal   73
   3.6.2   An illustration of the proposal   75
   3.6.3   Deriving the properties of verb doubling constructions   78
      3.6.3.1 The ordering of the functional projections in the CP periphery   78
      3.6.3.2 The movement properties in verb doubling constructions   79
      3.6.3.3 A syntactic explanation of Focus Intervention Effects   80
3.7   Alternative analyses to a head movement approach   83
   3.7.1   Non-movement approaches   83
      3.7.1.1 Base generation   83
      3.7.1.2 Base generation plus operator movement   85
   3.7.2   Phrasal movement approaches   87
      3.7.2.1 Remnant VP movement   87
      3.7.2.2 VP movement with subsequent deletion   88
3.8   Discussions and implications   90
   3.8.1   Reformulating the Head Movement Constraint   90
   3.8.2   A parallel analysis with phrasal movement   92
   3.8.3   Focus Intervention Effects in phrasal movement   94
3.9   Conclusions   96

CHAPTER 4. Scope effects: Movement of quantificational heads   **97**
4.1   Introduction   97
4.2   (Non-)occurrence of semantic effects with head movement: An ongoing debate   99
   4.2.1   A lack of semantic effects?   100
   4.2.2   Discourse effects of head movement   103
   4.2.3   Scope effects of head movement   104
      4.2.3.1 Movement of (quantificational) determiners   105
      4.2.3.2 Movement of negation   106
      4.2.3.3 Movement of modal verbs   110
      4.2.3.4 Movement of aspectual verbs   112
   4.2.4   Interim summary   112
4.3   The distribution of aspectual verbs and modal verbs   113
   4.3.1   The (restricted) high position   113
   4.3.2   Verbs that can appear in the high position   115
      4.3.2.1 Aspectual verbs   115
      4.3.2.2 Modal verbs   116
      4.3.2.3 Interim summary   118

4.3.3 Quantificational elements   118
4.3.4 Focused elements   122
4.3.5 Interim summary   124
4.4 Proposal: Scope-shifting head movement   124
    4.4.1 Two components of the proposal   124
        4.4.1.1 Overt scope-shifting head movement   125
        4.4.1.2 Scope Economy   127
    4.4.2 Deriving the properties of movement of quantificational heads   129
        4.4.2.1 Deriving the quantificational scope effects   129
        4.4.2.2 Deriving the focus scope effects   131
        4.4.2.3 Deriving the restriction on verbs   134
    4.4.3 Remarks on the landing site and the trigger   137
        4.4.3.1 The landing site   137
        4.4.3.2 The trigger   140
4.5 Further evidence for the proposal   142
    4.5.1 Stacking of quantificational heads in the high position   142
    4.5.2 Shortest Move   143
    4.5.3 Movement out of coordinate structures   147
    4.5.4 A remark on the indeterminacy of island sensitivity   148
4.6 Alternative analyses to a head movement approach   150
    4.6.1 Multiple base positions of aspectual verbs and modal verbs   150
    4.6.2 An in-situ approach to aspectual verbs and modal verbs   152
    4.6.3 A remnant movement approach   153
    4.6.4 Movement of aspectual verbs and modal verbs as phrasal movement   154
4.7 Discussions and implications   156
    4.7.1 Semantic effects of head movement   156
    4.7.2 A parallel observation with phrasal elements   156
    4.7.3 The trigger of head movement   158
4.8 Conclusions   161

CHAPTER 5. Linearization: Doubling effects of heads and phrases   **162**
5.1 Introduction   162
5.2 Asymmetries in doubling in Cantonese   165
5.3 Proposal: Cyclic Linearization and Copy Deletion suspension   167
    5.3.1 Cyclic Linearization   167
    5.3.2 Copy Deletion suspension   169
5.4 Deriving the asymmetries in doubling   172
    5.4.1 Licit and illicit cases in topic constructions   172

Table of contents   **XI**

    5.4.2   Licit, illicit and optional cases in right dislocation   174
         5.4.2.1 Licit cases   174
         5.4.2.2 Illicit cases   176
         5.4.2.3 Optional cases   178
    5.4.3   A remark on differences in acceptability   182
    5.4.4   Resolving a further asymmetry in doubling   183
5.5   Alternative explanations to the doubling effects   184
5.6   Extension: Verb movement without doubling   186
5.7   Conclusions   192

CHAPTER 6. Conclusions   **194**

References   **195**

Index   **213**

Acknowledgments

My foremost thanks goes to Audrey Li, Andrew Simpson, Roumyana Pancheva, and Stefan Keine, for discussions at different occasions over the years. 'This monograph would not have been possible without the people who share with me their judgment on Cantonese sentences. I thank Ka-Wing Chan, Kenith Chan, Sheila Chan, Mei-Ying Ki, Yik-Po Lai, Esther Lam, Chaak-Ming Lau, Margaret Lee, Tommy Li, Summer Mut, Carmen Tang, Oscar Wong, and Ka-Fai Yip, for the time and patience.

Earlier versions and portions of this monograph are presented at different venues, which led to substantial improvements, including Yue 22, FoCaL 1, LSA 93, GLOW in Asia XIII and SICOGG XXI, WCCFL 38, NACCL 32, and NELS 51, as well as at reading groups/seminars at Stanford University, University of California, Los Angeles, University Connecticut, and Yale University. I thank the audience at the above occasions. I must also thank the people who selflessly shared their ideas with me.

I would like to acknowledge, to the best of my memory, Željko Boškovic, Kenyon Branan, Lawrence Cheung, Colin Davis, Michael Yoshitaka Erlewine, Robert Frank, Vera Gribanova, Boris Harizanov, Hajime Hoji, Khalil Iskarous, Paul Law, Winfried Lechner, Peppina Po-lun Lee, Travis Major, Victor Junnan Pan, Luis Miguel Toquero Pérez, David Pesetsky, Ethan Poole, Ian Roberts, Deniz Rudin, Barry Schein, Sze-Wing Tang, Haley Wei Wei, Alexis Wellwood, Ka-Fai Yip, and Raffaella Zanuttini. This list is probably incomplete. I apologize to the people who I have talked to but are not on the above list.

I also want to thank the members of the Cantonese/Chinese online reading groups during the pandemic, which kept me company throughout the difficult times (although we are in different parts of the world): Zhuo Chen, Jiahui Huang, Ka-Wing Chan, Sheila Chan, Esther Lam, Margaret Lee, Minqi Liu, Jia Ren, Carmen Tang, Huilei Wang, Bo Xue, and Ka-Fai Yip.

For my family and my wife Ellie, it is all beyond words.

List of tables

2.1	Summary of evidence of scope effects with head movement	18
3.1	The word order patterns illustrated in (27) and (28)	28
3.2	The schematic pattern of topic constructions of verbs	43
3.3	The schematic pattern of 'even'-focus constructions of verbs	45
3.4	The schematic pattern of copula focus constructions of verbs	46
3.5	The schematic pattern of dislocation copying of verbs	47
3.6	The schematic patterns of verb doubling constructions	47
3.7	The discourse effects of the verb doubling constructions	55
3.8	The intervention effects observed with verb doubling constructions	69
3.9	Feature specification of the focus and defocus features in Cantonese	74
3.10	Distribution of the uninterpretable focus/defocus features and their realizations	75
3.11	The discourse effects of the verb doubling constructions (repeated)	78
3.12	The word order patterns illustrated in (27), (28) and (146)	93
4.1	Summary of evidence of scope effects with head movement	104
4.2	Two scenarios of exam results in a class of three	114
4.3	A parallel quantificational analysis of aspectual verbs and modal verbs	127
5.1	Doubling asymmetries in Cantonese	167
5.2	Verb doubling and remnant movement across languages	192

Abbreviations

ACC accusative (case)
CL classifier
CON contrastive marker
CONT continuative (aspect)
COP copula verb
DAT dative (case)
DECL declarative
DEL delimitive (aspect)
DIS disposal marker
EXP experiential (aspect)
FOC focus marker
IMP imperfective (aspect)
INF infinitive
MASC masculine (gender)
MOD modifier marker
NEG negation
NOM nominative (case)
PST past (tense)
PERF perfective (aspect)
PROG progressive (aspect)
Q question particle
REL relative marker
RES resultative
SFP sentence-final particle
SG singular
TOP topic marker

Abstract

Tommy Tsz-Ming Lee

Displacement (of linguistic expressions) is a ubiquitous phenomenon in natural language. In the generative tradition, displacement is modeled in terms of *transformation*, or more precisely, *movement*, which establishes dependencies among syntactic constituents in a phrase structure. This volume probes the question regarding to what extent movement theories can be unified. Specifically, I address issues surrounding the debate of the distinction between *head movement* and *phrasal movement* over the past few decades. The distinction presupposes that structural complexity of the moving element is correlated with its movement properties. The goal of this volume is to show that this is an unwarranted assumption. Based on a number of case studies on verb displacement phenomena in Cantonese, I attempt a unified theory of movement by abandoning the head/phrase distinction in movement theories. Particularly, I show (i) that verbs in Cantonese can undergo syntactic movement to the peripheral position of a sentence and is subject to general locality/minimality constraints on movement, and (ii) that their movement may affect semantic interpretation, leading to discourse effects and scope effects that are commonly observed in phrasal movement. I further argue, with evidence from linearization, that head movement and phrasal movement in Cantonese are subject to the same mechanism when determining the pronunciation of the movement chains. These observations converge on the conclusion that the phrase structure status of syntactic constituents bears a minimal role in theorizing displacement phenomena in natural language. This volume represents a minimalist pursuit of a unified theory of movement.

Preface

Chapter 1 sets up the research question and establishes the major arguments in this volume. The central idea is that movement operations do not make reference to phrase structural differences between heads and phrases. The empirical evidence comes from various cases of verb displacement in Cantonese.

Chapter 2 traces the origin and development of the notion of head movement since the 1970s. While the notion of head movement has proved empirically useful in capturing various linguistic phenomena, it also led to debates relating to theoretical and empirical issues since the early minimalist period. I review recent responses to the issues surrounding head movement.

Chapter 3 examines potential intervening elements in head movement. The discussion builds on four verb doubling constructions that come with (different) discourse effects. It is first argued that the verbs in these constructions undergo movement to the specifier position of a functional head in the left periphery. It is further shown that, while a head does not block the verb movement, a focused element may lead to intervention (i.e., Focus Intervention Effects). This property is argued to follow from a minimality condition of the operation Agree that makes reference to syntactic features (Chomsky 2000, 2001). The findings reveal that the Head Movement Constraint does not apply to all instances of head movement, and that syntactic intervention effects are observed with head movement, on a par with phrasal movement.

Chapter 4 diagnoses an instance of head movement that induces scope effects. I argue that quantificational heads such as aspectual verbs and (a subset of) modal verbs in Cantonese can undergo (overt) head movement to achieve scope enrichment. Furthermore, this movement is constrained by an economy condition, Scope Economy, which is independently observed with movement of phrasal quantifiers (Fox 2000). The findings suggest that head movement is no different from phrasal movement in terms of the potentials to induce semantic effects, and that Scope Economy constrains both head and phrasal movement.

Chapter 5 discusses the issue of how movement chains of heads are pronounced and linearized.

It concerns the doubling effects of head and phrasal movement in Cantonese. Empirical data reveal that the doubling effects are not specific to moving heads and that head movement does not always lead to doubling effects. It is suggested that doubling effects arise from the fact that the operation responsible for erasing copies in a movement chain is regulated by phonological requirements that follow from a version of Cyclic Linearization (Fox and Pesetsky 2005). Such an account derives the Cantonese doubling pattern of heads and phrases without recourse to the phrase structure status of the (non-)doubling elements. I maintain that the mechanism that determines copy pronunciation is the same for head chains and phrase chains.

Chapter 6 concludes the volume.

CHAPTER 1

Introduction

1.1 The theoretical goals and empirical domains of the volume

The theoretical goal of this volume is to contribute to our understanding of movement theories of natural language. I pick up ongoing debates of the theoretical status and empirical properties of head movement, and explore the possibility of a unified theory of movement that does not make reference to structural types such as heads and phrases. The distinction between head movement and phrasal movement presupposes that structural complexity of the moving element is correlated with its movement properties. I argue that this is an unwarranted assumption. Specifically, I argue that the role of the head-phrase distinction is minimal in movement theories: both types of constituents are targeted by the same movement operation. Supporting evidence comes from observations that movement of heads and phrases are subject to the same set of syntactic principles, which constrain (i) how they move in the syntax, (ii) how they contribute to interpretation, and (iii) how their chains are phonologically realized. To the extent that head movement can be assimilated to phrasal movement, this volume sets the basis of a movement theory that does not discriminate heads from phrases, hence a unified theory of movement.

The empirical domains of this volume are constituted by a number of verb displacement cases in (Hong Kong) Cantonese. The first type concerns what I refer to as *verb doubling constructions*, where an additional copy of a verb appears in the (left or right) peripheral position of a sentence, and conveys different discourse effects (e.g. topic- or focus-related interpretations). These constructions are exemplified in (1). The sentences in (1a–c) are often regarded as predicate cleft constructions. The analytical questions posited by these constructions concern the derivation of these sentences and the relationship between the verb in the base position and the verb in the peripheral position. These issues are discussed in details in Chapter 3 and Chapter 5.

2 The Unity of Movement

(1) Examples of verb doubling constructions
  a. $\boxed{V}$ SVO: Topic constructions of verbs
     Maai keoi hai **maai**-gwo go-bun syu.
     buy s/he COP buy-EXP that-CL book
     'As for buying, s/he has bought that book (but...).'
                                    (cf. Cheng and Vicente 2013, p. 13)
  b. *Lin-*$\boxed{V}$ SVO: 'Even'-focus constructions of verbs
     Lin **tai** keoi dou m-**tai** ni-bun syu.
     even read s/he also not-read this-CL book
     'S/he didn't even READ this book.'   (cf. Cheng and Vicente 2013, p. 2)
  c. *Hai-*$\boxed{V}$ SVO: Copula focus constructions of verbs
     Hai **dim** Aaming m-gam **dim** ni-zek dungmat ze1.
     COP touch Aaming not-dare touch this-CL animal SFP
     'Aaming dare not to TOUCH this animal only.'
  d. SVO SFP $\boxed{V}$: Right dislocation/dislocation copying of verbs
     Zoengsaam gammaan **fan** ni-zoeng cong aa3 **fan**.
     Zoengsaam tonight sleep this-CL bed SFP sleep
     'Zoengsaam (will) sleep on this bed tonight.'
                                    (K. K. Chan 2016, p. 18, adapted)

Another type of verb displacement discussed in this volume concerns aspectual verbs and a subset of modal verbs. In the sentences in (2), *hoici* 'begin' can appear a low position (following the subject) or a high position (preceding the subject). The two sentences convey different scope interpretations. They beg the question of whether the two sentences are derivationally related, and what are the relative constraints on the alternation of word order. These sentences are examined in depth in Chapter 4.

(2) The low and high positions of *houci* 'begin'
  a. <u>Dak</u> Aaming **hoici** haau-dou   'only' > 'begin' / *'begin' > 'only'
     only Aaming begin get-able
     hou singzik.
     good result
     'Only Aaming is such that he begins to get good results.'
  b. **Hoici** <u>dak</u> Aaming haau-dou   *'only' > 'begin' / 'begin' > 'only'
     begin only Aaming get-able
     hou singzik.
     good result
     'It begins to be the case that only Aaming is getting good results.'

As a note on the methodology, the judgment of the Cantonese sentences throughout this paper come from five (Hong Kong) Cantonese speakers (unless specified otherwise). Sentences without marking or marked by OK show that all the speakers find the sentences acceptable. An asterisk symbol * indicates that all/most speakers find the sentences unacceptable, whereas question marks ?/?? indicate that the speakers find the example unnatural or degraded, but not entirely unacceptable.

1.2 A unity approach to movement

In the generative tradition, phenomena relating to displacement of linguistic elements are modeled as (independent) transformational rules, or movement operations. In the course of theorizing displacement phenomena, there is a constant tension between the theoretical desire for unification and empirical challenges rooted from the diverse nature of the phenomena relating to head movement.

On one hand, the desire for unification underlies the efforts of reducing (different, construction-specific) transformational rules that apply to verbs to a single syntactic process. This gives rise to the first characterization of *Head Movement* (i.e., the adjunction approach to head movement) in the 1980s, in works by Koopman (1984), Travis (1984), and Baker (1988), among others. Head Movement under the Government and Binding Framework (Chomsky 1981, 1986) can be further subsumed under the notion of *Move-α* (i.e., move anything anywhere), which represents the most unspecified form of movement operation (and it also applies to phrases). In the later minimalist framework, movement is modeled as a sub-type of the operation *Merge*, namely, *Internal Merge* (Chomsky 1995b, 2000, 2001), which, again does not distinguish heads from phrases in terms of movement.

However, on the other hand, the attempts to unification face both theoretical and empirical challenges.[1] Head movement, or more precisely, the adjunction approach to head movement, violates a number of syntactic principles that movement operations are expected to obey, including the Extension Condition, the Empty Category Principle, and so on. Additionally, head movement appears to be qualitatively different from phrasal movement in terms of empirical properties. For example, head movement is said to obey a stricter locality constraint (i.e., the Head Movement Constraint, Travis (1984)) and it is also said to fail to induce semantic effects in the same way as phrasal movement (e.g., Chomsky 2000). These differences invite proposals that adopt a non-unity approach to movement, where head movement is substantially reformulated in a way that departs from the mechanism held responsible for phrasal movement.

---

1. See Chapter 2 for an extensive discussion.

In spite of the diverse nature of the phenomena concerning head movement, I suggest that it does not necessarily reflect the non-uniform nature of *movement operations* in syntax. The diverse nature of the head movement phenomena may be attributed to the fact that the displacement properties of heads are resulted from different operations in different components of the grammar. This volume puts itself along the line of (the continuation of) the minimalist pursuit of a movement theory that does not differentiate heads from phrases, which, to different extents, underlines the spirit in works by Fukui and Takano (1998), Toyoshima (2000, 2001), Takahashi (2002), Matushansky (2006), Lechner (2007), Vicente (2007), Roberts (2010), Szabolcsi (2010, 2011), Hartman (2011), Funakoshi (2014), Lee (2017), Matyiku (2017), Harizanov and Gribanova (2019), Harizanov (2019), Preminger (2019), Landau (2020), and Sato and Maeda (2021), among others.

The rest of this volume is dedicated to the pursuit of a unified theory of movement. The empirical evidence in favor for such an approach comes from different cases of verb displacement in Cantonese. The three main claims are as follows, which corresponds to the three main chapters in this volume.

(3) Arguments for a unified approach to movement from Cantonese verb movement

    a.   Chapter 3: Head movement is constrained by the same set of locality/minimality requirements as phrasal movement (cf. Chomsky 1995b; Rizzi 1990, 2001, 2004);

    b.   Chapter 4: Head movement exhibits the same range of possible interpretive effects as phrasal movement, and is also constrained by Scope Economy (Fox 2000);

    c.   Chapter 5: Head movement chains are linearized by the same mechanism as phrasal movement chains, i.e., Cyclic Linearization and copy deletion (Fox and Pesetsky 2005).

These three arguments focus on different aspects of head movement, namely, its syntactic properties (in Narrow Syntax), its interpretive properties (in the syntax-semantic interface), and the linearization of its chain (in the syntax-phonology interface). They constitute converging evidence from different components of the grammar for the proposal that head movement can be treated on a par with phrasal movement.

The theoretical consequence of a unified theory of movement is two-fold. First, it allows us to maintain the formulation of the structure-building operation, *Merge*, in its simplest form. Internal Merge applies to syntactic constituents without the need to distinguish heads from phrases, in a way comparable to External Merge, which applies equally to both heads and phrases. Second, it opens up questions of whether and how other reported differences between movement of heads and phrases can be attributed to components of the grammar other than the movement mechanism. It should be stressed that the accounts proposed for different cases of head movement in this volume does not involve any new machinery or principles of movement. Instead, the crucial ingredients in these accounts are independently motivated by phrasal movement, maximizing the explanatory power of our existing theory of (phrasal) movement.

A few remarks on what this volume is *not* about are in order. First, while this volume focuses on head movement, it does not attempt a *global* alternative to various cases of head movement. It does not invent new technology or theoretical apparatus specifically designed for head movement either.

Second, since the thesis focuses on the minimal component of movement theories, rather than about a particular approach to head movement/displacement in language, some important issues in head movement such as noun/verb incorporation and word formation are not discussed.

Finally, while this volume stresses the role of the head-phrase distinction is minimal in formulating *movement theories*, it does not aim at eliminating the primitive notions of heads and phrases in the grammar, which remain important in the study of, for example, phrase structure, projection, labeling algorithm, and so on.

1.3   The outline of this volume

This rest of this volume is structured as follows.

Chapter 2 traces the origin and development of the notion of head movement since the 1970s. While the notion of head movement has proved empirically useful in capturing various linguistic phenomena, it also led to debates relating to theoretical and empirical issues since the early minimalist period. I review recent responses to the issues surrounding head movement.

Chapter 3 examines potential intervening elements in head movement. The discussion builds on four verb doubling constructions that come with (different) discourse effects. It is first argued that the verbs in these constructions undergo movement to the specifier position of a functional head in the left periphery. It is further shown that, while a head does not block the proposed verb movement, a focused element may lead to intervention (i.e., Focus Intervention Effects). This property is argued to follow from a minimality condition of the operation Agree that makes reference to syntactic features (Chomsky 2000, 2001). The findings reveal that the Head Movement Constraint does not apply to all instances of head movement, and that syntactic intervention effects are observed with head movement, on a par with phrasal movement.

Chapter 4 diagnoses an instance of head movement that induces scope effects. I argue that quantificational heads such as aspectual verbs and (a subset of) modal verbs in Cantonese can undergo (overt) head movement to achieve scope enrichment. Furthermore, this movement is constrained by an economy condition, Scope Economy, which is independently observed with movement of phrasal quantifiers (Fox 2000). The findings suggest that head movement is no different from phrasal movement in terms of the potentials to induce semantic effects, and that Scope Economy constrains both head and phrasal movement.

Chapter 5 discusses the issue of how movement chains of heads are pronounced and linearized. It concerns the doubling effects of head and phrasal movement in Cantonese. Empirical data reveal that the doubling effects are not specific to moving heads and that head movement does not always lead to doubling effects. It is suggested that doubling effects arise from the fact that the operation responsible for erasing copies in a movement chain is regulated by phonological requirements that follow from a version of Cyclic Linearization (Fox and Pesetsky 2005). Such an account derives the Cantonese doubling pattern of heads and phrases without recourse to the phrase structure status of the (non-)doubling elements. I maintain that the mechanism that determines copy pronunciation is the same for head chains and phrase chains.

Chapter 6 concludes the volume.

CHAPTER 2

Approaching head movement

2.1 Introduction

This purpose of this chapter is to trace and review the ongoing debates relating to head movement. In §2.2, I discuss the adjunction approach to head movement under the Government and Binding framework (Chomsky 1981, 1986). In §2.3, I review the debates relating to both the theoretical status and empirical properties of head movement under minimalist framework (Chomsky 1995b, *et seq.*). Then, I discuss two major responses to the issues relating to head movement. In §2.4, I briefly overview approaches that discriminate head movement from phrasal movement (what I refer to as *non-unity approaches*). In §2.5, I turn to recent pursuits of a unified theory of movement.

2.2 The origin of head movement

2.2.1 From independent transformation rules to Move-α

It is well observed that a verb may appear beyond its projected verb phrase or combine with elements outside the verb phrase. To capture the derived position of verbs, early proposals model verb displacement by positing independent transformational rules. Some examples are given in (4).

(4) Transformation rules proposed to capture the displacement property of verbs
   a. Chomsky (1957): Affix Hopping in English
      a rule that allows tense affixes to be realized on the main verb
   b. Emonds (1970, 1976): *have/be*-raising in English
      a rule of "AUX movement" that replaces the modal *do* with a following auxiliary verb
   c. Aissen (1974): V-V movement in causative constructions (e.g., in Turkish)
      a rule that "extracts the embedded V from its clause and moves it into the matrix clause so that it forms a verb unit with the matrix" (p. 333)
   d. Emonds (1978): V-T movement in French (building on observations in Kayne (1975))
      a rule of "Finite Verb Raising" that moves the verb before negation and adverbs

e. den Besten (1983): Germanic verb-second phenomenon, French subject-clitic inversion and English subject-auxiliary inversion
a rule of "Verb Preposing" that moves constituents to the complementizer

Under the approaches to *head movement* in Koopman (1984), Travis (1984), and Baker (1985, 1988), transformation rules relating to verbs are examined under a different perspective. Particularly, head movement is characterized as an adjunction rule, allowing a head X to be (left-)adjoined to another head Y and form a complex head containing both X and Y. This idea is illustrated in (5). I refer to this characterization as *the adjunction approach to head movement.*

(5) Head movement as head-to-head adjunction

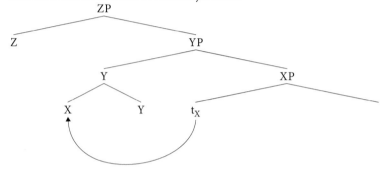

This characterization is primarily motivated by morphological considerations which allow a head to "pick up" additional morphemes via movement. Empirically, this mechanism has proved useful in capturing many different phenomena, roughly classified into two main types (for an overview, see Roberts (2001)).

(6) a. Morphological growth of heads
    i. noun/verb incorporation
    ii. verb movement to T (e.g. in French), and to C (e.g. in verb-second languages)
  b. Surface word order of heads
    iii. auxiliary inversions of different sorts in Romance and Germanic languages
    iv. the surface position of verb in VSO languages
    v. word order of NP/DP-internal elements in the nominal domain

As such, the conception of head movement in (5) marks an important step towards unification of movement operations, shifting the discussions from construction-specific transformation rules to an instance of a movement operation (adjunction), and from movement of elements of a particular category to movement of elements in a particular structural position. More generally, an implicit idea behind these approaches is (7), where the notion *Move-α* represents the theoretic pursuit of movement theory that reduces transformational rules to a single process.

(7) Head movement is the case of Move-α where α is X°.   (Roberts 2011, p. 196)

In other words, (7) do not only reflect the attempt to unify different cases of verb movement, but also the idea that head movement can be treated in a parallel fashion with phrasal movement.

2.2.2 Constraints on head movement

The suggestion in (7) is further supported by the observation that head movement as formulated in (5) is constrained by general well-formedness conditions that apply to movement operations and their outputs. I briefly discuss three of them.

First, head movement obeys Structure Preservation, which is later known as the Chain Uniformity Condition. Chomsky (1986) suggests (8) as a general condition on movement, where movement operations do not alter the structural status of the moving elements (following the spirit of Structure Preservation Principle in Emonds 1970, 1976).

(8) a. Only a head can be adjoined to a head.
     b. Only a maximal projection can be merged as a specifier.

It is suggested that (8) follows from some other principles. Chomsky (1986, p. 4) suggests that (8a) "would follow from an appropriate form of Emonds' Structure-Preserving Hypothesis (Emonds (1976))," and (8b) would follow "on the X-bar theoretic assumption that heads cannot be base-generated without a maximal projection so that a bare head cannot appear in the specifier position to receive a moved X° category." The formulation of head movement in (5) satisfies Structure Preservation, since a head moves to another head position.

Second, head movement is said to be subject to locality conditions, with the central one being the Head Movement Constraint (HMC, Travis 1984). It requires head movement to be applied in a highly local way. Informally, it means that head movement cannot skip an intervening head. A formulation of the HMC under the Government and Binding Theory (Chomsky 1981, 1986) is given in (9).

(9) The Head Movement Constraint (Travis 1984, p. 131)
     A head X may only move into the head Y that properly governs X.

Accordingly, the step in (10) is illicit, since Z does not properly govern X. Instead, it forces head movement to be cyclic, as in (11).[1]

---

1. For simplicity, head adjunction is indicated by the "+" sign between heads.

(10) Illicit cases of head movement

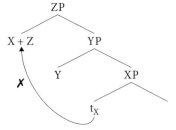

(11) Cyclic head movement

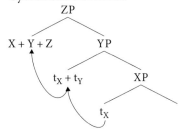

Third, the trace of head movement is subject to the Empty Category Principle (ECP), a well-formedness condition on traces. The ECP suggests that empty categories such as traces must be properly governed.

(12) The Empty Category Principle
 A nonpronominal empty category must be properly governed.
 (Lasnik and Saito 1984, p. 240)

In effect, this requires that (head) movement proceed in an "upward" fashion, and that XP be the structural complement of Y in case of movement of X to Y.

Accordingly, head movement as characterized in Koopman (1984), Travis (1984), and Baker (1985, 1988) is recognized as a core movement operation, hence an instance of Move-α.

One complication, however, is that the HMC appears to be specific to head movement, in the sense that phrasal movement does not exhibit a similar strictly local nature. While the HMC is motivated based on empirical evidence in different phenomena, it is less clear why it should hold in the grammar. In order to eliminate the particular nature of the HMC as a specific constraint on head movement, Baker (1988) proposes to derive the HMC effects from the ECP, where he suggests that "there must be no *barrier* category that intervenes between the two [heads]" (original emphasis, p. 55). For example, in the structure in (10), Y is "an intervening theta assigner [that] breaks a government path" (p. 56), such that X is not *directly theta-connected* to its trace, hence does not properly governs it. This suggestion highlights the importance of theta-connection in deriving the local nature of head movement.[2]

A different line to derive the HMC suggested by Rizzi (1990) makes reference to the notion of structural types. He proposes to relativize minimality effects to structural types. *Relativized Minimality* thus provides an unified account of both the local nature of head movement and minimality effects observed in phrasal movement. A version of Relativized Minimality is given in (13).

(13) Relativized Minimality (Rizzi 1990; a version taken from Rizzi 2011, p. 221–222)
    a. In the configuration … X … Z … Y …, a local relation cannot connect X and Y if Z intervenes and Z is of the same structural type as X.
    b. Structural types: (i) A′ positions, (ii) A positions, and (iii) heads.

In effect, the structure in (10) is disallowed because the head Y, being the same structural type as X, "intervenes" between X and its trace. As such, the HMC can be subsumed under the general minimality conditions on movement operations.

2.3 The debates surrounding head movement

While the adjunction approach to head movement may be a self-contained notion in the GB-era, the notion of head movement becomes controversial since the minimalist period. On one hand, head movement does not fit nicely with the minimalist pursuit started in the 1990s. The particular implementation of head movement (as adjunction) violates syntactic principles that head movement is expected to obey. On the other hand, certain empirical properties of head movement are often highlighted because it does not pattern nicely with phrasal movement (such as the locality effects and the (lack of) interpretive effects). I discuss some theoretical concerns in §2.3.1, followed by the (alleged) empirical differences between head movement and phrasal movement in §2.3.2.

2.3.1 Theoretical concerns of the adjunction approach to head movement

The theoretical concerns for the adjunction approach to head movement are well-known in the literature (Chomsky 2001; Toyoshima 2000; Mahajan 2003; Toyoshima 2001; Surányi 2005; Matushansky 2006, among many others). I repli-

---

2. While this captures the local nature of cases of incorporation, it appears to be too strict in cases of verb movement of the Romance/Germanic kind, where, for example, negation and adverbs may intervene the moving head and its trace.

cate the major theoretical concerns under the minimalist assumptions in Chomsky (1995b, 2000, 2001).

Before I start, it should be remarked that many of these concerns (if not all) are theory-internal. They may cease to exist under a different set of theoretical apparatus and assumptions (see, e.g., discussions in Funakoshi (2014), Chapter 1). However, most theoretical principles or conditions discussed in the following subsections are independently motivated by our understanding of (phrasal) movement. So the primary purpose of this subsection is not to shows how much the adjunction approach deviates from a particular theoretical framework, but to show how much the theoretical appearances of head movement differ from that of phrasal movement. This directly shapes how subsequent proposals on head movement respond to these issues.

2.3.1.1 *The Extension Condition*

First, the adjunction approach to head movement apparently violates the Extension Condition, which is a minimalist reformulation of the Strict Cycle Condition (Chomsky 1973). The condition requires movement to extend the structure, or to be effected at the root node. In (5), repeated below in (14), the movement of X does not extend ZP; rather, it is effected at Y in a counter-cyclic fashion (as Y is internal to a previously built structure).

(14)   Head movement as head-to-head adjunction = (5)

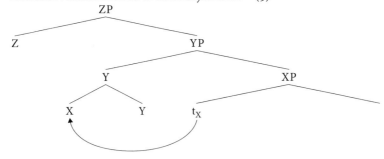

However, it should be noted that the version formulated in Chomsky (1995b) indeed exempts head movement (or more general, adjunction) from this condition, as it applies only to substitution.[3]

---

3. This is in line with his later suggestion that "[h]ead adjunction ... provides some reason to weaken the Extension Condition" (Chomsky 2000, p. 137), so as to allow head adjunction in syntax. He proposes a relaxed version of Extension Condition (i.e. the Least Tampering Condition), but it arouses other issues. For discussions, see Surányi (2005).

Chapter 2. Approaching head movement   **13**

(15) The Extension Condition (Chomsky 1995b, p. 190)
   a. [Generalized Transformation] and Move-α extend K to K′, which includes K as a proper part.
   b. Substitution operations always extend their target.

Another exempted case is covert movement (e.g. Quantifier Raising), but the covert syntactic cycle is no longer assumed in the subsequent minimalist framework (Groat and O'Neil 1996; Pesetsky 1998; Chomsky 2000, 2001; Bobaljik 2002). This renders head movement being the only exception, or one of the very few exceptions to the Extension Condition (cf. Tuck-in movement, N. Richards (1997)).

More specifically, allowing head movement to be an exception yields two kinds of asymmetries in structure-building (especially, if substitution and adjunction are to dissolve into one single *Merge* operation). On one hand, head movement is different from phrasal movement, which typically targets the root.[4] On the other hand, it differs from External Merge of a head, which always targets the root (i.e., a head cannot be adjoined to another head directly from the Numeration). This renders head movement in (14) a particular case of structure-building.

2.3.1.2 *The Empty Category Principle/ Proper Binding Principle*

Second, the adjoined head X in (14) does not c-command its trace t_X in a straightforward way, where *c-command* is defined as "X c-commands Y iff the first branching node dominating X dominates Y." This suggests that head movement would violate the Empty Category Principle (ECP) or the Proper Binding Condition (PBC).

To ensure that head movement obeys the ECP or the PBC, it is necessary to redefine the notion of *c-command*, for example, by introducing a distinction between containment vs. dominance or between segment vs. category.

(16) C-command, based on Baker (1988, p. 36, adapted)
   X c-commands Y iff X does not dominate Y and for every maximal projection ZP, if ZP dominates X then ZP dominates Y.

(17) C-command, based on Kayne (1994, p. 16)
   a. X c-commands Y iff *X and Y are categories* and X excludes and every category that dominates X also dominates Y (emphasis in original).
   b. X excludes Y if no segment of X dominates Y

---

4. But see Pesetsky (2013), Funakoshi (2012, 2014), and Yuan (2017) for proposals that some instances of phrasal movement is *undermerged*/adjoined to another non-root phrasal element.

Either way would however complicate our definition of c-command. Chomsky (2000) suggests that they do not "fall under the notion of *c-command* derived from Merge" (p. 116), which is transitive closure of sisterhood and containment.

(18) C-command, based on Chomsky (2000), p. 116, adapted
    a. K contains X if K immediately contains X or immediately contains L that contains X;
    b. X is a term of K if K contains X;
    c. X c-commands Y if X is the sister of K that contains Y.

2.3.1.3 *The non-successive cyclic nature*

Third, head movement cannot proceed in a successive cyclic fashion, as opposed to phrasal movement (e.g., successive cyclic *wh*-movement, Chomsky (1973, 1977)). It must "pick up" all the morphemes in the head position along its movement path. In other words, excorporation is suggested to be impossible for head movement.[5]

(19) The Ban on Head Extraction/ The Ban on Excorporation (cf. Baker 1988)
    If a head X moves to Y, then { X + Y } acts as one constituent, i.e., X cannot move out of the head complex.

(20) An illustration of the Ban on Head Extraction/ the Ban on Excorporation

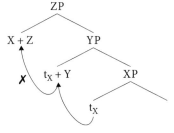

While such constraint is empirically supported by cases of incorporation and verb inflection, Roberts (2001) points out that it does not follow from GB conception of head movement. In other words, this ban must be stipulated in the adjunction approach to head movement. Note that it is suggested that (19) may be derived from the Lexical Integrity Hypothesis, which states that morphological structure cannot be targeted by syntactic operation.

(21) Lexical Integrity Hypothesis   (Lapointe 1980, p. 8)
    No syntactic rule can refer to elements of morphological structure.

---

5. But see Roberts (1991) for an opposite view.

This builds in a morphological character in head movement, but it then raises an architectural issue concerning the boundary between the syntactic component and the morphological component.

2.3.1.4 *Locality constraints*

Fourth, as far as locality is concerned, head movement is subject to a different, stricter locality condition compared to phrasal movement. The HMC requires head movement to be strictly local, but phrasal movement need not be so. While the HMC effects are suggested to be subsumed under general conditions on minimality (Relativized Minimality), the unification with other instances of movement operations may be superficial, since the typology of structural types involves "at least two irreducible distinctions" (Rizzi 2001, p. 90–91).

(22) Two distinctions in structural types
   a. a distinction between heads and phrases, and in the latter class,
   b. a distinction between positions of arguments (A-positions) and of non-arguments (A'-positions).

In other words, Relativized Minimality still implicates that the locality constraint on head movement is substantially different from phrasal movement, as heads in general blocks head movement, which is not relativized to another dimension (as in the cases of phrasal movement).

2.3.1.5 *The Chain Uniformity Condition*

Fifth, with the advent of Bare Phrase Structure (BPS, Chomsky 1994), syntactic projection levels are not explicitly assigned to X'-theoretic categories, and minimal and maximal projections are defined in terms of structural relation, as in (23).

(23) A relational definition on projection levels under BPS   (Chomsky 1994)
   a. A category that does not project any further is a maximal projection XP;
   b. One that is not a projection at all is a minimal projection X°;
   c. Any other is an X', invisible at the interface and for computation.

This arouses a non-trivial concern on the adjunction approach to head movement, as it violates the Chain Uniformity Condition (Nunes 1998; Toyoshima 2000, 2001).

(24) Chain Uniformity Condition   (Chomsky 1995b, p. 253)
   A chain is uniform with regard to phrase structure status.
   (where the phrase structure status of an element is its (relational) property of being maximal, minimal, or neither)

16   The Unity of Movement

For example, under (23), a head (before movement) is a non-maximal projection (as it projects). However, an adjoined head is a maximal projection, as it does not project further.[6]

2.3.2   Empirical differences with phrasal movement?

Apart from the theoretical concerns of the adjunction approach to head movement, there are non-trivial controversies over the empirical properties of head movement, which substantially affect the way head movement is modeled in the grammar.

2.3.2.1   *The locality constraints on head movement*

First, whether the HMC applies to all instances of head movement is not uncontroversial. It is observed that a substantial amount of cases involve local head movement, but it is also reported that head movement can be long-distance, in violation to the HMC. The first type of cases concerns a construction where a verb/participle is argued to be fronted before an intervening auxiliary verb. This construction is often referred to as *Long Head Movement* (LHM, Lema and Rivero 1990; Rivero 1991; 1993; 1994; Roberts 1994; Wilder 1994; Borsley, Rivero, and Stephens 1996, among others).

(25)   Examples of Long Head Movement
    a.   *Bulgarian*
        Pročel sum   knigata
        read   have+PRES+1SG book+the
        'I have read the book (completely).'   (Lema and Rivero 1990, p. 334)
    b.   *Breton*
        Lennet en   deus Yann al levr.
        read   3SG.MASC has Yann the book
        'Yann has read the book.'   (Borsley, Rivero, and Stephens 1996, p. 53)

Another type of cases comes from predicate cleft or verb fronting constructions. Typically, in these constructions, a verb is doubled and an extra verb appears on its own in the initial/periphery position.

---

6. To avoid this issue, Chomsky (1995b) proposes *Word Interpretation*, processes that are not constrained by syntactic principles, but see criticisms in Nunes (1998) and Toyoshima (2000, 2001) on the stipulative nature of Word Interpretation.

Chapter 2. Approaching head movement   **17**

(26) Examples of predicate cleft/ verbal fronting constructions
  a. *Vata*
     yī Ò wà [nā à yī   ]
     come s/he want NA we come
     'S/he wants us to come.'   (Koopman 1984, p.159)
  b. *Spanish*
     Comprar, Juan ha dicho [que María ha **comprado** un libro]
     buy.INF   J   has said that M   has bought   a book
     'As for buying, Juan has told me that María has bought a book.'
                                                  (Vicente 2007, p.79)

It is an empirical question as to whether these cases involve head movement. If they do, then the HMC must be weakened. If they do not, the HMC can be retained as an important property that needs to be captured by any proposals on head movement.[7]

2.3.2.2 *The interpretive effects of head movement*

Another difference between head and phrasal movement concerns the interpretation of movement in the syntax-semantics interface. It is suggested that head movement is semantically inert, as it does not affect interpretation. For example, there is no scope or reconstruction effects in case of head movement (Chomsky 2001; Harley 2004; Platzack 2013).[8] This is especially true for verb movement cases in the inflectional system in the sense of Germanic/Romance languages (see Chapter 4 for more discussions). Chomsky (2001) points out that "the semantic effects of head-raising in the core inflectional system are slight or nonexistent" (p.37). If head movement in general does not affect interpretation, this would represent a substantial difference from phrasal movement to the extent that the mechanism held responsible for phrasal movement might be considerably different from the one for head movement.

However, a number of cases of head movement have been reported to be able to bring along semantic effects. Table 2.1 summarizes some recent proposals in support of this view.

The analyses in these proposals are not uncontroversial. Debate continues as to whether head movement is indeed involved in these cases. So whether the lack of semantic effects is an inherent property of head movement is an unsettled empirical question. The answer to this question affects how head movement should be modeled in movement theories.

---

7. For discussions of the locality constraints on head movement, see Chapter 3.

8. The same criticism recurs in Chomsky (2015, 2019, 2021).

Table 2.1 Summary of evidence of scope effects with head movement

Types of heads	Language	Scope effects	Reference(s)
Determiner	Japanese	enhanced restriction	Takahashi (2002)
Negation	English	NPI licensing	Roberts (2010) and Szabolcsi (2010)
	Japanese	NPI licensing	Kishimoto (2007)
	English varieties	outscope subjects	Matyiku (2017) and Landau (2020)
	Korean	outscope objects	Han, Lidz, and Musolino (2007)
	Japanese	outscope objects	Sato and Maeda (2021)
Modal verb	English	outscope subjects	Lechner (2007, 2017)
	English	outscope negation	Iatridou and Zeijlstra (2013) and Homer (2015)
Aspectual verb	Shupamem	outscope subjects	Szabolcsi (2010, 2011)

2.3.2.3 *The morpho-phonological realization of head movement*

As opposed to phrasal movement, there is an important morphological character in head movement. For example, head movement is usually motivated by word formation or affixation, as in cases of incorporation and verb inflection.[9] However, it is also suggested that such morphological character may not be unique to head movement. Some instances of phrasal movement may lead to word formation, such as the Saxon genitive marker *'s* (Giorgi and Longobardi 1991). Also, the so-called "snowball movement" in Finnish involve phrases "rolling up" along the movement path (Huhmarniemi 2012), in a way similar to head movement. These cases suggest that the morphological character may not be unique to head movement.

In terms of phonological realization, especially in the discussions of predicate clefts, head movement commonly leads to double pronunciation of the movement chains. This is in contrast with phrasal movement, where double pronunciation is far less common (though not unattested). On one account, a doubled head is suggested to be a consequence of *morphological fusion* with another head (Nunes 1995, 2004), such that the two members in a head chain have to be pronounced as they are distinct syntactic objects (provided the copy deletion operation only

---

9. But this is not necessarily so, since T-to-C movement in many cases does not lead to increased morphological complexity. See also discussions in Harizanov and Gribanova (2019).

targets identical objects). Whether these issues should be taken into consideration in a theory of head movement is a non-trivial issue.

2.4 Non-unity approaches to head and phrasal movement

There are two major responses to the issues surrounding head movement, to be discussed in this section (§2.4) and the next (§2.5). The first type of responses acknowledges the theoretical and empirical differences between head movement and phrasal movement, and treat head movement different from phrasal movement. I call approaches along this line *non-unity approaches*. Either head movement is eliminated from the syntax or head movement is radically reformulated.

In light of recent comprehensive assessments and discussions of the different approaches to head movement, as in Roberts (2011) and Dékány (2018), the discussion in this subsection is intentionally brief, with the aim of showcasing the major directions of the development of head movement in the literature.

2.4.1 Eliminating head movement from the syntax

2.4.1.1 *Post-syntactic movement/operations*

Since the theoretical concerns of head movement arise due to violations of *syntactic* principles, a possible solution is that head movement is resulted from operations that are not in narrow syntax, but in the post-syntactic component (i.e., in the PF branch of grammar).

There are at least two ways to implement this idea. The first one is to posit some post-syntactic movement operation in the PF branch (Chomsky 2001; Boeckx and Stjepanović 2001; Schoorlemmer and Temmerman 2012; Harizanov and Gribanova 2019).[10] For example, the implementation in Harizanov and Gribanova (2019), resorts to post-syntactic head Raising/Lowering (cf. Embick and Noyer 2001). Essentially, it transplants the adjunction approach to head movement to the PF branch.

Another way of implementation denies the existence of movement in the PF branch. Instead, the displacement property of a head is resulted from the way syntactic structure is linearized, i.e., the linearization instructions to phonology (Brody 2000; Adger 2013; Platzack 2013; Ramchand and Svenonius 2014; Hall 2015; Svenonius 2016; Chomsky 2021). For example, this could be achieved by

---

10. Harizanov and Gribanova (2019) do not deny the presence of syntactic head movement, however.

the operation AMALGAMATE that amalgamates the inflectional elements the and verb along the clausal spine (or the like) (as in Chomsky (2021)), but this would also involve a substantially different mechanism to capture displacement property, when compared to phrasal movement (see Dékány 2018, for discussions).

2.4.1.2 *Remnant phrasal movement*

A different line of approaches seeks to reanalyze head movement as remnant phrasal movement, such that a head does not move on its own, but a phrase containing only a head does. In other words, what is said to be head movement is actually phrasal movement in disguise.

These approaches maintain that the mechanism responsible for head movement/displacement is syntactic, but there is no syntactic head movement at all, since the head does not move. This idea is adopted by Koopman and Szabolcsi (2000), Massam (2000), Rackowski and Travis (2000), Mahajan (2003), Nilsen (2003), and Müller (2004), among many others. In terms of implementation, a remnant phrasal movement approach head movement relies heavily on the mechanism that evacuates the elements within a phrase (but stranding a head). It is only after other phrase-internal elements have moved out that the phrase moves as if the head moves on its own.

2.4.2 Reformulating head movement in the syntax

Other proposals seek to reformulate the syntactic implementation of head movement such that it obeys the syntactic principles that movement operations are expected to obey. In other words, in these approaches, heads do move in the syntax, but they move in a way different from phrases.

For example, Nunes (1995, 2004), Bobaljik and Brown (1997), and Uriagereka (1998) propose a *sideward movement* approach to head movement, where movement occurs across two parallel workspaces. This specifically avoids the violation to the Extension Condition (but other concerns remain, e.g., the violation to the ECP and the CUC).

Another implementation is suggested in Koeneman (2000), Bury (2003), Fanselow (2003), Surányi (2005, 2008), and Donati (2006), who propose that head movement involves *reprojective movement*. The core idea is that a head moves into another empty head position, and projects a second time there. This simultaneously avoids violations to the Extension Condition, the CUC and the ECP.

Yet another type of approaches propose a syntactic operation/movement that allows the displacement of the phonological features of a head, such as *Conflation* (Harley 2004; cf. Hale and Keyser 2002), and (syntactic) phonological movement in the sense of Zwart (2001). A similar but not identical operation, *Generalized*

Head Movement, is recently proposed in Arregi and Pietraszko (2021), allowing the specific parts of a single complex head to be associated with different terminal nodes.

On the other hand, Roberts (2010) proposes that head movement is achieved via *Agree*, followed by an incorporation(-like) operation. This approach is also adopted in Aelbrecht and den Dikken (2013) and Iorio (2015). The idea of this approach is that, by Agree-ing with a lower head, a higher head acquires all the formal features of the lower head. By virtue of this, the lower head becomes defective, and is subsequently incorporated into the higher head.

2.4.3 Interim summary

It should be remarked that the validity and legitimacy of these approaches are both an empirical question and a theoretical question. It might be that one of these approaches turns out to be a global alternative to head movement, or that these different approaches are all needed for different head displacement/movement phenomena. Evaluation of these approaches is beyond the scope of this thesis.

The relevance of these approaches to this volume, however, is that a conceptual question for the non-unify approaches remains: what prevents head movement in syntax, or more specifically, what prevents a head, being a constituent, from undergoing movement in a way similar to phrases. Put differently, it begs the question of how the differences between head and phrasal movement follow from general principles of the grammar.

2.5 Recent pursuits of a unified theory of movement

The second type of responses to the issues relating to head movement is to assimilate head movement to phrasal movement as much as possible, maintaining that head movement is an instance of Move-α or is achieved by Internal Merge (Chomsky 2001). The general idea is that if head movement is problematic because it involves a mechanism that deviates from the one for phrasal movement, this can be avoided if head movement is achieved via the same mechanism. The pursuit of a unified theory of movement is reflected on recent re-evaluations of the differences between head movement and phrasal movement (Toyoshima 2001; Matushansky 2006; Lechner 2007; Vicente 2007; Hartman 2011; Funakoshi 2014; Harizanov and Gribanova 2019; Harizanov 2019; Preminger 2019, among others). In what follows, I briefly discuss some of them.

2.5.1 Head movement to the specifier position

One straightforward way to avoid the theoretical concerns of head movement is to allow a head to move into the specifier position, in a way similar to phrasal movement. This possibility has its root in Koopman (1984), where a verb is suggested to be able to move into a V'-position (cf. A'-position). This is further discussed in Fukui and Takano (1998), Toyoshima (2000, 2001), Matushansky (2006), and Vicente (2007).

Recall that the theoretical space for formulating head movement is severely restricted in the GB-era. A head-to-head adjunction approach is almost the only possible formulation at that time.[11] Other implementations of head movement, such as head movement to a specifier position or head movement adjoining to a phrase, are ruled out due to the combined effects of the X'-theoretic assumption of phrase structure and the assumption of Structure Preservation (Emonds 1970, 1976; Chomsky 1986). In other words, movement operations are expected to obey the CUC.

However, with the BPS replacing the X'-theoretic phrase structure, the CUC even rules out the adjunction approach to head movement. It is suggested that the CUC should be abandoned from the grammar (Nunes 1998; Toyoshima 2000, 2001). This would not only allow (i) head-to-head adjunction, but also (ii) head-to-specifier movement and (iii) head adjoining to a phrases.[12]

On the other hand, Fukui and Takano (1998) suggest that the CUC can be maintained, if "uniformity" is based on *non-distinctness* (instead of identity). If so, head movement does not necessarily violate the CUC. This is because while the head in the launching position and the head in the landing position heads are not identical in terms of projection level, they are not *distinct*, as both of them are minimal projections (i.e., they are not projected). Likewise, this would not only allow head-to-head adjunction, but also head-to-specifier movement and head adjunction to a phrase.[13]

Either the abandonment or the revision of the CUC opens up new possibility to formulate head movement within the minimalist framework. The possibility

---

11. Head movement may be formulated as a substitution rule, as proposed in Rizzi and Roberts (1989).

12. Abandoning the CUC would also allow a phrase to project again after movement (which is previously ruled out by the CUC), but Nunes (1998) suggests that this can be ruled out independently.

13. This revision of the CUC would still rule out further projection of a phrase after movement (as intended by the CUC), since the phrase (re-)projecting in the landing site would be non-maximal and non-minimal, hence invisible, under the BPS. It is thus distinct from the phrase in the launching site.

of head-to-specifier movement is adopted in many subsequent works (e.g., Matushansky 2006; Vicente 2007; Cheng and Vicente 2013; Harizanov and Gribanova 2019; Harizanov 2019; B. Hsu 2021, to name just a few). It should be noted that head movement to the specifier position is often taken as the first step of deriving properties of head movement, which may be followed by some morphological operation as in Matushansky (2006) and Harizanov and Gribanova (2019), or another syntactic operation, e.g., *Coalescence* as in B. Hsu (2021).

2.5.2 No head-specific locality constraint

With regard to the particular locality constraint of head movement (i.e., the HMC), a growing body of evidence suggests that the local nature of head movement is not an inherent property of head movement in general, as briefly discussed in §2.3.2.1. Specifically, the rich literature of predicate cleft across languages show that many instances of head movement do not obey the HMC. More importantly, these instances of head movement are constrained in a way similar to phrasal movement, where they exhibit sensitivity to syntactic islands, while tolerating clausal boundaries, moving in a long-distance fashion (e.g., Vicente 2007; Hein 2018; Harizanov and Gribanova 2019; Preminger 2019, among many others).

On the other hand, the local nature of head movement may be due to C(ategory)-selection, as suggested in Matushansky (2006). Since C-selection is by definition local, the dependency between a head and the head that it C-selects must be local. Note that C-selection is also local between a head and its selecting complement. Accordingly, the local nature of head movement has nothing to do with the inherent property of movement operations. No special locality constraint need to be posited for head movement.[14]

2.5.3 The interpretation of head movement

While the lack of interpretative effects of head movement is often taken to motivate a non-syntactic approach, it does not necessarily rule out the syntactic nature of head movement. In other words, while the interpretative effects of head movement are evidence that head movement must reside in the syntactic component, their absence does not speak against the syntactic nature of head movement. Certain instances of phrasal movements may also lack interpretive effects for different reasons. Matushansky (2006) also suggests that the reason why verb movement

---

14. The locality issues relating to head movement will be discussed in greater details in Chapter 3.

usually lack interpretive effects is due to their semantic type, which does not affect interpretation no matter a verb is interpreted in the launching position or the landing position. Proposals that argue for the interpretive effects of head movement, as mentioned in § 2.3.2.2, are thus potential evidence for a unity approach to head and phrasal movement, where both of them are syntactic by nature.[15]

2.6 Summary

The ongoing debates of head movement implies that head movement/displacement may be a non-uniform phenomenon (see, especially, Harizanov and Gribanova (2019)). The diverse nature may be due to the fact that the displacement properties of heads can be attributed to different operations in different components of the grammar. However, I stress that this does not necessarily reflect the non-uniform nature of *movement operations* in syntax. The rest of the volume is dedicated to a minimal pursuit of the question of to what extent a unified theory of movement, specifically one that does not distinguish heads from phrases, is possible. I present evidence from Cantonese verb movement showing that at least some instances of head movement behave exactly the same as phrasal movement.

---

15. It should be acknowledged that the arguments present for the interpretive effects are not uncontroversial. See Chapter 4 for extensive discussions.

CHAPTER 3

Intervention effects
Verb movement to peripheral positions

This chapter examines potential intervening elements in head movement by investigating four cases of non-local verb displacement in Cantonese. In these cases, the verbs are doubled, and their copy appears in the initial or final position of the sentence. I propose that these four cases uniformly involve head movement to a specifier position in the CP periphery, in a way identical to their phrasal counterparts. I further argue that elements of the same structural types (i.e., heads/verbs) do not necessarily block the proposed movement; instead, elements that possess the same syntactic feature are genuine interveners. The findings in the chapter challenge the status of the Head Movement Constraint as a general constraint on head movement. At the same time, I show that the proposed head movement exhibits the syntactic intervention effects that are observed with phrasal movement. I conclude that head movement is not constrained in a way different from phrasal movement with regard to intervention. Particularly, intervention effects are calculated in terms of syntactic features but not structural types. This conclusion necessitates a movement theory that does not distinguish head movement from phrasal movement in terms of locality.

3.1   Introduction

This chapter examines potential intervening elements in head movement by investigating four cases of non-local verb displacement in Cantonese. It is often suggested that head movement is subject to stricter locality requirements than phrasal movement, in the sense that an intervening head would block head movement. This is commonly known as the Head Movement Constraint (Travis 1984; Baker 1988; Rizzi 1990, among others). However, I will show that a head is not necessarily an intervener in head movement. From the perspective of a head movement analysis, the cases of non-local verb displacement in Cantonese show that head movement is intervened by elements possessing the same syntactic feature, but not elements of the same structural types (i.e., heads).[1]

---

1. Throughout this chapter, I use the term *structural types* to refer to *heads* and *phrases*.

I start with a brief introduction of the relevant constructions in Cantonese. The canonical word order in Cantonese is S(ubject)-V(erb)-O(object), and sentence particles typically appear at the end of the sentence. However, non-canonical word order is commonly found, and it is employed to convey different information structural meanings. Examples include (i) *topic constructions* (Matthews and Yip 2011; for Mandarin, Chao 1968; Li and Thompson 1981, i.a.), (ii) *'even'-focus constructions* (for Mandarin, Paris 1979, 1998; Shyu 1995; Badan 2007; Constant and Gu 2010); (iii) *copula focus constructions* (C. C.-H. Cheung 2015; for Mandarin, L. L. S. Cheng 2008; Pan 2014, 2017, 2019);[2] and (iv) *right dislocation* (L. Y.-L. Cheung 1997, 2005, 2009; Law 2003; B. H.-S. Chan 2013; Lee 2017, 2020; Lai 2019; K.-F. Yip 2020). An example of each construction is given in (27), respectively. For illustrative purposes, objects are chosen to demonstrate the change in word order, but these constructions are by no means exclusive to objects.

(27) Non-canonical word order with regard to objects
    a. $\boxed{O}$ SV: Topic constructions
        Zoeng zi   nei fong hai bin   aa3?
        CL   paper you put at where SFP
        'Where do/did you put the paper?'   (Matthews and Yip 2011, p. 84)
    b.   *Lin-* $\boxed{O}$ SV: 'Even'-focus constructions
        Lin **ni-bun syu** Aaming dou maai-zo.
        even this-CL book Aaming also buy-PERF
        'Aaming even bought this book.'   (cf. Shyu 1995, p. 6)
    c.   *Hai-* $\boxed{O}$ SV: Copula focus constructions
        Hai **nei ge** **taidou** keoidei m-zungji ze1.
        COP you MOD attitude they   not-like SFP
        'It is only your attitude that they do not like.'   (cf. Pan 2014, p. 19)
    d.   SV SFP $\boxed{O}$: Right dislocation
        Daaigaa dou m-zi   lo1 **ni-joeng je.**
        we   all not-know SFP this-CL thing
        'All of us don't know this thing.'   (L. Y.-L. Cheung 1997, p. 12, adapted)

This chapter focuses on the variants of these four constructions in Cantonese, all of which involve a doubled verb in a non-canonical position. An example of each construction introduced in (27) is given in (28).

---

2. In Victor Pan's work, these constructions are referred to as *ex-situ cleft constructions*. I avoided this name because it does not distinguish them from 'even'-focus constructions and it presumes a cleft structure. Since these constructions obligatorily involve a copula before the focus, I adopt a more descriptive name.

(28) Non-canonical word order with regard to verbs

    a. $\boxed{V}$ SVO: Topic constructions of verbs

        Maai keoi hai **maai**-gwo go-bun syu.

        buy   s/he COP buy-EXP   that-CL book

        'As for buying, s/he has bought that book (but...).'

                              (cf. Cheng and Vicente 2013, p. 13)

    b.   *Lin-* $\boxed{V}$ SVO: 'Even'-focus constructions of verbs

        Lin **tai** keoi dou m-**tai**   ni-bun syu.

        even read s/he also not-read this-CL book

        'S/he didn't even READ this book.'   (cf. Cheng and Vicente 2013, p. 2)

    c.   *Hai-* $\boxed{V}$ SVO: Copula focus constructions of verbs

        Hai **dim**   Aaming m-gam   **dim**   ni-zek dungmat ze1.

        cop touch Aaming not-dare touch this-CL animal   SFP

        'Aaming dare not to TOUCH this animal only.'

    d.   SVO SFP $\boxed{V}$: Right dislocation/dislocation copying of verbs

        Zoengsaam gammaan **fan**   ni-zoeng cong aa3 **fan**.

        Zoengsaam tonight   sleep this-CL   bed   SFP sleep

        'Zoengsaam (will) sleep on this bed tonight.'

                              (K. K. Chan 2016, p. 18, adapated)

In these cases, a copy of the main verb appears in the left or right periphery of the sentence. All these sentences in (28) with the displaced verb are associated with different discourse effects. These variants have received limited attention in the Cantonese literature. Cases of verbs appearing in topic constructions as in (28a) and 'even'-focus constructions as in (28b) are discussed in Matthews and Yip (1998, 2011).[3] To the best of my knowledge, copula focus constructions of verbs as in (28c) are not discussed in the literature. The cases of right dislocation as in (28d) are sometimes referred to as *dislocation copying*, since the dislocated element is not associated with a "gap" in the original sentence, as opposed to ordinary right dislocation. Dislocation copying has received relatively more attention in the literature, as discussed in L. Y.-L. Cheung (2015), Tang (2015), K. K. Chan (2016), and Lai (2019).

The word order patterns of S, V and O illustrated in (27) and (28) can be summarized in Table 3.1. For convenience, I refer to these constructions targeting verbs as *verb doubling constructions*.[4]

---

3. Although the Mandarin counterparts of the sentences in (28) receive some attention, the discussion is still very limited. As far as I am aware, Paris (1998) and Liu (2004) focus on the information structural status of the doubled verbs, whereas Constant and Gu (2010), Cheng and Vicente (2013), and Yang and Wu (2019) offer some level of analytical analysis.

Table 3.1 The word order patterns illustrated in (27) and (28)

	(i) topic	(ii) 'even'-focus	(iii) copula focus	(iv) right dislocation
Object	[O] SV	*lin-* [O] SV	*hai-* [O] SV	SV SFP [O]
Verb	[V] SVO	*lin-* [V] SVO	*hai-* [V] SVO	SVO SFP [V]

Disregarding the doubling effects, which I will set aside throughout this chapter, Table 3.1 shows that phrasal dislocation of the object and verb dislocation pattern identically.[5]

After a description of the syntactic and semantic properties of these verb doubling constructions, I argue for two claims. First, I propose that they uniformly involve head movement to a specifier position in the CP periphery, in a way similar to their phrasal counterparts.[6] I justify a movement analysis with evidence from (i) lexical identity effects; (ii) island effects, and (iii) idiomatic expressions. Second, I argue that the proposed movement exhibits intervention effects that are calculated based on syntactic features, but not structural types. The evidence comes from the observation that the two verbs in verb doubling constructions do not tolerate an intervening *focused element*, but they allow an intervening *head*.

The findings in the chapter challenge the status of the Head Movement Constraint (Travis 1984) as a general constraint on head movement. Importantly, it reveals that head movement exhibits focus intervention effects that are also observed with phrasal movement (Rizzi 1990, 2001, 2004). I conclude that in terms of intervention locality, head movement is not constrained in a way different from phrasal movement. These necessitate a movement theory that does not distinguish head movement from phrasal movement in terms of locality.

This rest of this chapter is organized as follows. §3.2 reviews the discussions on the intervention effects on head movement. §3.3 offers a detailed description on the four verb doubling constructions. §3.4 presents evidence for a verb movement analysis. §3.5 examines the potential interveners in verb doubling constructions. §3.6 details the proposal. §3.7 discusses two families of alternative analyses

---

4. There are many other instances of verb doubling in Cantonese, but they do not necessarily give rise to discourse effects or do so in a similar way. I confine the discussion to these four cases.

5. The difference in doubling effects between objects and verbs is non-trivial and deserves an explanation. Chapter 5 is dedicated to this issue.

6. This is not to say that all instances of constructions with a displaced object necessarily involve movement. The surface object may be base generated there and associated with an empty category in the canonical object position (for example, see, Huang, Li, and Li 2009; Shyu 1995; C. C.-H. Cheung 2008, 2015).

to a head movement approach. §3.8 explores some consequences of the proposal. §3.9 concludes the chapter.

3.2 Intervention effects and head movement

This section reviews *intervention* effects in head movement. I adopt a working definition of intervention suggested in Rizzi (2011)).

(29) Intervention (Rizzi 2011, p. 220)
 A local relation is disrupted by the intervention of an element with certain qualities which make it a potential participant in the local relation.

One prominent quality of interveners in the discussion of head movement is one that concerns the structural type of an element. Specifically, movement dependencies between heads are said to be disrupted by intervening heads, commonly known as the Head Movement Constraint (henceforth HMC, Travis 1984). I discuss the empirical and conceptual motivations of HMC in §3.2.1. Then, I turn to its particular nature and potential exceptions to the HMC in 3.2.2. I further discuss proposals in defense of HMC in §3.2.3.

3.2.1 Intervention due to identical structural types

Head movement is formulated in Koopman (1984), Travis (1984), and Baker (1988) as a syntactic operation that involves head-to-head adjunction, where a lower head moves up and adjoins to a higher head, as in (30a). A head may be displaced over a long distance as long as the head move through all the intervening head positions (and pick up the heads), as in (30b).

(30) Head movement as head-to-head adjunction
 a.
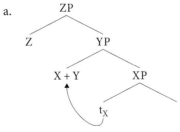

b.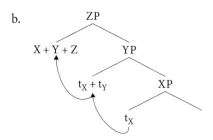

It is also suggested that head movement is subject to locality constraints that are stricter than phrasal movement. For example, head movement is said to be subject to the Head Movement Constraint (HMC, Travis 1984), which requires head movement to be highly local. A formulation of the HMC under the Government and Binding Theory (Chomsky 1981, 1986) is given in (31).

(31) The Head Movement Constraint, in Travis (1984, p. 131)
A head x may only move into the head y that properly governs x.

Since the notion of proper government has been abandoned in the modern minimalist models (Chomsky 1995b, et seq.), I adopt a version of the HMC reformulated in Roberts (2001). This version still captures the original insight of the HMC.

(32) The Head Movement Constraint, in Roberts (2001, p. 113)
Head movement of X to Y cannot skip an "intervening" head Z.
(where Z intervenes between Y and X iff Y asymmetrically c-commands both X and Z, while Z asymmetrically c-commands X)

Configurationally, cases that violate the HMC are illustrated in (33). In both cases, Y is "skipped" when X moves to Z.[7]

(33) Cases of head movement that violates of the Head Movement Constraint
a.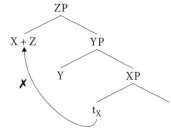

---

7. The way HMC as stated in (32) also prevents a head from moving out of a head complex, which is often referred to as an independent constraint on head movement, as given in (i).

(i) The Ban on Head Extraction/ The Ban on Excorporation (cf. Baker 1988)
If a head X moves to Y, then { X + Y } acts as one constituent, i.e., X cannot move out of the head complex.

b.

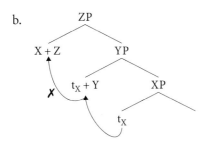

The empirical evidence of the HMC comes from verb/auxiliary movement in Germanic and Romance languages. For example, in English, an auxiliary can move to C as long as there is no intervening auxiliary. Thus, only the movement in (34b) is allowed, as opposed to (34b).

(34) English auxiliary movement (Rizzi 1990, p. 11)
    a. They could have left.
    b. **Could** they ⟨could⟩ have left?
    c. ***Have** they could ⟨have⟩ left?   *head movement skipping a T position*

Similarly, in Italian, while both auxiliaries and participles can move to C in certain non-finite clause, as in (35a–b), the participle cannot move across the auxiliary, shown in (35c).

(35) Italian verb movement to C (Rizzi 2001, p. 93)
    a. **Essendo** Mario ⟨essendo⟩ tornato a Milano, ...
       "Having Mario come back to Milan, ..."
    b. **Tornato** Mario ⟨tornato⟩ a Milano, ...
       "Come back Mario to Milan, ..."
    c. ***Tornato** Mario essendo ⟨tornato⟩ a Milano ...
       "Come back Mario having to Milan, ..."

The HMC is subsumed under *Relativized Minimality* (Rizzi 1990), which attempts to unify similar intervention effects observed with A-movement and A'-movement. Relativized Minimality specifically makes reference to structural types, which range over heads, A'-positions, and A-positions. A simplified formulation of Relativized Minimality is given in (36).

(36) Relativized Minimality (Rizzi 1990; a version taken from Rizzi 2011, p. 221–222)
    a. In the configuration ... X ... Z ... Y ...,
       a local relation cannot connect X and Y if Z intervenes and Z is of the same structural type as X.
    b. Structural types: (i) A'-positions, (ii) A-positions, and (iii) heads.

3.2.2 The particular nature of the HMC and exceptions to the HMC

While Relativized Minimality appears to successfully incorporate the HMC into a more general minimality condition in language, it remains unclear why the three structural types in (36b) should form a natural class. Rizzi (2001, p. 90–91) points out that the typology of structural types involves "at least two irreducible distinctions."

(37) Two distinctions in structural types
   a. a distinction between heads and phrases, and in the latter class,
   b. a distinction between positions of arguments (A-positions) and of non-arguments (A'-positions).

In other words, Relativized Minimality still implicates that head movement is substantially different from phrasal movement, in the sense that while a head is generally an intervener of head movement, a phrase is not always an intervener of phrasal movement (as it depends on whether a position is argument-related). Subsuming the HMC under Relativized Minimality does not remove the particular nature of the HMC: head movement is specifically constrained by stricter locality conditions compared to phrasal movement. Subsequent discussions and reformulation of Relativized Minimality focus on the featural encoding of potential phrasal interveners (Chomsky 1995b; Rizzi 2001, 2004). Head movement and the HMC receive relatively little discussion in the study of intervention.[8]

I stress that the particular nature of the HMC does not lie in whether they can be derived from more general principle of the grammar,[9] but in the suggestion that they represent a *general* constraint on movement of a particular structural type. It is true that some instances of phrasal movement may display similar effects, but the lack of generality marks a significant difference between the locality constraints on head and phrasal movement.

Empirically, the HMC appears to be too strict as a *general* locality constraint on head movement. Evidence reveals that there are many cases that constitute a violation to the HMC. The evidence comes roughly in two main types.[10] The first one concerns a construction where a verb/participle is argued to be fronted before

---

8. But see Koopman (1984) and Y. Li (1990) for discussions on an A- vs. A'-distinction on heads. See also Roberts (2001) for an operator vs. non-operator distinction on heads.

9. For example, Chomsky (1986), Baker (1988), and Rizzi (1990) suggest that the HMC can be derived from the Empty Category Principle (ECP). Baker (1988) also suggests that the ban of excorporation may be due to illicit trace within word.

10. I focus on cases in the verbal domain, but violation to the HMC has also been argued to be attested in the nominal domain, such as clitic climbing in Romance languages; see Roberts (1991, 2010) for discussions.

an intervening auxiliary verb. This construction is often referred to as *Long Head Movement* (LHM, Lema and Rivero 1990; Rivero 1991; 1993; 1994; Roberts 1994; Wilder 1994; Borsley, Rivero, and Stephens 1996, among others).[11] Two examples from Bulgarian and Breton are given in (38).

(38) Examples of Long Head Movement
    a. *Bulgarian*
        Pročel sum   knigata
        read   have+PRES+1SG book+the
        'I have read the book (completely).'   (Lema and Rivero 1990, p. 334)
    b. *Breton*
        Lennet en   deus Yann al levr
        read   3SG.MASC has Yann the book
        'Yann has read the book.'   (Borsley, Rivero, and Stephens 1996, p. 53)

It is reported that similar constructions are found in Old Romance, European Portuguese, Modern Romanian and many Slavic languages (Bulgarian, Serbo-Croatian, Czech, etc.) (Lema and Rivero 1990). Generally, LHM is said to display root effects, i.e., it is not available in embedded contexts. Languages may differ in the inflectional form of the fronted verb – they may be in infinitive forms or in participle forms. Languages may also differ in terms of the trigger and the interpretive effects. Without going into the details of language-specific properties of LHM, these cases typically involve fronting of the verb over the auxiliary verb. This constitutes a direct violation to the Head Movement Constraint. The general schema can be represented in (39).

(39) A schematic representation of LHM

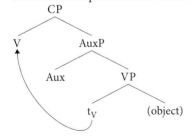

The other type of empirical evidence against the strictly local nature of head movement comes from predicate cleft or verb fronting constructions. Typically, in these

---

11. These cases earn their name as "long" in the sense that they are not strictly local, as opposed to "Short Head Movement" in Germanic languages that do not involve a verb crossing an auxiliary. Note that LHM is reported to be clause-bounded, and not to be confused with long-distance dependencies that may occur across clauses.

constructions, an additional copy of the verb appears on its own in the initial/ periphery position. These constructions are reported to convey discourse effects such as a focus reading or a topic reading of the verb, subject to language variations. The two copies of the same verbs can also be separated by clausal boundaries, establishing long distance dependencies. I give two examples from Vata and Spanish in (40), where the two verbs are separated by a clausal boundary.

(40) Examples of predicate cleft/ verbal fronting constructions
    a. *Vata*
        yī   Ò wà [nā à yī]
        come s/he want NA we come
        'S/he wants us to come.'   (Koopman 1984, p. 159)
    b. *Spanish*
        Comprar, Juan ha dicho [que María ha **comprado** un libro]
        buy.INF   J   has said that M   has bought   a book
        'As for buying, Juan has told me that María has bought a book.'
                                    (Vicente 2007, p. 79)

It has been argued that the two verbs are related by head movement and the movement is sensitive to syntactic islands (Koopman 1984; Vicente 2007). If this is the case, then when the verb moves to the initial position, it crosses at least a head along its path. These cases constitute violations to the HMC.[12] Similar behaviors are reported in predicate cleft/ verb fronting constructions in many other languages. A non-exhaustive list is given in (41). All these cases are argued to involve verb/head movement.

(41) A non-exhaustive list of predicate cleft/ verb fronting constructions[13]
    a. Vata (Koopman 1984)
    b. Bulgarian (Lambova 2004; Harizanov 2019)
    c. Hebrew (Landau 2006)
    d. Hungarian (Ürögdi 2006; Vicente 2007)
    e. Spanish (Vicente 2007)
    f. Haitian (Harbour 2008)
    g. Nupe (Kandybowicz 2008)
    h. Vietnamese (Trinh 2009)
    i. Brazilian Portuguese (Bastos-Gee 2009)
    j. Mandarin (Cheng and Vicente 2013)
    k. Asante Twi (Hein 2018)
    l. Russian (Antonenko 2019)
    m. Finnish (Brattico 2021)

---

12. The doubling effects of the verb are argued to be due to independent factors.

13. For extensive discussions on cross-linguistic verb/verbal fronting constructions, see Hein (2018).

As such, the cases of LHM and predicate cleft/verb fronting indicate that the HMC are too strict as a general locality constraint on head movement. On a weak thesis, the HMC must be revised such that it operates only on selected domains of head movement (in a way similar to a featural-based Relativized Minimality). On a strong thesis, the HMC may be non-existent in the first place, if the local nature of head movement (in the core cases in support of the HMC) follows from other principles in the grammar.

It should be remarked that cases of head movement as in LHM and predicate cleft/verb fronting are not entirely unconstrained. For example, LHM (in Bulgarian and Rumanian) cannot move across negation, as in (42).[14] Predicate clefts in Vata cannot span across a complex nominal, as in (43). These examples show that head movement is not exceptionally unconstrained in terms of locality.

(42) LHM in Bulgarian cannot cross negtion
      ***Pročel** ne sum   knigata
      read   not have+PRES+1SG book+the
      Int.: 'I have read the book (completely).'   (Lema and Rivero 1990, p.337)

(43) Predicate cleft in Vata cannot span across a complex nominal
      *tākā n̄ wà [fòtó mŪmÚ n̄ tākā-ɓÓ àbà]
      show you like picture ITIT   you showed-REL Aba
      Int.: 'You like the picture you showed to Aba.'   (Koopman 1984, p.159)

In sum, empirical evidence speaks against the HMC as a general constraint on head movement and calls for a more fine-grained locality theory of head movement that is not exclusively formulated with reference to structural types.

3.2.3 Base generation and remnant movement as alternatives

Efforts have been made in the literature to determine the correct analysis of LHM and predicate cleft/verb fronting. If it can be shown that in these cases no verb/head movement is involved, then the HMC can be maintained. In what follows, I briefly discuss two potential alternatives to a head movement analysis.

The first one is a base generation approach. For LHM cases, Embick and Izvorski (1997) suggest that the participle-auxiliary word order is not due to syntactic head movement but the enclitic nature of (certain) auxiliaries. In other words, the verb is base-generated in the low position, and the alternation in word order is due to a morphological merger that operates on heads. The idea is illustrated in (44).

---

14. See Roberts (2001) for a potential explanation based on the distinctions of operator heads and non-operator heads.

(44) An illustration of the base generation analysis of Bulgarian Participle-Auxiliary order
    a.   The verb base-generates at a low position:
         [Aux [V Obj]]
    b.   A morphological merger applies to affix the auxiliary to the participle:
         V-Aux Obj (where Aux is an enclitic)

A base generation analysis represents a potential alternative to a head movement approach.[15] If this is the case, no head movement is needed to derive the relevant order.

On a similar vein, a base generation analysis has been proposed for predicate cleft/verb fronting in Yiddish and Brazilian Portuguese in Cable (2004). Cable (2004) suggests that predicate cleft in Yiddish involves a base generated topic, which can be lexically non-identical to its verbal associate. In (45), the verb *forn* 'travel' is argued to be base-generated in the initial position, as it does not correspond to a gap or a copy in the lower clause.[16]

(45) A base generation analysis of Yiddish predicate cleft
    Forn   bin ikh gefloygn keyn Nyu-York
    travel.INF am I   flown   to   New-York
    'As for traveling, I've flown to New York.'

                  (Vicente 2007, p. 82; cf. Cable 2004, p. 9)

Another alternative to a head movement analysis is to posit remnant VP movement. In German, Participle-Auxiliary order is possible as with many cases of LHM. For example, den Besten and Webelhuth (1990) argue that instead of the verb moving on its own, the surface order results from VP movement. This VP, however, is a remnant created by object scrambling. The object has been moved out of the VP before VP movement. The VP thus contains only the verb.[17] When it moves, it appears that the verb is moving on its own. To illustrate, the Participle-Auxiliary order in (46) involves object scrambling (out of VP) and subsequent VP movement to the initial position.

---

15. See Fiantis (1999) for another phonological alternative to LHM in Bulgarian; see also Harizanov (2019) for a defense of a head movement analysis.

16. Indeed, Cable (2004) suggests that the initial verbal topic is base-generated in the minimal clause and may subsequently moves to its surface position in the periphery. If so, head movement is still needed.

17. Fanselow (2002) argues that, while remnant movement may be independently needed in other contexts in German, it has a number of shortcomings compared to a verb raising alternative in cases where a bare verb appears in the initial position.

(46) A remnant movement analysis of Participle-Auxiliary order in German
$[_{\text{VP}} \, t_i \, \text{Gelesen}]$ hat Hans [das Buch]$_i$ nicht t$_{\text{VP}}$
read has Hans the book not
'Hans has not read the book.'

Such a remnant movement approach has subsequently be applied to predicate cleft/verb fronting cases and other relevant structures (Koopman 1997; Koopman and Szabolcsi 2000; Mahajan 2003; Nilsen 2003; Müller 2004, among many others). For example, Koopman (1997) abandons her head movement analysis of Vata predicate cleft and proposes instead a remnant movement approach in a way similar to the German case.

The discussion in this subsection indicates that if the the HMC-violating cases of head movement can be alternatively analyzed as base generation or remnant movement, then the HMC can be maintained as a general constraint on head movement.

3.2.4 Interim summary

In summary, setting aside the particular nature of the HMC when compared to phrasal movement, the empirical validity of the HMC hinges on the correct analysis on the cases such as LHM and predicate cleft/verb fronting. In what follows, I present evidence from Cantonese and argue that a head movement approach is necessary to capture the empirical properties of the four verb doubling constructions. Crucially, I show that these constructions are not subject to the HMC, and thus the HMC cannot be maintained as a general constraint on head movement. However, I also show that head movement is not unconstrained. I show that it exhibits similar (focus) intervention effects as observed with phrasal movement.

3.3 Verb doubling constructions and discourse effects

In this section, I turn to verb doubling cases in Cantonese. In view of the little attention on these constructions in the literature, I present a detailed description of both the syntactic and semantic properties of these verb doubling constructions in Cantonese. The discussion serves as the empirical grounding for the proposed head movement analysis.

3.3.1 Types of verbs

Verb doubling constructions are productive in Cantonese. I illustrate the variety of verbs compatible with verb doubling constructions. While the examples given in (28) all involve a transitive verb, I show that transitivity of the doubled verbs does not affect the acceptability of the verb doubling constructions, on a par with semantic properties such as the stative/ eventive distinction and phonological properties such as the number of syllables.[18]

In topic constructions of verbs, the doubled verb can be an intransitive (unergative) verb, such as *siu* 'laugh', or a disyllabic (monomorphemic) verb, such as *pisen* 'present' (which is an English loan-word), as shown in the sentences in (47).

(47) Topic constructions of verbs
   a. **Siu** Aaming hai **siu**-dak hou daaiseng. Batgwo keoi gongje hou
      laugh Aaming COP laugh-RES very loud but he speak very
      saiseng.
      low.voice
      'As for laughing, Aaming laughs loudly. But he speaks very softly.'
   b. **Pisen** Aaming hai **pisen**-gwo ni-pin man. Batgwo keoi zinghai
      present Aaming COP present-EXP this-CL paper but he only
      gong-zo ng fanzung.
      talk-PERF five minute
      'As for presenting, Aaming has presented this paper. But he only talked for
      five minutes.'

In 'even'-focus constructions, sentences in (48) show that the targeted verb can be an unaccusative verb such as *zoek* 'be.turned.on' or a disyllabic transitive verb such as *daamsam* 'worry'.

(48) 'Even'-focus constructions of verbs
   a. Lin **zoek** bou dinnou dou m-**zoek**. Zanhai waai-dak hou citdai.
      even on CL computer also not-on really broken-RES very entire
      'This computer cannot even BE TURNED ON. (It has) really broken
      down completely.'
   b. Lin **daamsam** Aaming dou m-**daamsam** nei. M-hou waa ziugu nei.
      even worry Aaming also not-worry you not-good say take.care you
      'Aaming does not even WORRY about you, not to mention take care of
      you.'

---

18. Whenever appropriate, I include possible continuations after the target sentence to facilitate naturalness.

Paris (1998) observes that in Mandarin stative predicates like 'tired' and 'cheap' cannot be targeted in 'even'-focus constructions, as shown in the Cantonese counterpart in (49a). Matthews and Yip (1998) also observes a similar constraint in Cantonese, as in (49b).

(49) Illicit stative predicates in 'even'-focus constructions
    a. ^{??}Lin **gui** keoi dou m-**gui**.
        even tired s/he also not-tired
        'S/he is not even tired.' (cf. Paris 1998, p.146)
    b. *****Gwai** dou m-**gwai**. Janjan dou maai-dak-hei.
        expensive also not-expensive everyone all buy-able-up
        '(It is) not even expensive. Everyone can afford (it).'
        (Matthews and Yip 1998, p.184)

However, there are stative predicates that can be focused in 'even'-focus constructions, such as *zi* 'know' and *jit* 'hot', as shown in (50). I therefore suggest that there is no general ban on stative predicates in 'even'-focus constructions, but focusing stative predicates may require a specific context to sound natural.

(50) Licit statives predicates in 'even'-focus constructions
    a. Ni-gin si lin **zi** keoi dou m-**zi**. M-hou waa bei
        this-CL event even KNOW s/he also not-know not-good say give
        jigin.
        comment
        'S/he did not even know this, not to mention comment (on it).'
    b. Lin **jit** go faanhap dou m-**jit**. Nei giu jan dim sik?
        even hot CL lunchbox also not-hot you tell person how eat
        'The lunchbox (i.e., the food in the lunchbox) is not even HOT. How can I eat (it)?'

Copula focus constructions of verbs display similar flexibility in the choice of verbs. Since the constructions, as far as I know, have not been documented in the literature, I illustrate the construction with four examples and provide a context for each of them.

(51) Copula focus constructions of verbs
    a. *Context: A Japanese teacher is talking about one of his student, Aaming:*
        Hai **gong** Aaming **gong**-m-dou tongseon ge jatman zel. Keoi
        COP speak Aaming say-not-able fluent MOD Japanese SFP he
        se-dak hou hou.
        write-RES very good
        'Aaming cannot SPEAK fluent Japanese only. He writes very well.'

40   The Unity of Movement

b.   *Context: A frequent traveler is talking about his attitude towards Japan:*
Hai **zyu** ngo m-soeng **zyu** hai Jatbun ze1. Ngo bunsan hai zungji heoi
COP live I   not-want live in Japan SFP I   self   COP like   go
Jatbun leoihan ge3.
Japan travel SFP
'I don't want to LIVE in Japan only. I like to travel to Japan.'

c.   *Context: A recruitment manager is talking about one of the interviewees,*
Aaming:
Hai **leng** Aaming m-gau   Aafan **leng** ze1. Keita je   dou hai
COP pretty Aaming not-enough Aafan pretty SFP other thing all be
Aaming sikhap di.
Aaming suitable a.bit
'Aaming is not as PRETTY as Aafan only. For other things, Aaming is
more suitable.'

d.   *Context: A professor is talking about one of his students, Aaming:*
Hai **pisen** keoi mou   seonsam **pisen**-dak hou ze1. Se   peipaa
COP present s/he not.have confidence present-RES good SFP write paper
gewaa keoi gokdak se-dou.
if   s/he think write-able
'S/he lacks the confidence to PRESENT well only. If (s/he is) to write
paper, s/he thinks (s/he) can write (it).'

Lastly, for dislocation copying of verbs, possible verbs range from transitive verbs
to the copula verb and (disyllabic) attitude verbs, illustrated in (52).[19]

(52)   Dislocation copying of verbs

a.   **Coeng** matje aa3 **coeng**?
sing   what SFP sing
'What are (you) singing?'/ 'Why are (you) sing?'

(Matthews and Yip 1998, p. 186)

b.   Hungsaudou wui **hai** mou   je   hok go3 lo1 **hai**.
karate   club COP not.have thing learn SFP SFP COP
'The karate club offers nothing for us to learn.' (L. Y.-L. Cheung 1997, p. 9)

c.   Ngo **gokdak** nei zoengloi wui hou meimun aa3 **gokdak**.
I   think you future   will very fruitful SFP think
'I think your future will be very fruitful.'   (K. K. Chan 2016, p. 19)

---

19. Matthews and Yip (1998) notes that sentences like (52a), where an *wh*-expression is
involved, conveys an "idiomatic" meaning, though admitting that it is productive in colloquial
Cantonese. The "idiomatic" meaning can be regarded as a rhetorical meaning or a touch of
whining force that is attributed to the *wh*-expressions (Tsai 2021).

So far, all the above examples show that verb doubling constructions are productive. There is, however, a restriction on the choice of verbs. For example, some modal verbs cannot be targeted in the topic constructions and the two focus constructions. However, dislocation copying is able to target these verbs. Compare (53) and (54):

(53) Some modal verbs cannot be targeted in topic and focus constructions
    a. ??**Honang** Aaming hai **honang** m-lai   ge2.
       possible Aaming COP possible not-come SFP
       'As for whether it is possible, it is possible that Aaming does not come.'
    b. ??**Lin** **wui** Aaming dou m-**wui** heoi.
       even will Aaming also not-will go
       Int.: 'Aaming is not going – there is even no possibility that he will go.'
    c. ??**Hai** **jinggoi** Aaming m-**jinggoi** heoi ze1.
       COP should Aaming not-should go   SFP
       Int.: 'Aaming SHOULD not go only.'

(54) Dislocation copying of modal verbs
    a. Aaming **honang** m-lai   laa3 **honang**.
       Aaming possible not-come SFP possible
       'It is possible that Aaming is not coming.'
    b. Keoi **wui** zoeng gaan uk   maai-ceot-heoi gaa3 laa3 **wui**.
       s/he will DIS   CL   house sell-out-go   SFP SFP will
       'S/he will sell the house.'   (L. Y.-L. Cheung 2015, p. 248)
    c. Nei **jinggoi** tung jan   gong ge2 **jinggoi**.
       you should with person talk SFP should
       'You should tell others.'   (Lai 2019, p. 259)

As for why dislocation copying of verbs is allowed to target a larger set of verbs, I suggest that the difference lies in the discourse effects brought along by these constructions. Anticipating the discussion of their corresponding discourse effects in §3.3.3, the topic and focus constructions involve contrastive interpretation of the verbs in the periphery, whereas dislocations copying differs in marking the verb as defocused or given. I suggest to connect the split in discourse effects to the range of possible targets in these constructions. I suggest that only verbs that denote a proper eventuality can be contrasted or focused, whereas all verbs can be defocused.[20] This suggestion is in line with the observation that dislocation copying can even target adverbial elements that cannot be topicalized or focused. These examples include *jiging* 'already' and *dou* 'all.'

---

20. This is supported by the observations that auxiliary verbs fail to be targeted in predicate clefting in Spanish (Vicente 2007) and participle fronting in Bulgarian (Harizanov 2019).

42 The Unity of Movement

(55) Dislocation copying of adverbial elements
    a.   Keoi **jiging** heoi-gwo laa3 **jiging**.
          s/he already go-EXP   SFP already
          'S/he has already been there.'   (L. Y.-L. Cheung 2015, p. 234)
    b.   Keoi **dou** lai   gaa3 **dou**.
          s/he also come SFP   all
          'S/he also comes.'   (L. Y.-L. Cheung 2015, p. 236)

As a final remark, the verb in these verb doubling constructions cannot be regarded as a nominalized verb, a possibility mentioned in passing in Shyu (1995, p. 14, fn. 11).[21] This is because verbs cannot appear after *jau* 'have' in existential constructions (see, e.g., Huang 1987) or after the focus-marking *dak* 'only' (Tang 2002), both of which can only take nominal elements. If verbs were able to be nominalized, we would expect that they could appear in constructions that can only target nominals, contrary to facts. I therefore maintain that the doubled elements in verb doubling constructions are genuine verbs but not derived nominals.

(56) Existential constructions with *jau* 'have' cannot target verbs
    a.   Jau **jat-bun syu** ngo soeng maai.
          have one-CL book I   want buy.
          'There is a book that I want to buy.'
    b.   *Jau **maai** ngo soeng **maai** jat-bun syu.
          have buy I   want buy one-CL book
          Int.: 'There is a book that I want to buy.'

(57) Focus constructions with *dak* 'only' cannot target verbs
    a.   Dak Hoenggong ngo zyu-gwo.
          only Hong.Kong I   live-EXP
          'I have only lived in Hong Kong.'
    b.   *Dak **zyu** ngo **zyu**-gwo Hoenggong.
          only live I   live-EXP Hong.Kong
          Int.: 'I have only lived in Hong Kong.'

3.3.2 Morpho-syntactic properties and variants

3.3.2.1 *Topic constructions of verbs*

In topic constructions of verbs, there is no obligatory morpho-syntactic marking on the topicalized verb. A verb appears in its bare form. While the lower verb is often associated with the copula, it is not obligatory either, especially in shorter

---

21. This possibility is not implausible. For example, predicate cleft in Bùlì is obligatorily marked by an overt nominalizing suffix (Hiraiwa 2002).

sentences. Note that I assume with C. C.-H. Cheung (2015) and Erlewine (2020b) that the copula verb *hai* serves as a focus particle instead of a genuine verb, when it is used to mark focus position (for discussions, see § 3.3.2.3).

(58)   The copula before the lower verb is optional
       Zou keoi (hai) wui **zou** ge2.
       do   s/he COP   will do   SFP
       'As for doing, s/he will do.'

Typically, the construction has a concessive character (Matthews and Yip 1998). It usually comes with the sentence-final particle *ge2*, which conveys concession or reservation. Alternatively, a *but*-clause in the continuation is preferred. Note that the concessive sense does not disappear even in the absence of *ge2* or a *but*-clause, as pointed out by Matthews and Yip (1998, p. 179).

(59)   The sentence-final particle *ge2* is optional
       Jam keoi wui **jam**. Batgwo m-wui jam   hou dou.
       drink s/he will drink but   not-will drink very much
       'As for drinking, s/he will drink. But s/he will not drink much.'

The schematic pattern of topic constructions of verbs is summarized in Table 3.2.

Table 3.2 The schematic pattern of topic constructions of verbs

Type	Left periphery	S	Marker	V_{base}	O	SFP	Right periphery
Topic-V	**V**	S	(*hai*)	**V**	O	(*ge2*)	–

Note that in the discussions of verb fronting in Matthews and Yip (1998) and Matthews and Yip (2011, p. 88–89), they present cases with *zau* 'then' (except a few examples with *dou* 'all', which is an instance of 'even'-focus constructions, under the classification in this chapter). For example,

(60)   Topic constructions of verbs with *zau* 'then'
       Leng zau **leng**. Batgwo zau gwai-zo   di.
       pretty then pretty but   then expensive-PERF a.bit
       '(If it is about whether it is) pretty, then it is pretty. But (it is) a bit expensive.'
                                                   (Matthews and Yip 2011, p. 89)

I exclude these cases in the discussions for a few reasons. First, these sentences may involve a biclausal structure, since *zau* 'then' signals the presence of a conditional clause.[22] The doubled verb may be a significantly reduced form of a

---

22. This possibility is also mentioned in Matthews and Yip (1998), but they suggest that this is the case for verb doubling in imperative sentences. I suggest that this applies to all *zau*-sentences.

44   The Unity of Movement

conditional clause, conveying a non-contrastive topic reading, e.g., 'if it is about whether it is *beautiful*' in (60).[23] Second, the initial verb need not have an exact copy in the original clause, as in (61).

(61)   No doubling effects with *zau* 'then'
       Context: in reply to the question of whether the speaker knows a lot of Chinese.
       Gong zau hai. **Tai** zau m-hai.
       speak then be   read than not-be
       '(If it is about) speaking, then yes. (If it is about) reading, then no.'
       (Matthews and Yip 2011, p. 88–89, adapted)

As will be discussed in greater details in §3.4.1, lexical identity effects are crucial to diagnose syntactic dependencies. For the rest of the chapter, I focus on cases with doubling effects only.

3.3.2.2   *'Even'-focus constructions of verbs*

Turning to 'even'-focus constructions, despite its name, the focus particle *lin* 'even' can be dropped.[24] What is obligatory in these constructions is the adverb *dou*, in addition to the verb doubling effects.

(62)   The obligatory *dou* and the optional *lin*
       (Lin) **tai**   aaming *(dou) m-**tai**   ni-bun syu wo4.
       even read Aaming also   not-read this-CL book SFP
       'Aaming didn't even READ this book (to my surprise).'

The construction is compatible with different sentence-final particles, such as the mirative *wo4* that conveys speakers' surprise, and the questions particle *me1*. It is also compatible with their absence (as in (28b)).

(63)   Compatibility with different SFPs
       Lin **tai** Aaming dou m-**tai**   ni-bun syu me1?
       even read Aaming also not-read this-CL book SFP.Q
       'Is it that case that Aaming didn't even READ this book?'

The schematic pattern of 'even'-focus constructions of verbs can be summarized as follows. The notation (any sfp) in the table indicates its optionality and unselectivity.

---

23. This is in line with the suggestion in Liu (2004) for Mandarin and Shanghainese that verb doubling (or identical topics in his term) may be grammaticalized from reduced conditionals.

24. The categorial status of *lin* 'even' is not uncontroversial. Here I assume Cantonese *lin* patterns with Mandarin *lian* in being a focus particle instead of a verb or other lexical categories (Tsai 1994; Shyu 2004; Badan 2007).

Chapter 3. Intervention effects   45

Table 3.3 The schematic pattern of 'even'-focus constructions of verbs

Type	Left periphery	S	Marker	V_{base}	O	SFP	Right periphery
'Even'-V	(*lin*)-V	S	*dou*	V	O	(any SFP)	–

Note that as with the object/phrasal counterparts, the *lin*-marked verb can appear in a clause-internal position after the subject, in addition to the clause-initial position. Throughout the discussion, I will not address the potential differences between these two positions of 'even'-focus (for discussions, see Shyu (1995), among others).

(64)   Clause-internal *lin* is possible
Aaming lin   **dim**   dou m-gam   **dim**   ni-zek dungmat.
Aaming even touch also not-dare touch this-CL animal
'Aaming doesn't even dare to TOUCH this animal.'

3.3.2.3   *Copula focus constructions of verbs*

The signature property of copula focus constructions of verbs is the obligatory presence of *hai* in the clause-initial position.[25]

(65)   Obligatory *hai*
*(Hai) **gong** Aaming m-sik   **gong** jatman ze1.
COP   speak Aaming not-know speak Japnese SFP
'Aaming does not know how to SPEAK Japanese only.'

Copula focus constructions should not be conflated with the more discussed *hai...ge3* cleft constructions (the Mandarin counterpart of *shi...de* cleft constructions). As observed in L. L. S. Cheng (2008), the copula focus constructions (= her bare-*shi* sentences) are incompatible with the sentence-final *de* in Mandarin, or *ge3* in Cantonese.

(66)   Incompatible with sentence-final *ge3*
*Hai **gong** Aaming m-sik   **gong** jatman ge3.
COP speak Aaming not-know speak Japnese SFP
Int.: 'Aaming does not know how to SPEAK Japanese only.'

There is a requirement on the choice of sentence-final particles. The sentence is degraded in the absence of restrictive/focus-related particles such as *ze1* or *zaa3* (cf. Fung 2000).[26]

---

25. Note that the categorial status of the copula verb is a matter of debate. C. C.-H. Cheung (2015) and Erlewine (2020b) argues that it is a focus marker, whereas L. L. S. Cheng (2008) and Pan (2019) suggest that it is a genuine copula verb (and involves a bi-clausal structure). The distinction does not bear on the discussion.

The Unity of Movement

(67) Obligatory restrictive sentence-final particles
Hai **gong** Aaming m-zik   **gong** jatman   [??](ze1/ zaa3).
COP speak Aaming not-know speak Jaapnese SFP   SFP
'Aaming does not know how to SPEAK Japanese only.'

The schematic pattern of copula focus constructions of verbs is summarized below.

Table 3.4 The schematic pattern of copula focus constructions of verbs

Type	Left periphery	S	Marker	V_{base}	O	SFP	Right periphery
Copula-V	*hai-V*	S	–	**V**	O	*ze1/zaa3*	–

Similar to the case of topic constructions of verbs discussed in §3.3.2.1, there appears to be a variant of copula focus constructions which involves *zau* 'then'. I (again) suggest that these cases may involve a reduced verbal conditional clause in a bi-clausal structure. Also, there are no lexical identity effects, as illustrated in (68). I exclude this type of constructions in the discussion and focus on the verb doubling cases.

(68) Copula focus constructions with *zau* 'then'
a. Hai **zau** nei zau faaidi   zau laa1.
   COP go you then quickly go SFP
   '(If it is decided to) go, then you should go quickly.'
b. Hai **zau** nei zau mai lam gam do   laa1.
   COP go you then not think too much SFP
   (If it is decided to) go, then you should not think too much.'

3.3.2.4 *Dislocation copying of verbs*

The defining property of dislocation copying of verbs is the final position of the doubled verb. In addition, sentence-final particles are obligatory in the construction. This applies to cases of right dislocation/dislocation copying in general (L. Y.-L. Cheung 1997; Lai 2019; K.-F. Yip 2020).

(69) Sentence-final particles are obligatory in dislocation copying of verbs
Ngo **jiu**   lok   gaai maai di je   *(aa3) **jiu**.
I   need down street buy CL thing SFP   need
'I need to go out to buy something.'

---

26. This is different from the clause-internal *hai*, where there is no such requirement on sentence-final particles. Note also its compatibitlity with *ge3*.

(i) Aaming hai m-sik   gong jatman   (ze1/ zaa3 / ge3).
    Aaming COP not-know speak Japanese SFP/ SFP/   SFP
    'Aaming (only) doesn't know how to speak Japanese.'

One related variant of dislocation copying of verbs is that the base verb may be dropped, and thus the doubling effects are not obligatory. This contrasts with the previous three constructions.

(70) Right dislocation/dislocation copying of verbs
    a. Ngo (**hai**) Hoenggong jan   aa3 **hai**.
        I   be   Hong.Kong person SFP be
        'I am a Hongkonger.'
    b. Aaming tingjat   (**hoji**) lai   aa3 **hoji**
        Aaming tomorrow may   come SFP may
        'Aaming may come tomorrow.'

Right dislocation of verbs of this kind is specifically discussed in Lee (2017, 2021a). I suggest that the two constructions are the same constructions and optionality in doubling arises as a consequence of phonological linearization (see Chapter 5 for further discussions). This issue, however, should not concern us in the current discussion of the locality issues of head movement. In the rest of this chapter, I focus on dislocation copying of verbs.

The schematic pattern of dislocations copying of verbs is represented below.

Table 3.5 The schematic pattern of dislocation copying of verbs

Type	Left periphery	S	Marker	V_{base}	O	SFP	Right periphery
DC-V	–	S	–	(V)	O	any SFP	V

3.3.2.5 *Interim summary*

The properties of the verb doubling constructions discussed this far are summarized in Table 3.6.

Table 3.6 The schematic patterns of verb doubling constructions

Type	Left periphery	S	Marker	V_{base}	O	SFP	Right periphery
Topic-V	V	S	(*hai*)	V	O	(*ge2*)	–
'Even'-V	(*lin-*)V	S	*dou*	V	O	(any SFP)	–
Copula-V	*hai*-V	S	–	V	O	*ze1/zaa3*	–
DC-V	–	S	–	(V)	O	any SFP	V

In terms of morpho-syntactic marking on the verb in the peripheral position, both topic constructions of verbs and dislocation copying of verbs require no marking, but the latter involve a verb in the *right* periphery. Morpho-syntactic marking is optional in 'even'-focus constructions of verbs (i.e., *lin*), but it is obligatory in copula focus constructions of verb (i.e., *hai*). This illustrates that the four verb doubling constructions are distinctive in morpho-syntactic term. As will be discussed shortly, they are also distinguishable in terms of discourse effects.

3.3.3 Discourse effects

As far as interpretation is concerned, the four verb doubling constructions are not discourse-neutral, when compared to the non-doubled counterparts. They are generally incompatible with out-of-the-blue contexts or the beginning of a story. This subsection describes the different discourse effects associated with these constructions in terms of information structure.

3.3.3.1 *Contrastive verbal topics*

In addition to topicality, it is suggested that topic constructions of verbs are used "to place two verbs in contrast" (Matthews and Yip 2011, p. 88). It is natural to have a continuation that contrasts the verb in the previous sentence.

(71) Contrasting two verbs in topic constructions of verbs
Maai keoi hai **maai**-zo ni-bun syu. Batgwo mei   tai.
buy   s/he COP buy-PERF this-CL book but   not.yet read
'As for buying, s/he has bought this book. But (s/he) have read (it).'

If a verbal alternative is contextually unavailable or pragmatically odd, a contrastive reading in topic constructions of verbs is difficult to obtain, resulting in infelicity.[27] This can be illustrated with the copula verb *hai* or the verb *sing* 'have.surname'.

(72) Verbs that fail in topic constructions of verbs
a. [#]**Hai**, Aaming **hai** daaihoksaang.
   COP Aaming COP university.student
   'Aaming is a university student.'
b. [#]**Sing**,   Aaming hai **sing**   Lei.
   have.surname Aaming COP have.surname Lee
   'Aaming has "Lee" as his surname.'

This suggests that the doubled verb serves as a contrastive topic in the construction. Cheng and Vicente (2013, p. 5, and fn. 5) note that this construction usually carries *verum focus*, which affirms the truth of the proposition. This can be attributed to the presence of the copula *hai* before the verb. Combining these ideas, the interpretation of (71) is that (i) the action of buying is contrasted with reading,

---

27. I thank Ka-Fai Yip for discussions.

and (ii) the sentence focuses on the truth of the proposition (i.e., 's/he has bought this book').

I discuss a piece of evidence from the ordering with regard to topics in support of the contrastive topic status of the doubled verb. The sentences in (73) show that the doubled verb has to follow a (non-contrasting) discourse topic.[28]

(73) A topic must precede a contrastive (verbal) topic
    a.   Gaauzi   ne1, **sik**, ngo hai **sik** ge2.
          dumpling TOP eat I   COP eat SFP
          'Dumplings, as for eating, I eat (them).'
    b. ??**Sik**, gaauzi   ne1, ngo hai **sik** ge2.
          eat dumpling TOP I   COP eat SFP
          'As for eating, dumplings, I eat (them).'

This follows if contrastive topics are indeed a sub-type of focus (topic foci, following Büring (1997) and Krifka (2008)), and if genuine topics have to precede foci in the CP periphery in Cantonese, i.e., the topic field is higher than the focus field (as argued for in C. C.-H. Cheung 2015).

3.3.3.2 *Additive verbal foci*

It is suggested that the 'even'-focus constructions in Mandarin convey an addictive focus reading with scalar interpretation, similar to English *even* (Shyu 1995; Badan 2007). This idea can be applied to 'even'-focus constructions of verbs. For example, in (74), *lin* picks out an eventuality, i.e., *mong* 'look', which represents one of the extremes on the scale of things that Aaming does not dare to do. The speaker asserts that this eventuality holds true among the things that Aaming does not dare to do to Aafan. It implies that all other non-extreme eventualities on the same scale, for example, talking to Aafan, are also true.

(74) Addictive focus in 'even'-focus constructions of verbs
    Lin **mong** Aaming dou m-gam **mong** Aafan. M-hou   waa tung keoi
    even look   Aaming also not-dare look   Aafan not-good say with her
    gongje.
    talk
    'Aaming doesn't even dare to LOOK AT Aafan, not to mention to talk to her.'

In the discussions of Mandarin cases, Cheng and Vicente (2013) observe that many cases of 'even'-focus constructions of verbs tend to occur with negation, which is not observed with the phrasal counterparts. They suggest that this is due to the scalarity requirement imposed on verbs, as it requires the verb to be

---

28. Similar examples are discussed briefly in Cheng and Vicente (2013, p. 5, fn.4).

connected to a scale. A scale can be established by polatrity (e.g., negation), or superlatives, as illustrated with the Cantonese in (75).

(75) Scalarity satisfed by a superlative expression
lin **jam** Aaming dou jiu **jam** zeoi peng ge jejam.
even drink Aaming also want drink most cheap MOD drink
'Aaming even wants to DRINK {the cheapest drink.'

However, there are cases of 'even'-focus construction of verbs that involve neither negation or superlatives. Matthews and Yip (1998) note that a verb suffixed by a potential particle -*dou* can also license 'even'-focus constructions of verbs.

(76) Verbs with a potential suffix
Haang dou **haang**-dou laa1. Gam kan!
walk also walk-able SFP so close
'We can even WALK there. So close!' (Matthews and Yip 1998, p. 183)

Additionally, replacing the superlative in the sentence in (75) with a definite expression is indeed possible.[29] The verb in (77) is not associated with negation or potential suffix either. I therefore suggest that there is no specific requirement on 'even'-focus constructions of verbs.

(77) Verbs with no marking
Lin **jam** Aaming dou jiu **jam** ni-zek paaizi. M-daanzi sik.
even drink Aaming also want drink this-CL brand. Not-only eat.
'Aaming even wants to DRINK (products of) this brand, not (p.c. Ka-Fai Yip)
just eating (products of this brand).'

Without going into the precise semantic formulation of 'even'-focus constructions, I follow Shyu (1995) and Badan (2007) and assume that the 'even'-focus constructions convey both additivity and scalarity. Particularly, the additiviy can be attributed to the focus particle *lin* (Cheng and Vicente 2013), whereas the scalarity derives from the maximality operator *dou*, which provides a scalar extreme (Giannakidou and Cheng 2006; Xiang 2008; Shyu 2016).

Similar to verbal topics, the verbs marked by *lin* have to follow discourse topics (cf. Badan 2007), further confirming their focus nature.

---

29. I thank Ka-Fai Yip for pointing out this to me.

(78) A topic must precede the *lin*-marked verb
    a. Ni-bou dinnou lin **jung** Aaming dou mou   jung-gwo.
       this-CL computer even use Aaming also not.have use-EXP
       'This computer, Aaming didn't even USE (it).'
    b. *Lin **jung** ni-bou dinnou   Aaming dou mou   jung-gwo.
       even use this-CL computer Aaming also not.have use-EXP
       Int.: 'This computer, Aaming didn't even USE (it).'

3.3.3.3 *Exhaustive verbal foci*

The signature feature of copula focus constructions is the exhaustive identification function (Paris 1998; C. C.-H. Cheung 2015; Pan 2019). Descriptively, when a verb is targeted in the construction, an exhaustive set of eventualities is presupposed. The sentence asserts that a given proposition holds true of the eventuality denoted by the verb, and all other alternatives in the set are false (C. C.-H. Cheung 2015; Zubizarreta and Vergnaud 2017, among others). This idea can be illustrated with the conjunction tests, which diagnose exhaustivity (C. C.-H. Cheung 2015; Zubizarreta and Vergnaud 2017). In (79), the first sentence indicates that the eventuality of touching is the *only* one that holds true among things that Aaming does not dare to do to the animal. It is incompatible with the follow-up clause that asserts another eventuality (i.e., 'look') that also holds true.[30]

(79) Conjunction tests as a diagnostic for exhaustivity
    Hai **dim** Aaming m-gam **dim** ni-zek dungmat ze1. *Keoi zung m-gam
    COP touch Aaming not-dare touch this-CL animal   SFP he   also not-dare
    mong tim1.
    look SFP
    'Aaming dare not to TOUCH this animal only. He also dare not to look at (it).'

Pan (2019) notes that there is a restriction on episodicity in copula focus constructions in Mandarin, which precludes episodic eventualities in copula focus constructions. However, no such restriction is observed with copula construction of verbs in Cantonese.[31]

---

30. The exhaustive identification may be attributed to the copula *hai* or to the SFP *ze1*. One possibility is that the SFP *ze1* supplies the exhaustive semantics (Fung 2000), and the copula *hai* restricts the focus scope to the immediately following constituent, e.g., the verb *dim* in (79). The choice does not bear on the discussion, however.

31. In fact, the restriction does not seem to hold in Cantonese in general.

    (i) No restriction on (non-)episodicity in copula focus construction of objects
        Hai **ni-bou dinnou** Aaming camjat   zing-laan-zo   ze1. Keita dinnou   dou
        COP this-CL computer Aaming yesterday make-broken-PERF SFP other computer all
        mou   mantai.
        not.have problem
        'It is only this computer that Aaming has broken yesterday. Other computers are fine.'

(80) No restriction on (non-)episodicity
Hai **fan** Aaming **fan**-zo singjat ze1. M-hai waan-zo singjat.
COP sleep Aaming sleep-PERF whole.day SFP not-COP play-PERF whole.day
'Aaming only SLEPT the whole day. He didn't hang out the whole day.'

As a final remark, ordering restrictions with respect to discourse topics show that *hai*-marked verbs are similar to verbal topics and *lin*-marked verbs: they must follow the discourse topic.

(81) A discourse topic must precede the *hai*-marked verb
   a. Tungseon ge jatman hai **gong** Aaming **gong**-m-dou ze1.
      fluent MOD Japanese COP speak Aaming speak-not-able SFP
      'Aaming cannot SPEAK fluent Japanese only.'
   b. *Hai **gong**, tungseon ge jatman, Aaming **gong**-m-dou ze1.
      COP speak fluent MOD Japanese Aaming speak-not-able SFP
      'Aaming cannot SPEAK fluent Japanese only.'

3.3.3.4 *Defocused verbs*

The discourse effects brought along by dislocation copying, as suggested in L. Y.-L. Cheung (2015), concern "emphasis, clarification and repair", but he also notes that "these pragmatic functions are relatively weak" (p.262). The precise information structural status of the doubled verbs, or more generally, the doubled elements, remains unclear in the literature. There are two apparently conflicting views. On one hand, L. Y.-L. Cheung (2015) and K. K. Chan (2016) suggest that the doubled elements receive minor emphatic interpretation (or a special kind of contrastive interpretation). On the other hand, Lee (2017, 2020) suggests that the post-sentence-final particle position is designated for defocused elements. Likewise, Lai (2019) mentions in passing that the dislocated elements are marked as given.

In what follows, I first show that the dislocated elements are not topics or informational focus. I then suggest how the two views are indeed compatible with each other. Particularly, I suggest that the doubled elements are defocused, and the reported emphatic effects come from the pragmatic effects of repetition of expressions.

Recall the observation in §3.3.1 and §3.3.3.1 that dislocation copying of verbs can target modal and the copula verb, which cannot be topicalized. This suggests that the verb in dislocation copying is qualitatively different from that in topic constructions, speaking against their status as verbal topics.

Furthermore, adopting the question-answer pair test in L. Y.-L. Cheung (1997) and K. K. Chan (2016), the question-answer pairs in (82) and (83) show that the doubled verb cannot serve as the answer to a question that focuses on the verb in as (82a), whereas the same sentence can felicitously answer a question that focuses, for example, the object, as in (83a). This suggests that the doubled verbs cannot serve as informational focus either.

(82) Verbs cannot serve as answers in dislocation copying of verbs
    a. Nei gammaan fan-m-fan   ni-zoeng cong aa3?
       you tonight   sleep-not-sleep this-CL bed SFP
       'Will you sleep on this bed tonight?'
    b. #Ngo gammaan **fan**   ni-zoeng cong aa3 **fan**.
       I   tonight   sleep this-CL bed SFP sleep
       'I (will) sleep on this bed tonight.'

(83) Objects can serve as answers in dislocation copying of verbs
    a. Nei gammaan fan   bin-zoeng cong aa3?
       you tonight   sleep which-CL bed SFP
       'Which bed will you sleep on tonight?'
    b. Ngo gammaan **fan**   ni-zoeng cong aa3 **fan**.   = (82b)
       I   tonight   sleep this-CL bed SFP sleep
       'I (will) sleep on this bed tonight.'

Furthermore, the doubled elements are unlikely to be interpreted as contrastive focus, at least in the standard sense, since they resist contrastive stress, as observed in L. Y.-L. Cheung (2015, p. 261). I illustrate this point with dislocation copying of verbs (where stress is indicated with capitals).

(84) No stress of the doubled verb
    #Ngo gammaan **fan**   ni-zoeng cong aa3 **FAN**.
    I   tonight   sleep this-CL bed SFP sleep
    'I (will) sleep on this bed tognight.'

In light of these observations, L. Y.-L. Cheung (2015) explores the possibility that the doubled elements mark a minor emphasis, or a special type of contrastive focus (that resists contrastive stress), whose function is "to highlight to the hearer a discrepancy between the assertion of the host clause and the speaker's supposition that the hearer is unlikely to take the assertion into the common ground" (p. 263). K. K. Chan (2016) similarly suggests that it is the background assumptions, instead of the focus, that is contrasted in dislocation copying.

Instead of positing a fine-grained distinction on the nature of contrastive focus, I suggest that the position following the sentence-final particles is designated for hosting defocused/given elements (Lee 2017, 2020; Lai 2019). The primary function of defocusing an element is to "enable a constituent to escape the focus domain and to realize its discourse linking in formal terms" (Molnárfi 2002, p. 1132). I suggest that defocus/antifocus is the counterpart notion of focus and can be marked grammatically (for discussions and cross-linguistic evidence, see Lee 2020).[32] This not only explains why the doubled elements resist focus (and topic) interpretation, but also uniformly accounts for the discourse functions of dislocation copying and right dislocation, which can be regarded as instantiations of a single process of defocalization.

As for the observed emphatic effects, I suggest that it is a pragmatic consequence of the repetition of expressions in general: when the same expression appear more than once, it naturally gives rise to a sense of emphasis, but it need not be prominent or contrastively focused.[33] This is why the doubled elements do not pattern with contrastive focus (as they resist focus stress). Indeed, the minor emphatic effects as depicted in L. Y.-L. Cheung (2015) are general enough to apply to other verb doubling constructions as well, all of which displays some level of emphatic effects on the verb. I therefore conclude that the verb in dislocation copying of verbs is defocused, a discourse function that is different from the other three verb doubling constructions.

Lastly, concerning the relative order between a defocused verb and a discourse topic, while a discourse topic can appear in the right periphery as in (85a), it cannot precede or follow a defocused verb as in (85b) and (85c).[34]

(85) A discourse topic cannot precede the defocused verb
    a.   ngo soeng maai gaa3, ni-bun syu
          I   want buy SFP this-CL book
          'I want to buy this book.'
    b. *ngo **soeng** maai gaa3, ni-bun syu, **soeng**
          I   want buy SFP this-CL book want
          'I want to buy this book.'
    c. ??ngo **soeng** maai gaa3, **soeng**, ni-bun syu
          I   want buy SFP want this-CL book
          'I want to buy this book.'

3.3.3.5 *Interim summary*

Taking stock, while the four verb doubling constructions convey different discourse effects, contrastiveness is a common property among the first three con-

---

32. It is not uncommon that defocused elements end up in the sentence-final position. See, for example, Takano (2014) for discussions in Japanese.

33. This possibility is also mentioned in passing in Lai (2019). Indeed, Martins (2007) discusses similar cases of verb doubling in European Portuguese and suggests that the constructions convey *emphatic affirmation*.

34. The unacceptability in (85c) is relatively less severe, especially when a pause is inserted between the verb and the topic, but a pause does not improve the sentence in (85b).

structures. This is correlated with the ordering restriction with discourse topics, i.e., contrastive elements must follow discourse topics. On the other hand, verbs in dislocation copying display an opposite pattern, where they receive a non-contrastive interpretation and they cannot follow a discourse topic. The observations in this subsection are summarized in Table 3.7.

Table 3.7 The discourse effects of the verb doubling constructions

Type	Discourse effects	Contrastiveness	Relative order with topics
Topic-V	contrastive topic	✓	Topic > V / *V > Topic
'Even'-V	additive focus	✓	Topic > V / *V > Topic
Copula-V	exhaustive focus	✓	Topic > V / *V > Topic
DC-V	defocused/given elements	✗	*Topic > V / ??V > Topic

I stress that these discourse effects observed in verb doubling constructions are largely similar, if not identical, to their phrasal counterparts in (27), as described in the literature. The only difference is the types of elements (i.e., heads vs. phrases) that are targeted.

3.4 Evidence for verb movement

In this section, I present evidence in favor of a movement analysis of verb doubling constructions. I suggest that the verb in the peripheral position and the verb in the base position are derivationally related by movement dependencies. Evidence comes from (i) lexical identity effects, (ii) island effects, and (iii) idiomatic expressions.

3.4.1 Lexical identity effects

This subsection reports the lexical identity effects in verb doubling constructions. Particularly, the verb in the (left or right) periphery must be identical to the verb in the base position. I argue that such identity effects reveal a dependency relation between the two verbs. More specifically, the dependency relation is *syntactic*, rather than *semantic*, i.e., two verbs must be the same lexical item, instead of sharing identical meaning, or standing in an entailment relation. Following much work in verb doubling/clefting (especially, Cable 2004; Vicente 2007; Cheng and Vicente 2013), I argue that lexical identity effects are a direct consequence of syntactic movement. It follows straightforwardly from the copy theory of movement

(Chomsky 1995b, *et seq.*), where syntactic movement creates a chain of multiple copies of the moving elements in the structure.[35]

In order to confirm the identity effects are by nature syntactic, instead of semantic, it is instructive to see whether non-identical verbs can appear in verb doubling constructions. Especially in topic constructions, two elements may display the so-called *genus-species effects*, where an element stands in an asymmetric entailment relation with another. For example, a base-generated (frame-setting) topic bears such a relation with a (more specified) nominal in the sentence, as in (86), where *tuna* entails *fish*.

(86) No lexical identity effects with base generated topics
Jyu ngo zungji sik tannaa.
fish I   like   eat tuna
'As for fish, I like eating tuna.'

If verb doubling constructions display a similar pattern, it can be taken as a piece of evidence against a movement dependency between the two verbs (cf. Cable 2004). I employ four pairs of verbs that are in genus-species relation, listed in (87).

(87) Pairs of verbs in asymmetric entailment relations
a. *caau* 'to fry' entails *zyu* 'to cook'
b. *paau* 'to run' entails *juk* 'to move'
c. *mo* 'to pet' entails *dim* 'to touch'
d. *fei* 'to fly to' entails *heoi* 'to go to'

Applying these verbs to the verb doubling constructions, it is observed that the more general verb cannot appear in the peripheral position. This speaks against a base generation analysis.

(88) Lexical identity, but not semantic entailment, is crucial
a. {**caau**/ *zyu} ngo hai soeng **caau** coi   ge2.
fry   cook I   COP want fry   vegetable SFP
'As for frying/ cooking, I want to fry the vegetables.'
b. Lin {**paau**/ *juk} Aaming dou m-gam   **paau**.
even run   move Aaming also not-dare run
'Aaming doesn't even dare to RUN/MOVE.'
c. Hai {**mo**/ *dim} Aaming m-gam   **mo** ni-zek dungmat ze1.
COP pet   touch Aaming not-dare pet this-CL animal   SFP
'Aaming dare not to PET/TOUCH this animal only.'

---

35. The doubling effects are not commonly observed with other instances of phrasal movement. I argue in Chapter 5 that this results from independent phonological requirements.

d. Aaming haanin **fei** Meigwok aa3 {**fei**/ *heoi}.
Aaming next.year fly US   SFP fly/ go
'Aaming (will) fly to US next year.'

Note that no lexical identity effects are observed with sentences with *zau* 'then'.
As suggested in §3.3.2.1, these sentences may involve a bi-clausal structure with
the first clause being a reduced conditional minimally containing a verb. This suggests the absence of syntactic dependencies between the two verbs.

(89) No identity effects in sentences with *zau* 'then'
     a. *Context: the interlocutors are discussing whether to cook at home or dine*
         out.
         Hai **zyu** ngo zau jigaa caau coi.
         COP cook I   then now fry vegetable
         '(If it is decided to) cook (at home), then I fry the vegetables now.'
     b. *Context: the interlocutors are discussing whether to go to the cinema.*
         Hai **heoi** ngo zau ceotfat laa3.
         COP go   I   then depart SFP
         '(If it is decided to) go, then I depart now.'

On the other hand, it is also instructive to consider another dimension of the
identity effects, namely, semantic identity. Here I adopt pairs of verbs that are
(nearly) semantically identical to each other. Three of them involve English loan-
words which have been phonologically adapted to the phonotactics in Cantonese.
For example, *cek1* is for 'check', *kip1* for 'keep' and *pi6sen1* for 'present' (with tones
indicated by the number). Another pair concerns two verbs of selling, namely,
fong 'let.go' and *maai* 'sell'. They are semantically identical in the context of, for
example, stock markets (but not all other contexts). Applying these verbs to verb
doubling constructions, it is observed that the verbs in the periphery have to be
lexically identical to the verb in the base position. Their semantically identical
counterparts are not acceptable in the same position.

(90) Lexical identity, but not semantic identity, is crucial
     a. {**caa**/ *cek} ngo hai **caa**-gwo ni-go jan.
         check/ check I   COP check-EXP this-CL person
         'As for checking, I have checked this person.'
     b. Lin {**kip**/ *bougun} Aaming dou m-soeng **kip**.
         even keep keep   Aaming also not-want keep
         'Aaming dones't even want to KEEP (it).'
     c. Hai {**pisen**/ *bougou} keoi mou   seonsam **pisen**-dak hou ze1.
         COP present present   s/he not.have confidence present-RES good SFP
         'S/he lacks the confidence to PRESENT well only.'

58 The Unity of Movement

    d.   Aaming tingjat   wui **fong** ni-di   gupiu aa3 {**fong**/ *maai}.
        Aaming tomorrow will see this-CL stock SFP sell   sell
        'Aaming will sell these stocks tomorrow.'

However, in sentences with *zau* 'then', the lexical identity effects disappear.

(91) No identity effects in sentences with *zau* 'then'
    a.   Hai **cek**   ngo zau tingjat   faan-heoi caa-haa   ngo bun geisibou.
        COP check I   then tomorrow back-go check-DEL my CL notebook
        '(If it is decided to) check, then I go back and check my notebook tomorrow.'
    b.   Hai **kip** ngo zau jigaa bougun-zyu sin1.
        COP keep I   then now keep-CONT SFP
        '(If it is decided to) keep, then I keep it for now first.'

I conclude that the lexical identity effects in verb doubling constructions reveal syntactic dependencies, rather than semantic dependencies, between the two verbs. Under the copy theory of movement, the doubling effects are a natural consequence of movement, where multiple copies may be phonologically realized in a movement chain. I take this as evidence for a movement analysis of verb doubling constructions.

Before I leave the discussions of lexical identity effects, there is an intriguing but puzzling difference among the four verb doubling constructions. Verbs in topic constructions, 'even'-focus constructions and copula focus constructions only allow doubling of the verb in bare form, to the exclusion of verbal suffixes. However, the verb in dislocation copying requires doubling of both the verb and its associated suffixes. The difference is illustrated in the sentences in (92), which contrast topic constructions of verbs and dislocation copying of verbs.

(92) An asymmetry on lexical identity effects among verb doubling constructions
    a.   **Ngo**-(*dou) Aaming hai **ngo**-dou   wan laa3.
        hungry-RES Aaming COP hungry-RES dizzy SFP
        'As for being hungry, Aaming is so hungry that he feels dizzy.'
    b.   Aaming **ngo-dou**   wan laa3 **ngo**-*(**dou**).
        Aaming hungry-RES dizzt SFP hungry-RES
        'Aaming is so hungry that he feels dizzy.'   (cf. L. Y.-L. Cheung 2015, p. 229)

One possible explanation to this asymmetry is to connect the difference to the different discourse effects of these constructions. For example, it may be that verbs in contrastive interpretations can only represent the eventuality proper, and thus only the bare form of the verb is targeted for interpretation. On the other hand, in non-contrastive (i.e., defocused) interpretation, the restriction does not apply and thus a suffixed verb can be targeted as a whole.[36, 37]

3.4.2 Island effects

This subsection examines the possible structural distance between the verb in the peripheral position and the verb in the canonical position. Since Ross (1967), it has generally been agreed that certain structural domains are inaccessible for syntactic operations or dependencies. In this subsection, I show that the verbs in verb doubling constructions are sensitive to "island effects," a typical characteristic of movement dependencies. Furthermore, I show that the two verbs can occur at a distance and tolerate a clausal (CP) boundaries.

3.4.2.1 *Island sensitivity*

The verb in the peripheral position and the verb in the base position cannot be intervened by "island" boundaries. Typical "islands" include (i) complements of a noun phrase, (ii) relative clauses, (iii) adjunct clauses and (iv) sentential subjects. The first two can be subsumed under the Subjacency Condition (Chomsky 1973, 1981), whereas the last two fall under the Condition on Extraction Domain (Huang 1982). The following four sets of data show that the verb doubling constructions become unacceptable if the base verb originates in these domains, respectively illustrated in (93), (94), (95), and (96).

(93) NP complement
    a. *Tai ngo tungji go-go [keoi hai **tai**-gwo] ge jigin.
        read I agree that-CL s/he COP read-EXP MOD opinion
        Int.: 'As for reading, I agree with the opinion that s/he has read (it).'
    b. *Lin **zau** ngo gamjat dou tingdou [Aaming **zau**-dak maan-gwo jan].
        even leave I today also hear Aaming leave-RES slow-than person
        ge siusik.
        MOD rumor
        Int.: 'Today I heard that rumor that Aaming is slower than others even in LEAVING.'

---

36. This, however, does not explain why doubling of the suffix is obligatory, instead of optional, in dislocation copying. I have to leave this issue open.

37. Another possibility is to connect the asymmetry to the split between left and right periphery of the verb doubling constructions. I leave this possibility for future research.

60 The Unity of Movement

(94) Relative clauses
    a. *Hai **dim** ngo jicin gin-gwo ni-zek [Aaming m-gam **dim**] ge
        COP touch I   once see-exp this-CL Aaming not-dare touch MOD
        dungmat.
        animal
        Int.: 'I once saw this animal – one that Aaming dare not to TOUCH only.'
    b. *Aaming soeng hok [Aafan **hoji** gong] ge ni-saam-zung jyujin   aa3
        Aaming want learn Aafan can speak MOD this-three-CL language SFP
        hoji.
        can
        Int.: 'Aaming wants to learn these three languages that Aafan can speak.'

(95) Adjuncts
    a. *tai [hai Aaming hai **tai**-jyun bun syu zihau], ngo sin faan-dou
        read at   Aaming COP read-finish CL book after   I   first return-arrive
        ukkei.
        home
        Int.: 'As for reading, I was back after Aaming has already finished reading
        the book.'
    b. *Lin **zau**, [janwai Aaming dou **zau**-dak maan-gwo jan],   soji ngo
        even leave because Aaming also leave-RES slow-than person so   I
        mou   dang keoi.
        not.have wait him
        'Since Aaming is slower than others even in LEAVING, I didn't wait for
        him.'

(96) Sentential subjects[38]
    a. *Hai **gong** [Aaming **gong**-m-dou   jatman] ling   Aafan hou
        COP speak Aaming speak-not-able Japanese make Aafan very
        satmon.
        disappointed
        'That Aaming cannot SPEAK Japanese only disappoints Aafan.'
    b. *[Aaming gammaan **fan**   ni-zoeng cong] jiging   mouhobeimin laa3 **fan**.
        Aaming tonight   sleep this-CL bed   already unavoidable
        'That Aaming (will) sleep on this bed tonight is unavoidable.'

---

38. Matthews and Yip (1998) report that topic constructions of verbs can occur across sentential subject islands. They provide the following example, but my informants report that this
sentence is unacceptable, contrary to their observation.

(96)   Sentential subjects and topic constructions of verbs
     *Teoijau ngo gokdak 65 seoi   mei   **teoijau** mou   mantai.
     retire I   think   65 year.old not.yet retire not.have problem
     'As for retiring, I think not retiring at 65 years old is fine.'
                             (Matthews and Yip 1998, p. 181–182)

Since island sensitivity is typically taken as evidence for movement dependencies, I suggest that these observations support a movement analysis of verb doubling constructions.

3.4.2.2 *Long-distance/Cross-clausal dependencies*

While the two verbs in verb doubling constructions cannot be separated by island boundaries, they can be intervened by a clausal/CP boundary. In the sentences in (98), the clausal boundary is established by attitude verbs or verbs of saying, so the clausal boundary is presumably as large as a CP. Note that (98d) involves multiple CP boundaries.

(98) Cross-clausal dependencies in verb doubling constructions

    a. **Soeng** ngo lam [Aaming hai **soeng** heoi ni-go wuiji] ge2.
        want I   think Aaming COP want go this-CL meeting SFP
        'I think Aaming wants to go to this meeting.'

    b. Lin **maai** ngo gu [Aaming dou mei **maai** ni-bun syu].
        even buy I   guess Aaming also not.yet buy this-CL book
        'I guess Aaming has not even BOUGHT this book.'

    c. Hai **zou** ngo gokdak [Aaming m-soeng **zou** san lau] ze1.
        COP rent I   think Aaming not-want rent new house SFP
        'I think Aaming does not want to RENT a new house only.'

    d. Ngo ting [tinhei bougou waa [tingjat **honang** lokjyu wo5]] **honang**.
        I   hear weather report say tomorrow possible rain SFP possible
        'I heard from the weather report that it may rain tomorrow.'

Although long-distance/cross-clausal dependencies do not necessitate a movement analysis,[39] they are predicted by a movement analysis to be possible. Note that these case demonstrate the HMC-violating property of verb doubling constructions, since, the dependencies between the two verbs are intervened by overt heads, namely, the embedding attitude verbs or the verbs of saying.

3.4.2.3 *Interim summary*

The locality effects with regard to (im)penetrability can be summarized in (99). The dependencies between the two verbs in verb doubling constructions hold across CP boundaries, but not island boundaries.

---

39. This is because, for example, an unselective binding approach can also capture long-distance dependencies (Heim 1982). For proposal and application on interrogative clauses, see Tsai (1994), among others.

(99)   A schematic representation of the locality effects in verb doubling constructions

$$V_{periphery} \cdots \left\{ \begin{array}{l} \text{CP boundaries} \\ \text{*Island boundaries} \end{array} \right\} \cdots V_{base}$$

3.4.3   Idiomatic expressions

Separability of idiomatic expressions, is often taken as evidence for movement. The validity of this argument builds on a particular assumption on the analysis of idiomatic expressions in natural language. It is commonly assumed that an idiomatic expression must form a constituent, either in the lexicon (Jackendoff 1997) or in a local domain in the course of derivation (Marantz 1997). With either one of these assumptions, idiom chunks can be used to diagnose the base position of the displaced elements. In our cases of verb doubling, a movement analysis predicts that the verb in an idiomatic expression can occur in verb doubling constructions without losing its idiomatic meaning.[40] This is borne out in (100).

(100)   Idiomatic expressions in verb doubling constructions
a.   **Put** ngo hai honang **put**-zo   nei laang seoi. Batgwo ngo zihai soeng
      pour I   COP possible spill-PERF you cold   water but   I   only want
      giklai   nei ze1.
      encourage you SFP
      Idiomatic reading: 'I may have spoiled your pleasure, but I only want to encourage you.'
b.   Lin **ceoi** Aaming dou m-tung   ngo **ceoi** seoi. M-hou   waa king
      even blow Aaming also not-with me blow water not-good say discuss
      zingging je.
      serious   thing
      Idiomatic reading: 'Aaming didn't even CHIT-CHAT with me, not to mention discuss serious things.'
c.   Hai **duk** Aaming **duk**-gwo nei   buizek ze1. Keoi mou   dongmin
      COP poke Aaming poke   your back   SFP he   not.have face.to.face
      naau-gwo nei aa3.
      scold-EXP you SFP
      Idiomatic reading: 'Aaming has STABBED AT YOUR BACK only. He hasn't scold at you face to face.'

---

40. The same test is adopted to diagnose movement for copula focus constructions in C. C.-H. Cheung (2015).

d. Ni-zek laaihaamou **soeng** sik tinngo juk   aa3 **soeng**.
    this-CL toad   want eat swan   meat SFP want
    Idiomatic reading: 'This person is craving for what s/he is not worthy of.'

It should be noted that in (100a–c), the contrastive interpretation does not fall exclusively on the verb in the peripheral position. Instead, it is the whole VP that is focused. This can be illustrated by the continuing clauses that contrast the first clause with another VP. This observation is by no means unique to idiomatic expressions, as illustrated with the 'even'-focus construction of verbs below.

(101)   VP focus interpretation in 'even'-focus constructions of verbs
        Lin **sik** jau jan   dou **sik**-m-saai   ni-fan saaleot. M-hou   waa
        even eat have person also eat-not-finish this-CL salad   not-good say
        jam-maai bui gaafe.
        drink-also CL coffee
        'There is someone who cannot even FINISH THIS SALAD, not to mention drink the coffee.'

The more salient VP-focus reading (i.e., more salient than a V-focus reading) is presumably due to the fact that the idiomatic expressions are VP (V+O) expressions and that it is difficult, if not impossible, to focus on the verb to the exclusion of the object (while maintaining the idiomatic readings).[41]

3.5   Focus Intervention Effects

Before I turn to a movement analysis of the verb doubling constructions in Cantonese, I further show that the dependency between the verb in the base position and the verb in the peripheral position may be disrupted by intervention of an element with certain qualities. In what follows, I examine three types of potential intervening elements: verbs, focused elements, and quantificational elements. The empirical observations with regard to intervention effects are summarized in (102).

(102)   (Non-)intervening elements in verb doubling constructions
        a. Verbs/Heads do not cause intervention effects.
        b. Focused elements create intervention effects (except in dislocation copying of verbs).
        c. Quantificational elements do not cause intervention effects.

---

41. The mismatch between morpho-syntactic focus marking and the scope of focus interpretation falls into another interesting line of study concerning *anti-pied-piping* (Branan and Erlewine 2020), which does not bear on the discussion here, however.

The findings reveal that the verb doubling constructions exhibit intervention effects triggered by focused elements, but not elements of the same structural types (i.e., heads).

3.5.1 No intervention by heads

As discussed in §3.2, head movement is said to be constrained by the Head Movement Constraint (Travis 1984) or Relativized Minimality (Rizzi 1990). This suggests that intervention effects would be induced by intervening verbs/heads in case of verb movement. However, the following data show that verbs in the peripheral positions in verb doubling constructions tolerate intervening verbs. In all the cases in (103), the verbs in the base and peripheral positions are intervened by an (overt) head element, e.g., a control verb or a modal verb. Note that in terms of *linear order*, the modal verb *wui* in (103d) does not "intervene" the two copies of *heoi* 'go'. Anticipating a movement analysis of dislocation copying, where the dislocated verb is suggested to move across the modal verb at some point in the derivation, the verb in the peripheral position in (103d) is comparable to the other three constructions in terms of *hierarchy structure*.

(103) No intervention effects triggered by intervening verbs
    a. **Heoi**, Aaming hai <u>soeng</u> **heoi** Meigwok ge2.
        go   Aaming COP want go   US   SFP
        'As for going, Aaming wants to go to the US.'
    b. Lin **gong** Aaming dou m-<u>sik</u>   **gong**.
        even speak Aaming also not-know speak
        'Aaming doesn't even know how to SPEAK.'
    c. Hai **dim** Aaming m-<u>gam</u> **dim** ni-zek dungmat ze1.   =(28c)
        COP touch Aaming not-dare touch this-CL animal   SFP
        'Aaming dare not to TOUCH this animal only.'
    d. Aaming <u>wui</u> **heoi** maai ni-bun syu aa3 **heoi**.
        Aaming will go buy this- book SFP go
        'Aaming will go to buy this book.'

In other words, verb doubling constructions display a HMC-violating property. These cases are configurationally uniform (at least at some point of their derivation) with respect to the presence of intervening heads.

(104) (The absence of) intervention effects in verb doubling constructions, part 1

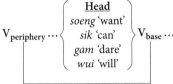

3.5.2 Intervention by focused elements

While heads do not cause intervention effects in verb doubling constructions, this subsection reveals that *focused elements* disrupt the relation between the verb in the peripheral position and the verb in the base position. To illustrate this point, I adopt two types of (in-situ) focused elements (i) focused elements associated with *dak* 'only' (Tang 2002), and (ii) *wh*-nominals, which bear inherent focus (Rochemont 1986; Horvath 1986; Shi 1994; S.-S. Kim 2006).

As a remark on the basic properties of *dak* 'only' in Cantonese, *dak* 'only' conveys an (exhaustive) focus reading on the constituent to its right (Tang 2002). It can appear in both preverbal and postverbal positions, exemplified in (105).

(105) The distribution of the focus operator *dak* 'only'
    a. Preveal *dak* and subject focus
        Dak [ngo]$_{Focus}$ faatbiu jigin.
        only I   express opinion
        'Only I express opinions.'   (Tang 2002, p,281)
    b. Postverbal *dak* and object focus
        Keoi tai-dak   [saam-bun syu]$_{Focus}$.
        s/he read-only three-CL book
        'S/he read only three books.'   (Tang 2002, p. 267)

In terms of syntactic category, Tang (2002) argues that the preverbal *dak* is a verb and the postverbal *dak* is a verbal suffix. He also observes that postverbal *dak* imposes a cardinality requirement on its associate, which is absent in preverbal *dak*. Since the discussion here focuses on the structural position of focused elements, these differences do not bear on the argumentation.

In what follows, I show that *dak* 'only' may cause intervention effects between the two copies of verbs in three out of four verb doubling constructions (with the exception of dislocation copying of verbs). Specifically, it causes intervention effects when it is associated with a pre-verbal element (e.g., a subject), but not with a post-verbal element (e.g., an object). First, in the topic constructions of verbs in (106), the *dak*-associate cannot appear in the subject position, as opposed to the object position.

66   The Unity of Movement

(106)   Subject vs. object focus in topic constructions of verbs
    a.   *__Heoi__ dak Aaming hai soeng **heoi** Meigwok.
        go   only Aaming COP soeng heoi US
        'As for going, only Aaming wants to go to the US.'
    b.   **Heoi** Aaming hai **heoi**-dak jat-go deifong.
        go   Aaming COP go-only one-CL place
        'As for going, Aaming has been to only one place.'

Note that the focus operator *hai* does not induce intervention effects in (106b), suggesting that it is the focused elements, but not the focus particles/operators that are responsible for the intervention effects. Indeed, it is possible to add another focus operator, *zinghai* 'only' (associating with the object), before the verb in (106b), and no intervention effects are observed (the same is also observed in (108b) and (110b)).

(107)   Focus operators do not trigger intervention effects
    Heoi Aaming hai zinghai **heoi**-dak jat-go deifong.
    go   Aaming COP only   go-only one-CL place
    'As for going, Aaming has been to only one place.'

Similarly, in 'even'-focus constructions of verbs, the *dak*-associate in the pre-verbal position leads to intervention effects, as in (108a), as opposed to the *dak*-associate in the post-verbal position, as in (108b).

(108)   Subject vs. object focus in 'even'-focus constructions of verbs
    a.   *Lin **haang** dak Aaming dou **haang**-m-dou sap fanzung. M-hou   waa
        even walk   only Aaming also walk-not-able ten minute   not-good say
        paau.
        run
        'Only Aaming cannot even WALK for ten minutes, not to mention run.'
    b.   Lin **haang** Aaming dou zinghai **haang**-dak sap fanzung. M-hou   waa
        even walk Aaming also only   walk-able ten minute   not-good say
        paau.
        run
        'Aaming can WALK only for ten minutes, not to mention run.'

One might suggest that the unacceptability of (108a) is due to the fact that the *dak*-associate intervenes the *lin*-V ... *dou* construction, instead of the V-V dependency. This is not the case, however, since the intervention effects persist even if *dou* occurs before the *dak*-associate. This is shown in (109), which involves a bi-clausal structure.[42] Crucially, *dou* surfaces in the matrix clause, whereas the *dak*-associate is in the embedded clause.

(109) Intervention effects induced between the two verbs, not *lin* and *dou*
    *Lin **haang** ngo dou jingwai [dak Aaming **haang**-m-dou sap fanzung].
    even walk I   also think   only Aaming walk-not-able ten minute
    M-hou   waa paau.
    not-good say run
    'I think that only Aaming cannot even WALK for ten minutes, not to mention run.'

In a parallel fashion, similar intervention effects are observed in copula focus constructions of verbs as in (110).

(110) Subject vs. object focus in copula focus constructions of verbs
    a. *Hai **maai** dak Aaming **maai**-m-hei ni-gaan uk   ze1. Keoi zou-dak-hei.
        cop buy   only Aaming buy-not-up this-CL house SFP he   rent-able-up
        'Only Aaming cannot BUY this house only. He can (afford) renting it.'
    b. Hai **maai** Aaming zinghai **maai**-dak jat-gaan uk   ze1. Zou gewaa keoi
        cop buy   Aaming only   buy-only one-CL house SFP rent if   he
        hoji zou gei-gaan.
        can rent several-CL
        'Aaming can BUY only one house only. If (it is about) renting, he can (afford) renting several houses.'

However, it is important to note that similar intervention effects do not replicate in dislocation copying of verbs, as in (111): both sentences are acceptable.

(111) Subject vs. object focus in dislocation copying of verbs
    a. dak Aaming gammaan **hoji** fan   baat-go zung zaa3 **hoji**.
        only Aaming tonight   can sleep eight-CL hour SFP can
        'Only Aaming can sleep for eight hours tonight.'
    b. Aaming gammaan zinghai **hoji** fan-dak   jat-go zung zaa3 **hoji**.
        Aaming tonight   only   can sleep-only one-CL hour SFP can
        'Aaming can sleep for only one hour tonight.'

I now turn to *wh*-expressions, which may induce similar intervention effects as *dak*-associates. Here, I follow Rochemont (1986), Horvath (1986), Shi (1994), and S.-S. Kim (2006) and assume that *wh*-expressions bear inherent focus (despite the absence of overt morpho-syntactic focus marking). *Wh*-expressions in the subject position are disallowed in verb doubling constructions, but they are acceptable

---

42. For discussions on the positions of *dou*, see Shyu (1995) for the Mandarin counterpart *lian...dou* constructions.

68 The Unity of Movement

in the object position. This is illustrated with topic constructions of verbs in (112) and 'even'-focus constructions verbs in (113).

(112) Subject vs. object *wh*-expressions in topic constructions of verbs
    a. ***Soeng** bingo hai **soeng** heoi Meigwok?
       want who COP want go US
       'Who wants to go to the US?'
    b. **Soeng** Aaming hai **soeng** heoi bindou?
       want Aaming COP want go where
       'Where does Aaming want to go?'

(113) Subject vs. object *wh*-expressions in 'even'-focus constructions of verbs
    a. *Lin **haang** bingo dou **haang**-m-dou sap fanzun?
       even walk who also walk-not-able ten minute
       'Who can't even WALK for ten minutes?'
    b. Lin **haang** Aaming dou **haang**-m-dou geidou fanzung?
       even walk Aaming also walk-not-able how.many minute
       'For how many minutes does Aaming even fail to WALK?'

Turning to copula focus constructions of verbs, there is a complication. The sentences are unacceptable regardless of the position of the *wh*-expressions, as in (114a–b). Indeed, in the absence of verb doubling, the sentence in (114c) is still unacceptable. This suggests that copula focus constructions of verbs are incompatible with *wh*-expressions in general. So there is no evidence for the intervention effects in copula focus constructions from *wh*-expressions.[43]

(114) Subject vs. object *wh*-expressions in copula focus constructions of verbs
    a. *Hai **maai** bingo **maai**-m-hei ni-gaan uk zaa3?
       COP buy who buy-not-up this-CL house SFP
       Int.: 'Who is person such that s/he cannot BUY this house only?'
    b. *Hai **maai** Aaming **maai**-m-hei bin-gaan uk zaa3?
       COP buy Aaming buy-not-up which-CL house SFP
       Int: 'Which is the house such that Aaming cannot BUY it only?'

---

43. The incompatibility between exhaustive/restrictive focus and *wh*-expressions has been noted in Mandarin (S.-S. Kim 2002a, 2002b, 2006; Soh 2005; Yang 2008, 2012; Li and Cheung 2012, 2015). Indeed, S.-S. Kim (2006) and Yang (2012) further note that additive focus is also incompatible with *wh*-expressions in Mandarin, but Cantonese is different in this regard, given the acceptability of (113) and the following sentence in (i).

  (i) Additive focus and *wh*-expressions
     lin Aaming dou soeng maai matje?
     even Aaming also want buy what
     'What is the thing such that even Aaming also wants to buy it?'

c. *Aaming maai-m-hei bin-gaan uk   zaa3?
   Aaming buy-not-up which-CL house SFP
   Int.: 'Which is the only house such that Aaming cannot buy it?'

(cf. S. P. Cheng 2015, p.169)

Finally, dislocation copying of verbs do not exhibit intervention effects due to the presence of *wh*-expressions. Both sentences in (115) are acceptable no matter whether the *wh*-expression is in the the pre-verbal or in the post-verbal position.

(115) Subject vs. object *wh*-expressions in dislocation copying of verbs
   a. Bingo gammaan **hoji** fan   baat-go zung aa3 **hoji**?
      who tonight   can sleep eight-CL hour SFP can
      'Who can sleep for eight hours tonight?'
   b. Aaming gammaan **hoji** fan   geinoi   aa3 **hoji**?
      Aaming tonight   can sleep how.long SFP can
      'How long can Aaming sleep tonight?'

Table 3.8 sums up the discussion above: focused elements in the subject/preverbal position induce intervention effects in three out of four verb doubling constructions. In (i) topic, (ii) 'even'-focus, and (iii) copula focus constructions of verbs, the relation between the verb in the peripheral position and the verb in the base position is disrupted by focused elements in the preverbal position. However, no similar intervention effects are observed in dislocation copying of verbs.

Table 3.8 The intervention effects observed with verb doubling constructions

Type	Preverbal *dak*-focus	Preverbal *wh*-expressions
Topic-V	*(106)	*(112)
Even-V	*(108)	*(113)
Copula-V	*(110)	N/A (cf. (114))
DC-V	OK(111)	OK(115)

Indeed, focus interveners are not restricted to *dak*-associates and *wh*-expressions. Subjects associated with *lin* 'even' or the copula *hai* are also potential interveners, as shown in (116).

(116) Intervention effects triggered by other focused elements
   a. ***Soeng**, lin   Aaaming dou hai m-**soeng** heoi Meigwok.
      want   even Aaming also COP not-want go US
      Int.: 'Even Aaming didn't want to go to the US.'

70 The Unity of Movement

b. *Lin **mong** hai Aaming dou m-gam **mong** Aafan.
   even look COP Aaming also not-dare look Aafan
   Int.: 'Only Aaming does not even dare to LOOK at Aafan.'

c. *Hai **dim** lin Aaming dou m-gam **dim** ni-zek dungmat.
   COP touch even Aaming also not-dare touch this-CL animal
   'Even Aaming does not dare to TOUCH this animal only.'

Furthermore, the interveners need not be in the subject position to block verb doubling. Elements associated with *dak* in the preverbal position also lead to intervention effects. In all the sentences in (117), the verb doubling constructions are blocked by a non-subject element associated with the preverbal *dak*. Note that the sentences are well-formed in the absence of these elements.

(117) Intervention effects triggered by focused elements in non-subject position

a. ***Soeng** dak ni-bun syu Aaming hai **soeng** maai.
   want only this-CL book Aaming COP want buy
   Int.: 'Aaming WANTS to buy only this book.'

b. *Lin **mong**, dak ni-go jan, Aaming dou m-gam **mong**.
   even look only this-CL person Aaming also not-dare look
   Int.: 'Only this person is such that Aaming does not even dare to LOOK at him/her.'

c. *Hai **gong**, dak Jatman, Aaming **gong**-m-dou ze1.
   COP speak only Japanese Aaming speak-not-able SFP
   Int.: 'Only Japanese is such that Aaming cannot SPEAK only.'

This allows us to generalize the intervention effects observed in verb doubling constructions in (118).

(118) Intervention effects in verb doubling constructions, part 2 (to be expanded)
Focused elements cannot intervene between the verb in the peripheral position and the verb in the base position in (i) topic, (ii) 'even'-focus, and (iii) copula focus constructions of verbs.

$$V_{periphery} \cdots \left\{ \begin{array}{c} \underline{\textbf{Preverbal position}} \\ \text{*Focused elements} \end{array} \right\} \cdots V_{base} \cdots \left\{ \begin{array}{c} \underline{\textbf{Postverbal position}} \\ \text{OKFocused elements} \end{array} \right\}$$

3.5.3 No intervention by quantificational elements

To delimit the range of intervening elements in verb doubling constructions, I discuss quantificational elements in verb doubling constructions. They are interveners in *wh*-questions involving *wh*-adverbs in Mandarin (Soh 2005; Yang 2008, 2012), and in other phenomena (Rizzi 2001, 2004). I show that elements such as existential markers, nominal quantifiers, modal verbs and negation, but no intervention effects are observed in any of the verb doubling constructions.

The sentences in (119) involve existential sentences in verb doubling constructions. The existential verb *jau* 'have' and its associating nominals can occur in the preverbal position without triggering any intervention effects.

(119) Existential *jau*-sentences in verb doubling constructions
    a. **Soeng** jau saam-go jan   hai **soeng** heoi Meigwok ge2.
        want have three-CL person COP want go US   SFP
        'There are three people who want to go to the US.'
    b. Lin **haang** jau   hoksaang dou **haang**-m-dou sap fanzung.
        even walk have student   also walk-not-able ten minute
        'There are students who cannot even WALK for ten minutes.'
    c. Hai **maai** jau di jan   **maai**-m-hei ni-gaan uk   ze1.
        COP buy have CL person buy-not-up this-CL hose SFP
        'Some people cannot afford BUYING this house only.'
    d. Jau jan   gammaan **hoji** fan   ni-zoeng cong aa3 **hoji**.
        have person tonight   can sleep this-CL bed SFP can
        'Someone can sleep on this bed tonight.'

As for other quantificational elements, I include both subject quantifiers (of various kinds) and modal verbs in the sentences in (120). Again, no intervention effects are observed. Note that (120a/c) also involve preverbal negation (i.e., the prefixal *m-* and the negative verb *mou* 'not.have'), but they do not cause intervention effects either.

(120) Subject quantifiers, modal verbs and negation in verb doubling constructions
    a. **Soeng** cyunbou hoksaang dou jinggoi hai m-**soeng** heoi Meigwok ge2.
        want every   student   all should COP not-want go US   SFP
        'Every students probably don't want to go to the US.'
    b. Lin **haang** houdou jan   dou honang **haang**-m-dou sap fanzung.
        even walk many   person also possible walk-not-able ten minute
        'Many people cannot even WALK for ten minutes.'
    c. Hai **maai** mou   jan   gam **maai** ni-gaan uk   ze1.
        COP buy not.have person dare buy this-CL house SFP
        'No one dare BUY this house only.'
    d. Daaiboufan jan   gammaan dou jatding   **hoji** fan baat-go zung aa3
        majority   person tonight   all necessary can sleep eight-CL hour SFP
        hoji.
        can
        'The majority of the people must be able to sleep for eight hours tonight.'

Summing up, various quantificational elements can freely occupy the subject/preveral position between the two verbs in verb doubling constructions, in contrast to focused elements.

(121) (The absence of) intervention effects in verb doubling constructions, part 3 (to be expanded)

$$V_{periphery} \ldots \left\{ \begin{array}{c} \underline{\text{Preverbal position}} \\ ^{OK}\text{quantificational elements} \end{array} \right\} \ldots V_{base} \ldots \text{(Object)}$$

3.5.4 Interim summary

Taking stock, it was first shown that verb doubling constructions tolerate intervening heads between the two verbs. Then it was revealed that verb doubling constructions disallow intervening focus elements in the subject or preverbal positions. On the other hand, quantificational elements in the same position do not induce similar intervention effects. A summary is given in (122).

(122) Focus Intervention Effects in verb doubling constructions (final)
Focused elements cannot intervene between the verb in the peripheral position and the verb in the base position in (i) topic, (ii) 'even'-focus, and (iii) copula focus constructions of verbs.

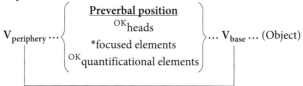

Put differently, the intervention effects observed with verb doubling constructions should be characterized as *focus intervention effects* (cf. S.-S. Kim 2002a, 2002b, 2006; Soh 2005; Yang 2008, 2012; Li and Cheung 2012, 2015), but not *quantifier intervention effects* (cf. Linebarger 1987; Beck 1996, 2006; Beck and Kim 1997).

3.6 Proposal: Head movement to the specifier position

In view of the empirical observations presented in previous sections, I propose that in all four verb doubling constructions, verb movement (head movement) is involved in their derivation. All of them are triggered by discourse features, and the verb moves to a specifier position of a functional head in the CP periphery.

I assume the minimalist framework of Chomsky (2000, 2001), where feature checking is achieved via an Agree operation. I also adopt the suggestion in Pesetsky and Torrego (2007) that feature interpretability and feature valuation are independent of each other, i.e., uninterpretable features may enter the syntax being valued or unvalued, and vice versa.[44]

(123) Feature checking/valuation and the operation Agree under a Probe-Goal system

    a. An unintrepretable feature F on a *probe* searches its c-command domain and Agrees with another instance of F, a *goal.*

    b. Agree between a probe and a goal is based on a Matching or non-distinctness relation (i.e., feature identity independently of value).

    c. Agree is subject to the locality condition of closest c-command.

    d. The value of a probe or a goal is assigned to the other.

    e. The uninterpretable feature on the probe is deleted upon Agree for LF convergence.

Furthermore, I adopt a split CP framework after Rizzi (1997), where the CP projection contains a number of functional projections responsible for discourse information and clause-typing. The precise components and orderings of these projections will be detailed in the proposal.

3.6.1 Details of the proposal

There are three components in the proposal: (i) feature specification, (ii) feature distribution, and (iii) head movement. First, I suggest that there are two discourse features that can be associated with syntactic constituents, namely the [Focus] feature and the [Defocus] feature.[45] Furthermore, I suggest that the uninterpretable [Focus]/[Defocus] features (henceforth [*u*Focus]/[*u*Defocus]) enter the syntax with a specific value, whereas the interpretable counterparts (i.e.,

---

44. In the proposal in Chomsky (2001, p.5), it is suggested that "the uninterpretable features, and only these, enter the derivation without values, and are distinguished from interpretable features by virtue of this property." Pesetsky and Torrego (2007) develops a theory of feature valuation and interpretability that relaxes this valuation-interpretability biconditional.

45. This amounts to saying that that defocused interpretation should be treated on a par with focus interpretation, in the sense that both notions have syntactic manifestations (as discourse features). This suggestion is defended in Lee (2020) based on cross-linguistic evidence. Similar features have been proposed for right dislocation in Japanese (Takano 2014) and scrambling in modern Afrikaans and West Germanic languages (Molnárfi 2002). A slightly different suggestion is proposed in Lai (2019), where a structure-building feature attracts a constituent to a position that is interpreted as given information in dislocation copying. I do not further distinguish a defocus feature and a structure-building feature responsible for attracting given information.

[*iFocus*]/[*iDefocus*]) are unvalued (cf. the feature system in Pesetsky and Torrego 2007). The value for [*uFocus*] can be CON for contrastive, ADD for additive, and EXH for exhaustive, but there is only one value for [*uDefocus*], i.e., DEF for defocus. The feature specification is summarized in Table 3.9.

Table 3.9 Feature specification of the focus and defocus features in Cantonese

Feature	Uninterpretable feature	Interpretable feature
Focus feature	[*u*Focus: CON/ADD/EXH]	[*i*Focus: _]
Defocus feature	[*u*Defocus: DEF]	[*i*Defocus: _]

As for the distribution of these features, I suggest that the interpretable features are assigned to constituents (e.g., verbs in our cases of verb doubling constructions), and that the uninterpretable features are held by different functional heads in the CP domain.[46] Specifically, I propose that there are different phonological realizations of the Focus heads, under different feature specifications.

Lastly, I suggest that movement of a constituent is independently triggered by an EPP feature on the focus/defocus heads. This EPP feature triggers movement upon successful establishment of an Agree relation between a probe and a goal. The movement of the goal targets the specifier position of the probe. Applying this to the verb doubling constructions in Cantonese, the verbs bearing the interpretable features would move to the specifier position of the Focus head or the Defocus head in the CP domain due to the presence of an EPP feature. This amounts to the suggestion of head-to-specifier movement in the sense of Toyoshima (2000, 2001), Matushansky (2006), Vicente (2007), and Harizanov (2019).[47]

---

46. This is similar to the suggestion in Li and Cheung (2012, 2015) that focus particles bear uninterpretable features, whereas focused phrases bear interpretable features. However, this is different from the suggestion in S.-S. Kim (2006), for example. For discussions, see §3.6.3.

47. A technical concern on head-to-specifier movement (as opposed to the head-to-head adjunction approach (Baker 1988, *et seq.*)) is that it violates the Chain Uniformity Condition (CUC), as stated in (i).

(i) Chain Uniformity Condition (CUC) (Chomsky 1995a, p.406)
A chain is uniform with regard to phrase structure status.

If phrase structure status is to be construed as the level of projection, the issue with head-to-specifier movement is that a head, which is projecting, moves to a specifier position and becomes non-projecting. In view of this, a strong thesis is to abandon CUC entirely (Nunes 1998; Toyoshima 2000, 2001). A weak thesis, following Fukui and Takano (1998), is to suggest that CUC only requires *non-distinctness*, instead of *uniformity*, with regard to phrase structural status. Substantially, the head in its base position and the head in the specifier are non-distinct

Table 3.10 Distribution of the uninterpretable focus/defocus features and their realizations

Construction	Head in the CP domain	Feature	Phonological realization
Topic-V	Focus	[*u*Focus: Con]	null (ø)
'Even'-V	Focus	[*u*Focus: Add]	*lin* or null (ø)
Copula-V	Focus	[*u*Focus: Exh]	*hai*
DC-V	Defocus	[*u*Defocus: Def]	null (ø)

Two remarks are in order. First, it should be noted that the proposal does not provide an explanation of the doubling effects in verb doubling constructions. I assume that the verb movement chains are exempted from the copy deletion operation (under the copy theory of movement, Chomsky (1995b, *et seq.*)). See some relevant discussions in §3.6.3.2. Chapter 5 is dedicated to this issue. Second, I stress that the proposal here is not restricted to verb doubling constructions. It also can readily be extended to the phrasal counterparts of the verb doubling constructions in (27) as discussed in §3.1, if the relavent features are associated with phrasal elements. I return to this issue in §3.8.2.

3.6.2 An illustration of the proposal

A schematic representation of the proposal is given in (124), which reflects a particular step of the derivation in verb doubling constructions (but *not* the ultimate structure). This is intended to illustrate the time when the probes (i.e., the Focus head and the Defocus head) have successfully located their matching goals in the c-command domain. Specifically, in verb doubling constructions, the first step is that the probe, [*u*Focus] or [*u*Defocus], finds the matching feature [*i*Focus: _] or [*i*Defocus: _] on the V in the VP. Then, the probe Agrees with its goal (value assignment and feature deletion not shown). Due to the presence of an EPP feature of the Focus/Defocus head, the V moves to the specifier of the corresponding head.

---

in the sense that both are not projected elements, despite the above noted difference. Indeed, the head-to-head adjunction approach to head movement also requires similar relaxation of CUC. I suggest that CUC cannot be maintained in its original form, although I do not commit myself to how it should be revised. For further justification of head-to-specifier movement, see Toyoshima (2001), Surányi (2005), Matushansky (2006), and Vicente (2007), among others.

(124) A schematic representation of the proposed head-to-specifier movement

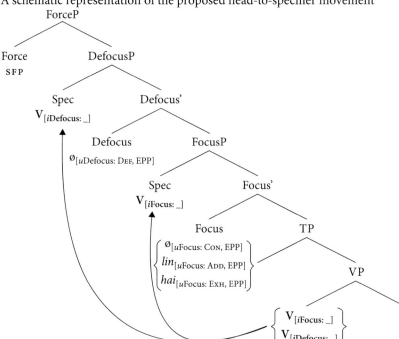

Two qualifications are in order. First, the structure in (124) is a halfway derivation of verb doubling constructions. The derivation continues with a subsequent phrasal movement into the specifier position of ForceP. Since ForceP is headed by sentence-final particles, I refer to this movement as *SFP-driven movement* for convenience.[48] By way of illustration, in topic constructions, 'even'-focus constructions and copula focus constructions, the FocusP undergoes this SFP-driven movement to Spec ForceP, deriving the verb-initial order, as depicted in (125a). On the other hand, in dislocation copying, the TP (but not the DefocusP) undergoes the SFP-driven movement, stranding the verb in Spec DefocusP, as depicted in (125b). Note that the proposed structure in (124) allows the co-occurrence of DefocusP and FocusP. In such case, FocusP undergoes SFP-driven movement, stranding (again) the DefocusP, as depicted in (125c).

(125) SFP-driven movement (to the specifier position of ForceP)

a.

FocusP movement

---

48. I return to the justification of this movement shortly.

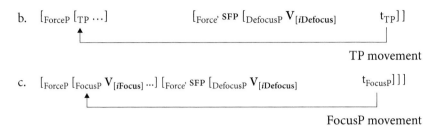

TP movement

FocusP movement

To see examples of (125c), consider the sentences in (126). In (126a), the verb *maai* 'buy' is topicalized (i.e., it bears the [*iFocus*] feature), whereas the modal verb *jinggoi* 'should' is right-dislocated and doubled (i.e., it bears the [*iDefocus*] feature). The SFP-driven movement strands the DefocusP. Similar can be said to (126b), where the verb *sik* 'eat' is focused and the verb *jiu* 'want' is defocused.

(126) Co-occurrence of DefocusP and FocusP
 a. **Maai**, Aaming **jinggoi** hai soeng **maai ge2 jinggoi**.
  buy Aaming should COP want buy SFP should
  'As for buying, Aaming probably wants to buy this book.'
 b. Lin **sik** Aaming dou **jiu** **sik** zeoi gai   ge je aa3 **jiu**.
  even eat Aaming also want eat most expensive MOD thing SFP want
  'Aaming even wants to EAT the most expensive thing.'

Turning to the nature of the SFP-driven movement, it is by no means an *ad hoc* movement operation to derive the word order in verb doubling constructions. It is a commonly assumed step for proposals that adopt a head-initial analysis of sentence-final particles in Chinese. The general idea is that in order to derive the final position of sentence-final particles, the main clause must move to a higher position, following the spirit of the Linear Correspondence Axiom (Kayne 1994). For example, in a regular declarative sentence, SFP-movement is still needed, schematized in (127).

(127) SFP-movement, in the absence of DefocusP and FocusP

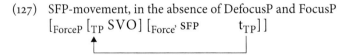

This movement step is not only proposed or assumed in works on right dislocation in L. Y.-L. Cheung (2009), Lee (2017), Wei and Li (2018), and Lai (2019), but also in works on the sentence-final particles, such as Tang (1998b), Sybesma (1999), Simpson and Wu (2002), Lin (2010), Hsieh and Sybesma (2011), and Pan (2020) (see also Simpson (2014) for overview and references therein). In other words, the SFP-driven movement is a step needed independently of verb doubling constructions.

78   The Unity of Movement

Second, for 'even'-focus constructions and copula focus constructions, there are ordering issues with regard to the surface position of the focus particles *lin* and *hai* and their focus associates. In the structure in (124), the word appears to be V-*lin/hai*, contrary to facts. I suggest that both *lin* and *hai* are prefixes in need of phonological support, and that they are prefixed on their focus associate in the specifier position upon Spell-Out such that they appear to the left of their focus associates.[49]

3.6.3   Deriving the properties of verb doubling constructions

3.6.3.1   *The ordering of the functional projections in the CP periphery*

Recall the section summary in §3.3.3, repeated below in Table 3.11. In the proposal, I suggested that a Focus head is involved in three out of four verb doubling constructions, with the exception that a Defocus head is designated for dislocation copying. I suggest that this distinction is made based on whether the verb in the relevant constructions involve a contrastive interpretation or not.

Table 3.11 The discourse effects of the verb doubling constructions (repeated)

Type	Discourse effects	Contrastiveness	Relative order with topics
Topic-V	contrastive topic	✓	Topic > V / *V > Topic
'Even'-V	additive focus	✓	Topic > V / *V > Topic
Copula-V	exhaustive focus	✓	Topic > V / *V > Topic
DC-V	defocused/given elements	✗	*Topic > V / ??V > Topic

Also, I have assumed that DefocusP is structurally higher than the FocusP. In effect, this ensures that verbs that receive a contrastive reading appear sentence-initially (when FocusP undergoes the SFP-driven movement), whereas those that do not appear sentence-finally (when the SFP-driven movement strands DefocusP).

A remaining issue is the relative order between DefocusP/FocusP and discourse topics. The relative order between the verbs and topics in Table 3.11 follows

---

49. Another possibility is that the focus particles, *lin* and *hai*, undergo a short head movement to a position above its specifier. This suggestion is made in the analysis of *dak* 'only' in Tang (2002). This option is plausible under the assumption that *dak* is a genuine verb and the head movement is indeed short verb movement that is common in Chinese (Huang 1994). I do not adopt this possibility, since I suggest that *lin* and *hai* are differnt from *dak* in this regard, and I treat them as functional categories, following Shyu (1995) and C. C.-H. Cheung (2008, 2015).

if we assume a TopicP that is sandwiched between DefocusP and FocusP. The clausal structure in the CP domain is depicted in (128).

(128)   The proposed left periphery in Cantonese
        ForceP > DefocusP > TopicP > FocusP > TP

This straightforwardly explains why a discourse topic must precede a verb in the left periphery: because TopicP is structurally higher the FocusP. On the other hand, it also accounts for why a topic cannot precded a verb in the right periphery: because DefocusP is higher than TopicP. As for why a defocused verb cannot precede a topic, I suggest that DefocusP has to be stranded when SFP-driven movement applies to the structure, whereas TopicP must undergo SFP-driven movement.[50]

Note that the suggestion here is consistent with the topography of CP periphery put forth for Cantonese in C. C.-H. Cheung (2015), where the focus "field" is located below the topic "field" (cf. Benincà Paola and Poletto 2004). With the introduction of DefocusP, it seems plausible to suggest that both DefocusP and TopicP fall into the topic "field," since they involve non-contrastive interpretations.

3.6.3.2   *The movement properties in verb doubling constructions*

The lexical identity effects discussed in §3.4.1 follow from a movement analysis, particularly from the copy theory of movement (Chomsky 1995b; Nunes 1995, 2004). Under this theory, movement chains create two identical copies of the moving elements (instead of leaving behind traces). Usually, the lower copy is deleted by a mechanism (i.e., copy deletion) in the interface system, and only the higher copy survives. However, it has been suggested that the mechanism of copy deletion is not hard-wired and can be disrupted or suspended due to independent reasons (Bošković 2007; Nunes 2011). I suggest that this is the case for verb doubling constructions. In other words, instead of taking "gapless" structures as evidence against movement, I suggest that "gapless" structures with lexical identity effects are indeed evidence *for* movement. The exceptional realization of the lower copy is due to independent constraints in the interface system responsible for linearization. For a detailed proposal on the doubling effects in verb doubling constructions, see Chapter 5.

The summary of the locality effects with regard to (im)penetrability is repeated in (129). While certain syntactic configurations constitute syntactic

---

50. It should be acknowledged that the basis of this suggestion is empirical. To the extent that the precise nature of SFP-driven movement is not entirely clear in the literature, I do not attempt a deeper explanation on this property of DefocusP.

"islands" and are inaccessible to movement operations, CP boundaries do not constitute syntactic islands.

(129) A schematic representation of the locality effects in verb doubling constructions

$$V_{periphery} \cdots \begin{Bmatrix} CP\ boundaries \\ *Island\ boundaries \end{Bmatrix} \cdots V_{base}$$

Such a locality profile is not unique to verb doubling constructions in Cantonese, but has been reported in many other cases of verb movement (Koopman 1984; Vicente 2007; Harizanov and Gribanova 2019, among many others; see discussions in §3.2).

To the extent that such a locality profile is similar to typical instances of A'-movement (Chomsky 1973, et seq.), I assume that the verb movement in the long-distance verb doubling constructions proceeds in a successive cyclic fashion, and stops at an intermediate position, i.e., the specifier position of CP, before exiting a CP. This is illustrated in (98) (cf. long-distance A'-movement (Chomsky 2000; 2001, among many others)).

(130) A schematic representation of long-distance verb doubling constructions
[$_{FocusP/DefocusP}$ V$_{periphery}$ [$_{TP}$ ... [$_{CP}$ V$_{intermediate}$ C [$_{TP}$ ... V$_{base}$ ...]]]]

3.6.3.3 A syntactic explanation to Focus Intervention Effects

In §3.5, I arrived at the generalization of Focus Intervention Effects, repeated in (131).

(131) Focus Intervention Effects in verb doubling constructions (final)
Focused elements cannot intervene between the verb in the peripheral position and the verb in the base position in (i) topic, (ii) 'even'-focus, and (iii) copula focus constructions of verbs.

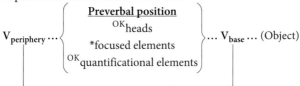

I suggest that Focus Intervention Effects are a natural consequence of the locality condition of Agree (Chomsky 2000, 2001), where Agree is subject to the locality condition of closest c-command. I illustrate this idea with the schematic structure in (132). I omitted the ForceP and the EPP features for their irrelevance.

(132) A configuration of Focus Intervention Effects in verb doubling constructions

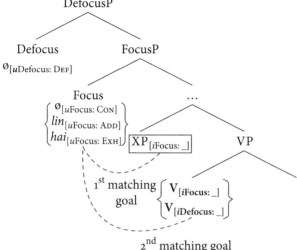

In (132), an focused element, XP, intervenes between the Focus head and the verb. Both the XP and the verb bear the [*i*Focus: _] feature. At the time when the Focus head searches its c-command domain for a matching feature, it encounters the structurally closer XP, before the verb in the VP. Under the locality conditions of Agree, the Focus head must Agree with XP instead of the verb. In other words, the verb cannot be successfully targeted for movement in the presence of a structurally higher focused element.

In contrast, no intervention effects are observed if the focused element is in the object/postverbal position, since it does not intervene between the Focus head and the verb. Also, a verb or a quantificational element would not intervene if they do not possess the [*i*Focus:_]. Additionally, Focus Intervention Effects do not arise in dislocation copying, since the [*i*Focus:_] on the XP is not a matching for the Defocus head. The [*i*Defocus:_] on the verb is the first matching Goal for the Defocus head. This delivers the Focus Intervention Effects. This explanation amounts to a featural characterization of the intervener for head movement. More generally, this can be regarded as a natural extension of the feature-based relativized minimality discussed in Rizzi (2001, 2004), which applies to both head and phrasal movement.[51]

The derivation in (132) would be well-formed if the Focus head Agrees with XP, instead of the verb. For example, in (133a), the focus head *lin* can be associated

---

51. A similar feature-based approach to constrain head movement is suggested in Roberts (2001, p.140–145), where he discusses Long Head Movement in Breton. This possibility is also mentioned in passing in Toyoshima (2001).

82 The Unity of Movement

with a preverbal *wh*-expression.[52] In (133b), the focus head *hai* is associated with *dak* and its associate.[53, 54]

(133) Focus heads Agree with intervening focused elements
    a. Lin bingo dou tai-gwo ni-bun syu?
       even who also read-EXP this-CL book
       'Even WHO has read this book?'
    b. Hai dak Aaming m-gam dim ni-zek dongmat ze1.
       COP only Aaming not-dare touch this animal SFP
       'Only AAMING does not dare to touch this animal.'

It should be remarked that the suggestion here amounts to a *syntactic* account to intervention effects along the line of Rizzi (2001, 2004), S.-S. Kim (2006), Yang (2008, 2012), and Li and Cheung (2012, 2015), instead of a *semantic* account to intervention effects (Beck 1996; 2006; Beck and Kim 1997, among many others). The motivation for the former comes from the observation that focus operators by themselves do not cause intervention effects, as discussed in §3.5.2. For example, in (107), repeated in (134), *zinghai* 'only' in the preverbal position does not cause intervention effects.[55]

(134) Focus operators do not trigger intervention effects
    Heoi Aaming hai zinghai. **heoi**-dak jat-go deifong.   (= (107))
    go Aaming COP only go-only one-CL place
    'As for going, Aaming has been to only one place.'

A semantic approach to intervention effects would predict that the lower focus operator (i.e., *zinghai*) would block a higher focus operator (i.e., the (null) Focus head), since the former consumes all the alternatives within its local domain, before the latter can locate its focus associate. However, the sentence is well-formed. The acceptability of (134) follows from the current proposal, if *zinghai* does not bear any [*u*Focus] feature, and thus does not intervene between the two verbs.[56]

---

52. Similar cases involving double association with focus and question operators are discussed in Li and Cheung (2012, 2015).

53. (133b) raises an issue of how double exhaustive focus marking is interpreted compositionally, on which I am agnostic. However, as far as syntactic dependencies are concerned, this configuration would be allowed if *dak* also bears a [*u*Focus] feature, and thus both *dak* and *hai* Agrees with the [*i*Focus] feature on *Aaming*.

54. In principle, movement to Spec FocusP is involved, but, as suggested, *lin* and *hai* are prefixal elements and would be linearized to the left of the focused elements, rendering the movement string-vacuous.

55. Similar examples include (108) and (110), as well as *dak* 'only' in (133b).

3.7 Alternative analyses to a head movement approach

Two types of alternative analyses of the kinds of patterns are considered here. Non-movement approaches might suggest that the two verbs in verb doubling constructions are not (directly) related by movement dependencies. Phrasal movement approaches would suggest that the moving constituent is not a head but a phrase. I discuss these two approaches (and their variants) in the following subsections, respectively.

3.7.1 Non-movement approaches

Since verb doubling constructions involve "gapless" structures, this provides some initial motivation to pursue a non-movement/base generation account. While, to the best of my knowledge, no base generation account has been proposed for verb doubling constructions, their phrasal counterparts have been independently argued to involve base generation, especially in "gapless cases". However, I will first show that a direct application of a base generation approach to verb doubling constructions fails to capture the properties observed in previous sections. For the sake of argument, I explore a more specific version of base generation, which is coupled with operator movement. I again show that this hybrid approach does not capture the relevant facts and leads to undesirable predictions.

3.7.1.1 *Base generation*

As far as discourse effects are concerned, each of the verb doubling constructions has a phrasal counterpart that does not involve a gap, illustrated in (135) (cf. their gapped counterparts in (27)).

---

56. This amounts to the suggestion that not all focus operators bear [*u*Focus]. One possible explanation for this split is that focus operators with [*u*Focus] trigger movement of the focused elements, whereas those without it do not. This is supported by that fact that *zinghai* can occur at a distance with its focus associate, i.e., *jat-go deifong* 'one place' in (134). Its contrasts with *lin*, *hai* and *dak*.

(135) Examples of "gapless" cases
- a. Topic constructions with an "aboutness" relation
  Seoigwo ngo zeoi zungji monggwo.
  fruit I most like mango
  'For fruits, I like mango the most.' (Chao 1968, among others)
- b. 'Even'-focus constructions with resumptive pronouns
  Lin **Aaming**$_i$ Aafan dou m-tai **keoi**$_i$ ge syu.
  even Aaming Aafan also not-read his MOD book
  'Aafan didn't even read AAMING's book.' (cf. Shyu 1995, p. 139)
- c. Copula focus constructions with resumptive pronouns
  Hai **ni-go doujin**$_i$ Mingzai zeoi zungji tai **keoi**$_i$ pak ge dinjing.
  COP this-CL director Mingzai most like watch s/he shoot MOD film
  'Mingzai like to watch the films directed by THIS DIRECTOR the most.'
  (cf. C. C.-H. Cheung 2015, p. 95, modified)
- d. Dislocation copying with non-identical copies
  Gam **keoi**$_i$ zau-m-zau hou ne1 **Fatgwok lou**$_i$?
  then he leave-not-leave good SFP France guy
  'Then should he, the French guy, leave?' (L. Y.-L. Cheung 2015, p. 230)

It is commonly suggested that these sentences involve base generation of a nominal phrase in the periphery position. The nominal phrase establishes a non-movement dependency with its associates, which may be a semantically related category in (135a) or a resumptive pronoun in (135b–d).[57] Applying this idea to verb doubling constructions, one may posit that a verb is base generated in the peripheral position and is associated with the verb in the base position via a non-movement dependency. As such, no (head) movement is needed.

However, such a base generation approach fails to account for the properties of verb doubling constructions. First, in the cases in (135), the base generated element need not be lexically identical to its associate, as long as they are semantically related. This differs substantially from verb doubling constructions which exhibit the lexical identity effects, as discussed in § 3.4.1.

Second, and more importantly, a signature property of base generation structures is their island insensitivity. For example, in the sentences in (135b) and (135c), the resumptive pronoun in both cases is embedded in a complex nominal structure. However, no island effects are observed. This is in sharp contrast with verb doubling constructions, since, they have been shown to be sensitive to syntactic islands in § 3.4.2.[58]

---

57. It is possible that resumption also involves movement (for recent discussions of Cantonese, see Yip and Ahenkorah (to appear).

Lastly, a base generation does not predict Focus Intervention Effects, as detailed in §3.5. It is unclear how the base generation of verbs in the peripheral position would be intervened by focused elements, given the lack of syntactic dependencies between the two verbs.

3.7.1.2 *Base generation plus operator movement*

Before a base generation approach is entirely dismissed, it is instructive to note that the issue of island sensitivity might be circumvented, if the base generation approach is equipped with operator movement, whose availability in Chinese is independently motivated.

In such an approach, it might be suggested that, while the verb in the peripheral position is base generated, movement of a null operator occurs in the lower clause. The dependency between the two verbs is thus indirect: it is mediated by a null operator that establishes a predication relation. Importantly, island sensitivity follows from the hypothetical operator movement, instead of head movement. Drawing largely on the analysis proposed for *dak* 'only' in Tang (2002), I suggest that a conceivable implementation of his idea to verb doubling constructions consists of two steps: first, a null operator (of the same semantic type as verbs) moves to the edge of the clause; second, the clause is predicated on the base generated verb in the periphery.[59] This idea is illustrated in (136).[60]

---

58. Pan (2019) argues that copula focus constructions (or ex-situ focus cleft constructions, in his terminology) in Mandarin involve base generation structures. His proposal is based on the observation that there is no island sensitivity in the copula focus constructions in Mandarin. Given the crucial difference in empirical observations, I suggest that the derivation for copula focus constructions are different in Cantonese and Mandarin.

59. Operator movements have been independently motivated on empirical grounds, including passive constructions (**Ting:1995**) and relative structures involving *wh*-adjuncts (e.g., Aoun and Li 2003). Although these proposals are proposed for Mandarin, as far as I can see, the argumentation largely be applied to Cantonese as well.

60. This approach is indeed similar to a suggestion in defense of a base generation analysis in Cable (2004) and Vicente (2007), where a verb may be base-generated in the edge of the lower clause (i.e., Spec CP). When this CP is is embedded in an syntactic island, movement of this base-generated verb to the matrix periphery position would violate island conditions. In this approach, verb movement is still needed, and the only difference with the proposed head movement approach lies in the base generation position of the verb. Furthermore, unlike the case in Yiddish, verb doubling constructions in Cantonese display lexical identity effects as shown in §3.4.1, and thus there is little motivation to posit a base generated verb at Spec CP.

(136) An illustration of a base generation plus operator movement analysis
[FocusP V [Focus' Focus [TP OP [TP Subject ... t_OP ... (Object)]]]]

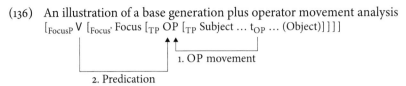

where OP is of the same semantic type as verbs

As a note on the legitimacy of operator movement, this can be construed as a syntactic correlate of a semantic operation, namely, *lambda conversion*, which converts a proposition/TP into a predicate that denotes a relation. Abstracting away from irrelevant details, the semantic denotation of the FocusP in (136) can be given in (137).

(137) The denotation of the TP in (136)
λR [R(x,y)] *where R denotes a relation, x is the subject and y the object (if any)*

Since this hybrid approach involves movement, it handles the locality effects better than a pure base generation approach. Island sensitivity follows, since operator movement should be constrained in a similar way. It is expected to violate island conditions if the operator is embedded in the relevant structures and undergoes movement into a higher clause. In order to derive Focus Intervention Effects, it must be assumed that the operator movement under discussion by nature is a kind of focus movement, such that it is sensitive to intervening focused elements. Although it remains unclear why this must be the case (given that not all cases of operator movement are focus-related), the assumption does not seem implausible.

However, there are a number of challenges to this approach. First, additional assumptions are needed to accommodate the lexical identity effects. For example, it must be assumed that, at the point of predication, the operator does not only absorb the semantic content of the verb, but also its phonological content (which is then transmitted to its trace/lower copy), resulting in verb doubling. This represents, as far as I know, an unprecedented way to derive doubling effects, and its validity hinges on a general theory of syntactic operators, which I cannot do justice here.

A more substantial challenge comes from the idiom chunks as discussed in §3.4.3. Under this base generation approach, the verb in an idiomatic expression enters into the structure independently of the rest of the expression. It is thus predicted that the idiomatic reading should be unavailable; however, this is not the case.

3.7.2 Phrasal movement approaches

Another alternative to the proposed head movement is to maintain that there are movement dependencies between the two verbs in verb doubling constructions, but the moving element is a phrase, instead of a head, and what occupies the peripheral position is a VP instead of a single V head. As such, what appears to be head movement is phrasal movement in disguise.[61]

(138) A hypothetical phrasal movement in verb doubling constructions

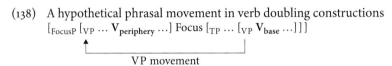

There are at least two conceivable ways to derive a VP that contains only a V head, which I explicate (and argue against) in the following two subsections.

3.7.2.1 Remnant VP movement

One way to create a VP that contains only a head is to posit independent movement operations that evacuate the VP before movement of the VP. To illustrate the idea, imagine a VP that consists of a verb and its object. Before the VP moves to the periphery position, the object moves out of VP for independent reasons. It could be an instance of object scrambling or object shift. Subsequently, when the VP moves at a later step in the derivation, it moves as if the verb alone is moving.

(139) A hypothetical *remnant* phrasal movement in verb doubling constructions, version 1

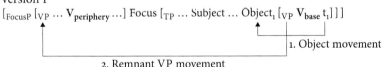

This approach is argued to be responsible for predicate fronting in German and Russian (see, for example, den Besten and Webelhuth 1990; Abels 2001, among many others), both of which has a considerably productive mechanism of (object) scrambling.

In order to apply this approach to verb doubling constructions in Cantonese, two issues have to be addressed. First, object movement (or any movement operation that evacuates the VP) must be independently motivated for each case of verb doubling constructions.[62] This is not implausible, since the object may be fronted

---

61. VP movement in the relevant constructions is allowed, although there is no doubling effects on the verbs; see discussions in §3.8.2.

for contrastive focus in Cantonese, giving a SOV word order.[63] If, in each case of verb doubling constructions, the object (if any) is fronted, then the object in verb doubling constructions must always be in contrastive focus. This is, however, not the case.

Second, and more critically, the word order depicted in (139), i.e., VSOV, is not the surface word order for verb doubling constructions. An extra movement step of the VP must be posited. Particular, after object movement, the VP must then move to a position before the object.

(140) A hypothetical *remnant* phrasal movement in verb doubling constructions, version 2

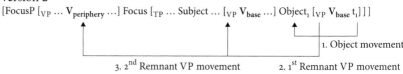

Furthermore, it has to be assumed that the lowest VP has to be deleted whereas the intermediate VP has to be pronounced, such that the sentences are only pronounced with two verbs but not three in verb doubling constructions. To the extent that the movement operation and th Spell-Out mechanism is not independently motivated, they appear to be *ad hoc* operations specifically designed for verb doubling construction to derive the word order.

3.7.2.2 *VP movement with subsequent deletion*

Another way to create a VP that contains a single verb is that the VP moves to the periperhal position and then a subsequent deletion operation erases everything but the verb, as depicted in (141).

(141) A hypothetical phrasal movement with deletion in verb doubling constructions

[$_{FocusP}$ [$_{VP}$ **V**$_{periphery}$ O̶b̶j̶e̶c̶t̶] Focus [$_{TP}$ Subject [$_{VP}$ **V**$_{base}$ Object]]]

VP movement + object deletion

---

62. Hinterhölzl (2002) suggests that the VP-evacuating movement can be regarded as *a licensing movement* for remnant movement. In other words, these movements need not correspond to other attested movement operations in the language, and are parasitic on remnant movement. This suggestion is criticized in Landau (2006) and Cheng and Vicente (2013). I do not pursue this possibility further.

63. But other kinds of object scrambling is highly restricted in Chinese, see Soh (1998) and Cheng and Vicente (2013).

The validity of this approach, thus, hinges on the validity of the precise nature of this deletion operation. There are a few possibilities for this deletion. First, since I have assumed the copy theory of movement and a mechanism of copy deletion, it might be that the object in (141) is deleted at the interface component. However, this requires non-standard positional deletion, i.e., deletion of the higher copy, instead of the lower copy.[64] Furthermore, the deletion must be *partial*, as it deletes only a subpart of the whole VP.[65] Based on the standard understanding of mechanisms of copy deletion, I reject this possibility.

Second, the deletion of the object in (141) might be regarded as an instance of *argument ellipsis*, where a missing argument does not leave behind a pronominal, variable or nominal trace.[66] However, it has been shown that the distribution of missing objects is restricted. For example, there are verbs that cannot take a null clausal object. I contrast the verb *gu* 'guess' and *soengseon* 'believe' in their ability to license a null clausal object. The contrast first observed and discussed in Mandarin in Y.-H. A. Li (2005) and Aoun and Li (2008).

(142)   Some verbs disallow null clausal objects
        Ngo gu/   soengseon Aaming lai.   Aafan dou {*gu/ soengseon}.
        I   guess believe   Aaming come Aafan also guess believe
        'I guess/ believe that Aaming (will) come. Aafan also guess/ believe (so).'

If verb doubling constructions involve argument ellipsis as a way depicted in (141), it is predicted that verbs like *gu* 'guess' cannot be used in verb doubling constructions, since it does not license a null clausal object. However, this is not the case.

(143)   Verbs that disallow null clausal objects are compatible in verb doubling constructions
        Gu   ngo zicin hai **gu**   Aaming wui lai   ge2. Batgwo keoi zeoihau
        guess I   before COP guess Aaming will come SFP but   he   at.last
        mou   lai.
        not.have come
        'I have guessed that Aaming will come. But he didn't come at last.'

---

64. This option is not impossible, as discussed as Nunes (2004) and Bošković (2007), but requires independent justification.

65. Partial deletion is argued to be possible, as in Fanselow and Cavar (2002). Again, it requires independent justification on why it is selectively employed in verb doubling constructions but not other phenomena.

66. Argument ellipsis is argued to be present in Japanese and Korean (Oku 1998; S. Kim 1999, among others). Its availability in Chinese is questionable, as discussed in Y.-H. A. Li (2005), Aoun and Li (2008), and Y.-H. A. Li (2014). Since I argue against this possibility, the precise characterization of this deletion operation does not bear on the discussion.

As such, in order to maintain the proposal in (141), it has to be assumed that the deletion operation is specific to verb doubling constructions. Indeed, Lai (2019) proposes a similar deletion operation in his analysis on dislocation copying, and suggests that a deletion operation specifically applies to dislocation copying. However, it is unclear why such a construction-specific mechanism has to be adopted, especially when there is a a more straightforward, head-to-specifier movement analysis.

I therefore conclude that the proposed head movement to specifier is superior to the alternatives discussed in these two subsections, primarily because its application does not rely on other mechanisms such as scrambling and deletion.

3.8 Discussions and implications

3.8.1 Reformulating the Head Movement Constraint

If the proposed head movement analysis is on the right track, then verb doubling constructions in Cantonese constitute empirical evidence against the Head Movement Constraint (HMC), since verb movement can skip intervening heads (alongside the examples discussed in §3.2). In other words, the HMC cannot be maintained as a general locality condition on head movement. Indeed, it has been suggested in passing that the locality constraint on head movement should be "attributed to the presence of relevant features on the intervening head(s)" (Toyoshima 2001, p.121). Likewise, Roberts (2001) also mentions in a footnote that "a featural characterization of the intervener for head movement seems more than justified in this context" (p.147, fn11).

If so, then the evidence previously taken to support the HMC is now in need of explanation. The question becomes why head movement is often short/local in V-T/ T-C movement in Romance and Germanic languages, for example. To derive the local nature of head movement, one possibility is to resort to categorial selection, or *C-selection*, as suggested in Matushansky (2006).

(144) Categorial selection (C-selection, Matushansky 2006, p.76)
A head may select the syntactic category (and the lexical content) of the head of its complement.

As proposed in Svenonius (1994), Holmberg (2000), and Julien (2002), C-selection is achieved via a set of C-features, which can be construed as (uninterpretable) counterparts of categorial features. Crucially, Matushansky (2006) suggests that head movement is based on C-selection and the local nature of head movement is not due to head movement *per se*, but it is a direct consequence of the local nature of C-selection. For example, a T head has an uninterpretable [*u*V] feature and C-selects a VP as its complement. Verbs, with the interpretable [*i*V] feature, move to T to check the feature on T.[67]

(145) Illusions of head movement triggered by C-selection/C-features

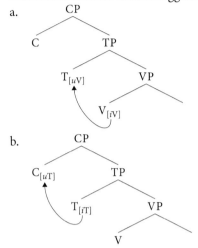

In other words, head movement is local because the attracting C-feature resides in the next higher head in the structure, but not because head movement cannot skip an intervening head.

This explanation of the local nature of head movement allows head movement to be non-local, if it is not triggered by C-features. This is precisely the cases of verb doubling constructions in Cantonese. As proposed, verb movement is triggered by the [*u*Focus]/[*u*Defocus] features, which occur at a distance from the verb (i.e., in the CP domain). Verb movement into the specifier position of these projections may skip heads along its movement path. However, it cannot skip an element that bears an identical [*i*Focus] feature. This locality requirement may be taken to motivate a featural reformulation of the HMC, which states that head movement cannot skip intervening (matching) *features*, instead of *heads*.[68] More generally, the locality requirement on head movement can be subsumed under the locality condition of Agree, as proposed in § 3.6. Provided that phrasal movement

---

67. This provides a partial explanation of why many cases of head movement seem to be semantically inert (Chomsky 2001, p. 37). This is because C-selection involves formal features, and thus it does not trigger interpretive effects.

68. A similar idea has been suggested in Roberts (2001), where Long Head Movement in Breton can move across non-operator heads such as auxiliaries but not operator heads such as negation.

92   The Unity of Movement

is also subject to the locality condition of Agree, a non-trivial implication of this suggestion is that head movement is constrained in a way similar to phrasal movement, and there is no head-movement-specific constraint such as the HMC.

Before I leave this subsection, I briefly discuss a complication pertaining to the suggestion that local head movement is connected to C-selection (or any featural trigger). This issue has been discussed in Matushansky (2006), Funakoshi (2014), and Preminger (2019). In the structure in (145), it is plausible that VP also bears the same $[iV]$ feature as V, which in turns constitutes a structurally closer goal for $[uV]$ on T. Consequently, VP should move instead of V. This problem can be generalized to any phrasal category XP, as it will block the movement of its own head X. As such, without further assumptions, deriving the local nature via C-selection undesirably rules out all instances of local head movement.

Different proposals have been made to dismiss the status of XP as an intervener of the movement of its own head X. For example, Funakoshi (2014) suggests that in the structure in (145), VP does not serve as an intervener because it cannot move to the specifier of TP, as it is too "local" (based on notion of *anti-locality* (Abels 2003; Grohmann 2003)). Alternatively, Preminger (2019) suggests that VP ceases to intervene due to a prior Agree relation with the T head. Movement of V out of VP does not violate locality constraints (specifically minimality constraints), since locality constraints only need to be satisfied once (following the spirit of Principle of Minimal Compliance, or PMC, N. Richards (1998)). To the extent that anti-locality and the PMC are independently motivated, the validity of these explanations hinges on the corresponding predictions on head movement, which I do not dwell on here.

3.8.2   A parallel analysis with phrasal movement

In addition to eliminating an asymmetry in locality constraints between head movement and phrasal movement, the movement analysis of the four verb doubling constructions further suggest that the relevant constructions do not distinguish their targets based on structural types (i.e., heads and phrases). Recall that the examples with a displaced object in (27), and consider also the examples in (146) with a displaced VP.

(146)   The constructions that can target verbs can also target verb phrases
a.   **Zigei zyu faan sik** Aaming hai m-hang   ge2. Daan keoi hang
self   cook rice eat Aaming COP not-willing SFP but   he   willing
bongsau sai   wun.
help   wash dish
'Cooking on his own, Aaming is not willing to (do so). But he is willing to help wash dishes.'

b. Lin **dim-haa ni-zek dungmat** Aaming dou m-gam.
   even touch-DEL this-CL animal Aaming also not-dare
   'Aaming does not even dare to TOUCH THIS ANIMAL.'
c. Hai **heoi haangsaan** Aaming m-soeng zaa3. Zou keita je keoi wui heoi.
   COP go hiking Aaming not-want SFP do other thing he will go
   'Aaming does not want to GO HIKING only. He will do other things.'
d. Aaming kyutding-zo gaa3 laa3 **heoi Meigwok duksyu**.
   Aaming decide-PERF SFP SFP go US study
   'Aaming has decided to go to the US for study.'

These cases suggest that the each of these constructions can target both heads (verbs) and phrases (nominal objects and verb phrases). The only difference concerns the size of the focused/defocused elements (and the doubling effects). An updated pattern including the VP cases is given in Table 3.12.

Table 3.12 The word order patterns illustrated in (27), (28) and (146)

	(i) topic	(ii) 'even'-focus	(iii) copula focus	(iv) right dislocation
Object	O SV	lin- O SV	hai- O SV	SV SFP O
Verb	V SVO	lin- V SVO	hai- V SVO	SVO SFP V
VP	VP SV	lin- VP SV	hai- VP SV	SV SFP VP

The parallels follow naturally from the proposal. As I stressed in the proposal in §3.6, the focus/defocus movement is due to the presence of an [*i*Focus]/[*i*Defocus] feature on constituents, which can be a head or a phrasal element. In other words, the movement under discussion is not designed specifically for verb movement; instead, it readily accounts for movement other verbs, if the relevant features are associated with phrasal elements.[69] This idea is schematically represented in (147), showing the relevant structure before merging with sentence-final particles (and the SFP-driven movement).

(147) A uniform movement analysis
   a. [*i*Focus]/[*i*Defocus] on verbs, as in (28)

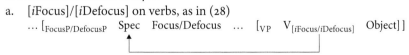

   ... [FocusP/DefocusP Spec Focus/Defocus ... [VP V[*i*Focus/*i*Defocus] Object]]

---

69. Island effects of constructions like (27) are reported in literature, which I do not repeat here. For topic constructions, see Huang, Li, and Li (2009), for an overview; for 'even'-focus constructions, see Shyu (1995); for copula focus constructions, see C. C.-H. Cheung (2008, 2015); for right dislocation/dislocation copying, see L. Y.-L. Cheung (2015) and Lee (2017).

94 The Unity of Movement

b. [*iFocus*]/[*iDefocus*] on verb phrases, as in (146)
… [FocusP/DefocusP Spec Focus/Defocus … [VP[*iFocus/iDefocus*] V Object]]

c. [*iFocus*]/[*iDefocus*] on objects, as in (27)
… [FocusP/DefocusP Spec Focus/Defocus … [VP V Object[*iFocus/iDefocus*]]]

If all these cases are derived uniformly via Agree on the Focus/Defocus feature, followed by subsequent movement, a prediction is that the VP movement cases and the object movement cases exhibit Focus Intervention Effects, in the same way as verb doubling constructions. I discuss this issue in the next subsection.

3.8.3 Focus Intervention Effects in phrasal movement

The prediction on Focus Intervention Effects in the phrasal movement cases are only borne out partially. First, in the VP, Focus Intervention Effects are observed in topic constructions, 'even'-focus constructions and copula focus constructions, to the exclusion of dislocation copying.[70] All the sentences in (148) contain a *dak*-associate in the subject position.

(148) Focus Intervention Effects observed with verb phrases
a. *Zigei zyu faan sik, dak Aaming hai m-hang   ge2.
self   cook rice eat only Aaming COP not-willing SFP
'Cooking on his own, only Aaming is not willing to (do so).'
b. ??Lin **dim-haa   ni-zek dungmat** ngo dou gokdak dak Aaming m-gam.
even touch-DEL this-CL animal I   also think   only Aaming not-dare
'I think that Aaming does not even dare to TOUCH THIS ANIMAL.'
c. *Hai **heoi haangsaan** dak Aaming m-soeng zaa3.
COP go   hiking   only Aaming not-want SFP
'Only Aaming does not want to GO HIKING only.'
d. Dak Aaming kyutding-zo zaa3 **heoi Meigwok duksyu**.
only Aaming decide-PERF SFP go   US   study
'Aaming has decided to go to the US for study.'

These cases are consistent with the proposed movement account, and Focus Intervention Effects are observed in both verb doubling constructions and their phrasal counterparts.

However, in the object cases, no Focus Intervention Effects are observed. The sentences in (149) contain either a *wh*-expression or a *dak*-associate in the subject

---

70. The absence of Focus Intervention Effects is expected for (148d), since the movement in right dislocation does not involve a [Focus] feature.

position, and they are all acceptable. The sentences in (149a–c) thus posit a challenge to a focus movement analysis.[71]

(149) No Focus Intervention Effects observed with objects

    a. **Ni-bun syu** bingo/ dak Aaming maai-zo.
       this-CL book who only Aaming buy-PERF
       'Who bought this book?/ Only Aaming bought this book.'

    b. Lin **ni-bun syu** ngo dou jingwai [dak Aaming tai-zo].
       even this-CL book I also think only Aaming read-PERF
       'Even for this book, I think only Aaming have read it.'

    c. Hai **ni-gaan uk** dak Aaming zou-m-hei ze1.
       COP this-CL house only Aaming rent-not-up SFP
       'It is only this house that only Aaming cannot afford renting.'

    d. dak Aaming m-zi zaa3 **ni-joeng je.**
       only Aaming not-know SFP this-CL thing
       'Only Aaming doesn't know this.'

I suggest that the absence of Focus Intervention Effects in sentences in (149) is due to the fact that these sentences have a non-movement derivation. In particular, I suggest that the displaced objects in these cases are base generated in the Spec FocusP and they are co-indexed with a null pronominal element (e.g., a *pro*, which in common in Chinese languages) in the base position. The possibility of a base generation approach in constructions like the ones in (148a–c) has been suggested in the literature (see the references in footnote 69), and is illustrated in the "gapless" structures in (135). As such, the structure in (150) does not involve movement, and the focused subject does not lead to Focus Intervention Effects.

(150) A base-generation approach to sentences like (149a–c)

$$[_{\text{FocusP}} \text{Object}_{i \, [i\text{Focus}]} \text{ Focus} \ldots [_{\text{TP}} \text{S}_{[i\text{Focus}]} \text{ V } pro_i]]$$

It should be noted that the availability of a non-movement derivation is contingent on the availability of the appropriate null elements. The reason why cases of verb doubling constructions and the sentences in (148) cannot circumvent Focus Intervention Effects in a similar way can be attributed to the fact that there is no corresponding verbal *pro* elements. In other words, the asymmetry between verb doubling constructions and (148) on one hand (149) on the other is due to the lexical resources of null elements in Cantonese.

If the discussion here is on the right track, then the verb doubling constructions can be analyzed on a par with their phrasal counterparts under the current movement-to-specifier proposal, and Focus Intervention Effects, as a result of the

---

71. Again, the acceptability of (149d) is expected, as it does not involve a [Focus] feature.

locality condition of Agree, are observed with both heads and phrasal elements in constructions that involve focus movement.

3.9 Conclusions

This chapter examined potential intervening elements in head movement by investigating four cases of non-local verb displacement in Cantonese. In these cases, the verbs are doubled, and their copy appears in the initial or final position of the sentence.

I proposed that these four cases uniformly involve head movement to a specifier position in the CP periphery, in a way identical to their phrasal counterparts. I further argued that elements of the same structural types (i.e., heads/verbs) do not necessarily block the proposed movement; instead, elements that possess the same syntactic feature are genuine interveners.

The findings in the chapter challenge the status of the Head Movement Constraint as a general constraint on head movement. At the same time, I show that the proposed head movement exhibits the syntactic intervention effects that are commonly observed with phrasal movement.

I conclude that head movement is not constrained in a way different from phrasal movement with regard to intervention. Particularly, intervention effects are calculated in terms of syntactic features but not structural types. This conclusion necessitates a movement theory that does not distinguish head movement from phrasal movement in terms of locality.

CHAPTER 4

Scope effects
Movement of quantificational heads

This chapter focuses on the semantic effects of head movement, which are often said to be absent from such movement. The primary goal of this chapter is to present a novel piece of evidence for head movement with semantic effects from Cantonese. An in-depth investigation into the distribution of quantificational heads such as aspectual verbs and modal verbs in Cantonese shows that these heads can occupy a non-canonical, high position in the sentence, if they are immediately followed by a quantificational element or a focused element. I propose that these quantificational heads can undergo overt head movement to a higher position and take scope in the landing site (i.e, scope-shifting head movement). Additionally, the proposed movement of quantificational heads is constrained by an independently motivated condition on interpretation, Scope Economy, which precludes semantically vacuous scope-shifting operations. The findings lend support to the claim that head movement can induce semantic effects. Importantly, head movement can shift scope relations, in a way similar to Quantifier Raising proposed for nominal quantifiers. Furthermore, Scope Economy is shown to be a general constraint on both phrasal movement and head movement. The conclusion of this chapter challenges the view that head movement does not result in any semantic effects – a view which has been said to claim that head movement is non-syntactic and occurs at PF. It is shown that head movement is no different from phrasal movement in the potential to induce semantic effects. This motivates a unified theory of movement of head movement and phrasal movement.

4.1   Introduction

This chapter focuses on the debate about semantic effects of head movement, which are often said to be absent (Chomsky 2001; Harley 2004, 2013; Platzack 2013). Such a lack of semantic effects appears to distinguish head movement from phrasal movement. This raises non-trivial concerns relating to the theoretical status of head movement in movement theories. A primary goal of this chapter is to present a novel piece of evidence for head movement with semantic effects from Cantonese.

The core empirical foundations come from the distribution of aspectual verbs and modal verbs in Cantonese. For example, the aspectual verb *hoici* 'begin' can appear in either a post-subject (low) position or a pre-subject (high) position, as illustrated in (151). It is significant to note that he different surface positions of *hoici* in (151a) and (151b) correspond to different interpretations with regard to the subject marked by the focus marker *dak* 'only'. In both cases, only the surface scope reading is available.

(151) The low and high positions of *hoici* 'begin'
    a. <u>Da</u>k Aaming **hoici** haau-dou hou.   'only' > 'begin' / *'begin' > 'only'
        only Aaming begin get-able   good
        singzik.
        result
        'Only Aaming is such that he begins to get good results.'
    b. **Hoici** <u>da</u>k Aaming haau-dou hou.   *'only' > 'begin' / 'begin' > 'only'
        begin only Aaming get-able   good
        singzik.
        result
        'It begins to be the case that only Aaming is getting good results.'

Importantly, the placement of *hoici* 'begin' is not unconstrained. In the absence of the focus particle *dak*, the high, pre-subject position is unavailable, as in (152b).

(152) The high position of *hoici* 'begin' unavailable in the absence of *dak* 'only'
    a. Aaming **hoici** haau-dou hou   singzik.
        Aaming begin get-able   good result
        'Aaming begins to get good results.'
    b. ***Hoici** Aaming haau-dou hou   singzik.
        begin Aaming get-able   good result
        Int: 'Aaming begins to get good results.'

Similar patterns are also observed with modal verbs like *hoji* 'may' and *wui* 'will'. The distribution of aspectual verbs and modal verbs and the restriction on the high position calls for an analysis of the paradigm in (151) and (152). As far as I know, this has not been documented in the Cantonese literature.[1]

Empirically, this chapter makes the novel observation that the distribution of aspectual verbs and modal verbs in Cantonese is correlated with the presence of

---

1. The structural position of modal verbs in Mandarin is not a new topic, but the discussions focus on the availability of the pre-subject position of epistemic modals, in contrast to other modal verbs (Lin 2011; Chou 2013; Tsai 2015). One exception is Y.-y. Hsu (2016, 2019), who discusses admissible cases of pre-subject deontic modals. But there is no discussion on the positional alternation of aspectual verbs, as far as I am aware.

quantificational and focused elements in the pre-verbal position. Analytically, I propose that these verbs can undergo overt head movement to a high position and take scope in the landing site. In other words, they can undergo scope-shifting head movement. Additionally, I suggest that the proposed movement is constrained by an independently motivated condition on interpretation, namely, Scope Economy, which precludes semantically vacuous scope-shifting operations (Fox 2000).

The findings lend support to claims recently found in the literature that head movement can impose semantic effects. Importantly, head movement can shift scope relations, in a way similar to Quantifier Raising proposed for nominal quantifiers. Furthermore, Scope Economy is shown to be a general constraint on both phrasal movement and head movement.

More generally, the conclusion of this chapter challenges the assumption that a lack of semantic effects is a general empirical property of head movement, a property that is taken as evidence for the non-syntactic status of head movement (an analytical position found in Chomsky 2001; Harley 2004, 2013; Boeckx and Stjepanović 2001; Schoorlemmer and Temmerman 2012; Platzack 2013; Hall 2015; McCloskey 2016). It is shown that head movement is no different from phrasal movement in its potential to impose semantic effects. Furthermore, the observation that head movement is constrained by an economy condition that was originally proposed to constrain (some instances of) phrasal movement (in particular Quantifier Raising) provides new evidence for the claim that the computational system of natural languages does not discriminate head movement from phrasal movement. This sets out the foundations of a unified theory of movement.

The organization of this chapter is as follows. In §4.2, I review the debate about semantic effects with head movement. In §4.3, I investigate the distribution of aspectual verbs and modal verbs in Cantonese. In §4.4, I detail the proposed head movement analysis, and, in §4.5, I provide further evidence for the proposed analysis. In §4.6, I discuss and argue against alternative analyses to a head movement approach. In §4.7, I discuss some consequences and implications of the proposal. I conclude in §4.8.

4.2 (Non-)occurrence of semantic effects with head movement: An ongoing debate

The debate about semantic effects with head movement (whether such effects occur or not) is part of the broader debate about the theoretical status of head movement in the generative/minimalist literature. Since the theoretical recognition of head movement as a syntactic operation in the grammar (Koopman

1984; Travis 1984; Baker 1985, 1988), its differences from other (phrasal) movement operations such as A-movement (movement to argument positions) and A'-movement (movement to non-argument positions) have supported a non-uniform analysis of head/phrasal movement dependencies. Among other differences, head movement is often said to lack semantic effects, as opposed to (many) instances of phrasal movement (Chomsky 2001; Harley 2013; Platzack 2013). This has stimulated a debate on whether the apparent lack of semantic effects with head movement is a general empirical property of the movement of heads.

The significance of the debate is that if head movement can impose semantic effects, this would constitute evidence against a non-syntactic analysis of head movement.[2] In fact, if it turns out that head movement cannot impose any semantic effects, treating head movement as a syntactic operation needs to develop a plausible account of why there should be this difference with phrasal movement (which can impose semantic effects). Additionally, the debate hinges on whether head movement should in general be distinguished from phrasal movement, since there is growing evidence that the occurrence of semantic effects does appear to crosscut both head movement and phrasal movement. In § 4.2.1, I review the evidence in support of assumptions that there is a lack of semantic effects with head movement. In § 4.2.2 and § 4.2.3, respectively, I review the debates and concerns on the arguments for the semantic effects of head movement based on (i) discourse effects and (ii) scope effects.[3]

4.2.1 A lack of semantic effects?

The primary observation of an apparent lack of semantic effects with head movement can be attributed to verb movement in Germanic and Romance languages (cf. Emonds 1978; Pollock 1989). For example, Harley (2004) notes that verb movement over negation in French does not create different scope readings between the verb and the negation (i.e., V > NEG/ NEG > V). In both sentences in (153), the negation takes scope over the verb.[4]

---

2. While it will not be the focus of this chapter, evidence for the syntactic nature of head movement also includes various *syntactic* effects of head movement. For example, head movement may license ellipsis (Gergel 2009); it may reformulate/void opaque syntactic domains (den Dikken 2006; Gallego 2010; Stepanov 2012); it may feed subsequent syntactic movement such as VP-fronting (Wiland 2008; Funakoshi 2014, 2019).

3. I have set aside a few studies, such as Benedicto (1998), Lechner (1998), Zwart (2001), Hartman (2011), Keine and Bhatt (2016), and Gribanova (2017) who discuss movement of heads that imposes semantic effects other than discourse effects and scope effects. For discussions of some of these studies, see Hall (2015) and McCloskey (2016).

Chapter 4. Scope effects   **101**

(153)   French V movement to T   (Harley 2004, p. 244)
    a.   *The main verb moves over negation*
        Jean ne **parlait**   pas français.   NEG>V
        Jean NE speak.IMP not French
        'John didn't speak French.'
    b.   *The main verb does not move over negation*
        Jean n'as pas **parlé**   français.   NEG>V
        Jean has not spoken French.
        'John hasn't spoken French.'

Harley (2013) also suggests that, in English, the position of the past tense morpheme does not affect the relative scope of tense and the universal quantifier in case of T-C movement, as shown in (154). Both sentences can have wide and narrow scope readings for the time variables introduced by tense.

(154)   English V/T movement movement to C   (Harley 2013, p. 117)
    a.   Everyone **left**.   everyone > PAST; PAST > everyone
    b.   **Did** everyone leave?   everyone > PAST; PAST > everyone

Additionally, Platzack (2013) examines minimal pairs of examples in different languages, where verb movement is available in one language but unavailable in the other. As she suggests, if verb/head movement has semantic effects, it is expected to cause different readings. However, this does not appear to be the case. For example, English lacks verb movement to the second position, as opposed to Swedish. However, the two sentences in (155) are semantically equivalent.

(155)   Languages with/without verb movement to the second position
                                      (Platzack 2013, p. 31)
    a.   This book, John **has** read.   (English, a non-V2 language)
    b.   Denna bok   **har** John läst.
        this   book has John read
        'This book, John has read.'   (Swedish, a V2 language)

---

4. In Italian, Cinque (1999, p. 184, fn.8) mentions that the different positions of past participle with regard to adverbs like *sempre* 'always' may have different interpretations. While the "always > participle" order only has a non-perfect reading, the "participle > always" order is compatible with both a perfect and non-perfect reading.

  (i)   Placement of participles in Italian
      a.   Gianni ha <u>sempre</u> **avuto** i capelli lunghi.   a non-perfect reading
          'Gianni still has long hair.'
      b.   Gianni ha **avuto** <u>sempre</u> i capelli lunghi.   a perfect or a non-perfect reading
          'Gianni had/still has long hair'

To see one more example, Platzack (2013, p. 32–33) argues that V2 movement of Negative Polarity Verbs in Norwegian and Swedish does not alter the c-commanding relation with the negative licensor. For example, in (156a), the verb *enset* 'notice' in Norwegian requires negative licensing (as the absence of negation leads to unacceptability). Assuming that the V2 position is higher than the negation *ikke* 'not', V2 movement of *enset* 'notice' is found not to affect the negative licensing of *enset*. This suggests that V2 movement does not impose syntactic/semantic effects. Similar conclusions can be drawn from the V2 movement of *gitter* 'bother' in Swedish in (156b).

(156) V2 movement of Negative Polarity Verbs
    a.   Hun **enset**   *(ikke) bråket.
          she sensed not   noise.def
          'She didn't notice the noise.'   (Norwegian, Platzack 2013, p. 32)
    b.   Han **gitter**   *(inte) göra det.
          he   bothers not   to.do it
          'He doesn't bother to do it.'   (Swedish, Platzack 2013, p. 33)

These cases of head movement substantiate the suggestion in Chomsky (2001, p. 37) that "semantic effects of head raising in the core inflectional system are slight or nonexistent, as contrasted with XP-movement, with effects that are substantial and systematic." In other words, the lack of semantic effects seem to be a characteristic, empirical property of head movement.[5]

However, all these cases concern verb movement in Germanic and Romance languages. This raises questions of generality, as head movement has been proposed for various phenomena in different languages. Also, there are at least two reasons for the consistent lack of semantic effects of in these cases.[6] The first one concerns the *trigger* of the movement. If a movement is triggered by categorial features (Svenonius 1994; Holmberg 2000; Julien 2002), such as a V feature on T heads (in V-T movement) or a T feature on C heads (in T-C movement), then the movement might not be expected to impose semantic effects, since categorial features are commonly assumed to be purely formal/syntactic. Another

---

5. Chomsky (2001, p. 37) sets aside cases of noun incorporation, which arguably involves head movement (Baker 1988). Harley (2013, p. 117, fn. 3) suggests that the semantic effects of noun incorporation "are not introduced by head movement, but rather a precondition on its occurrence." Since there are also debates on whether noun incorporation involves head movement (e.g., Barrie and Mathieu 2016), I set aside these cases and focus on cases of verb movement.

6. The lack of semantic effects is often taken to be evidence for a phonological approach to head displacement (Chomsky 2001; Harley 2004, 2013; Platzack 2013). However, as Platzack (2013, p. 34) also admits, phrasal movement may also lack semantic effects. Thus the lack of semantic effects does not necessitate a phonological approach to head displacement.

reason, as suggested in Matushansky (2006) and Vicente (2007), concerns the *semantic types* of the moving heads. The most discussed cases of head movement involve non-quantificational heads. Presumably, they are of semantic type $\langle e,t \rangle$ or $\langle e,\langle e,t \rangle\rangle$. Their interpretation should be the same in the launching site or the landing position.

These suggestions provide an explanation on why the cases in (153) through (156) lack semantic effects. Importantly, these suggestions also make a prediction on the availability of semantic effects of head movement, as described in (157).

(157) Head movement may impose semantic effects if
    a. the movement is triggered by features other than categorial/purely formal features; or
    b. the head is of a quantificational type (i.e., $\langle\langle\alpha,t\rangle,t\rangle$).

It is thus an empirical question as to whether such cases of head movement are attested in natural language. I review certain relevant cases in the next two subsections.

4.2.2 Discourse effects of head movement

Concerning (157a), it is indeed not uncommon to see verb movement being associated with discourse effects. For example, a verb may be interpreted as a topic or a focus in predicate cleft/ verbal fronting constructions (Vicente 2007; Cheng and Vicente 2013; Hein 2018; Harizanov 2019, among many others; see also references in Chapter 3). The verb doubling constructions in Cantonese discussed in Chapter 3 also fall into this category. Additionally, it has been proposed that verb movement to the second position/ the C position imposes illocutionary effects, e.g., declarative forces and interrogative forces (Wechsler 1991; Truckenbrodt 2006).

However, Harizanov and Gribanova (2019) suggest that the discourse effects accompanying movement operations may be (at least as a logical possibility) attributed to the featural encoding on the heads that trigger the movement, instead of the movement itself. These heads may be a topic head or a focus head in the CP domain bearing a [topic] or [focus] feature that triggers verb movement. Likewise, the illocutionary effects in V2 languages are suggested to be due to the trigger of the head movement, instead of a consequence of head movement (Wechsler 1991; Truckenbrodt 2006).[7] Accordingly, head movement with

---

7. Indeed, Wiklund (2010) argues that the illocutionary effects are not due to V2 movement.

104   The Unity of Movement

discourse effects or illocutionary effects may not serve as a knock-down argument for the existence of head movement with semantic effects.[8]

This shifts the spotlight onto cases relating to (157b), since head movement with scope effects is immune to alternative explanations of the type just described. The scope effects must accordingly be attributed to head movement *per se*, instead of the trigger.

4.2.3   Scope effects of head movement

With regard to (157b), there is a growing body of evidence for the scope effects of head movement, involving the movement of determiners, negation, modal verbs and aspectual verbs (Takahashi 2002; Han, Lidz, and Musolino 2007; Lechner 2007; Kishimoto 2007; Roberts 2010; Szabolcsi 2010, 2011; Iatridou and Zeijlstra 2013; Homer 2015; Matyiku 2017; Landau 2020; Sato and Maeda 2021). However, the reported evidence for scope effects of head movement is not uncontroversial. Among others, Hall (2015) and McCloskey (2016) critically point out that the arguments presented may build on unmotivated assumptions, and/or may have alternative analyses. For space reasons, for each case, I only present the core observations in support of scope effects of head movement. I then briefly mention potential concerns or alternative analyses discussed in the literature. This is meant to illustrate the controversial nature of these alleged cases of head movement with scope effects. Table 4.1 previews recent proposals arguing for the scope effects of head movement.

Table 4.1 Summary of evidence of scope effects with head movement

Head	Language	Scope effects	Reference(s)
Determiner	Japanese	enhanced restriction	Takahashi (2002)
Negation	English	NPI licensing	Roberts (2010) and Szabolcsi (2010)
	Japanese	NPI licensing	Kishimoto (2007)
	English varieties	outscope subjects	Matyiku (2017) and Landau (2020)
	Korean	outscope objects	Han, Lidz, and Musolino (2007)
	Japanese	outscope objects	Sato and Maeda (2021)
Modal verb	English	outscope subjects	Lechner (2007, 2017)
	English	outscope negation	Iatridou and Zeijlstra (2013) and Homer (2015)
Aspectual verb	Shupamem	outscope subjects	Szabolcsi (2010, 2011)

---

8. However, if this reasoning goes through for head movement, it should also apply to phrasal movement that is triggered by a topic or focus feature. This amounts to the suggestion that many instances of phrasal movement lack semantic effects in the same way as head movement.

4.2.3.1 *Movement of (quantificational) determiners*

Based on evidence from Japanese, Takahashi (2002) argues that determiner raising may enhance the restriction of quantificational scope. Assuming that the universal marker *mo* is a determiner and selects *wh*-expressions as its complement, Takahashi suggests that it may head-move to a higher position. For example, the base generated *mo* in (158a) is argued to undergo movement to a higher, NP-external position in (158b). Crucially, *mo* has an enhanced restriction in (158b), i.e., the restriction of *mo* is wider if it is adjacent to the matrix subject instead of the embedded subject.

(158) Japanese determiner raising   (Takahashi 2002, p.594)
    a. $[_{TP}[_{NP}$ Dare **mo**]-ga   kaikosareru] toyuu <u>uwasa</u>-wa hontoo datta.
          person every-NOM is-fired   that   rumor-TOP true   was
          'The rumor that everyone would be fired was true.'
    b. $[_{TP}[_{NP}$ Dare]-ga   kaikosareru] toyuu <u>uwasa</u> **mo**   hontoo datta.
          person-NOM is-fired   that   rumor every true   was
          Lit.: 'Every rumor that a person would be fired was true.'

This movement analysis is supported by the observation that the movement of *mo* is constrained by an economy condition that requires its movement to impose semantic effects (Scope Economy, cf. Fox 2000): it must cross a quantificational element along its path. Assuming that a noun/nominal category involves an implicit existential determiner, the high position of *mo* is unavailable if it only crosses a (non-quantificational) verb/verbal category, as shown in (159b).

(159) Japanese determiner raising, an illicit case   (Takahashi 2002, p.599)
    a. Taroo-wa $[_{VP}$ Hanako-ni $[_{NP}$ dare **mo**]-o   <u>sikari</u>] sae saseta.
          Taroo-TOP   Hanako-DAT   person every-ACC scold even made
          'Taroo made Hanako even scold everyone.'
    b. *Taroo-wa $[_{VP}$ Hanako-ni $[_{NP}$ dare]-o   <u>sikari</u> **mo**] (sae) saseta.
          Taroo-TOP   Hanako-DAT   person-ACC scold every (even) made
          'lit. Taroo made Hanako (even) every scold a person.'

However, Yatsushiro (2009, p.167–169) argues that such an approach incorrectly predicts additional positions for the landing site of *mo*, when there is more than one nominal category along the movement path. Also, the alleged scope effects can be alternatively derived without movement under an unselective binding approach, as discussed in Shimoyama (2006).

4.2.3.2 *Movement of negation*

There are three types of cases concerning the scope effects of negation movement in the literature, where negation interacts with (i) Negative Polarity Items, (ii) subject quantifiers, and (iii) object quantifiers.

(i)   *The licensing scope of negation*

The first type of cases concerns the licensing scope of negation. Assuming that Negative Polarity Items such as *any* in English must be c-commanded by an element that licenses it, Roberts (2010, p. 8–12) argues that the movement of the negative auxiliary in English may extend that scope of negative licensing. For example, the movement of *doesn't* (to the C position) licenses the subject *anybody* in (160b). Note that Roberts argues that *n't* optionally cliticizes to T from a lower position. When T moves to C, *n't* moves together with T.

(160)   English T-C movement in question formation and NPI licensing
   a.   *[$_{CP}$ Which one of them **does** [$_{TP}$ <u>anybody</u> **not** like?]]

(Harizanov and Gribanova 2019, p. 514)

   b.   [$_{CP}$ Which one of them **doesn't** [$_{TP}$ <u>anybody</u> like]] ?

(McCloskey 1996, p. 89)

Similarly, Szabolcsi (2010) reports that the movement of negation in imperatives creates an otherwise unavailable licensing context for subject NPIs, as illustrated in (161).

(161)   English T-C movement in imperatives and NPI licensing

(Szabolcsi 2010, p. 44)

   a.   *[$_{TP}$ <u>Any one of you</u> **don't** touch the money] !
   b.   [$_{CP}$ **Don't** [$_{TP}$ <u>any one of you</u> touch the money]] !

However, Hall (2015) points out two potential concerns with these arguments. On one hand, if *n't* cliticizes on T before movement to C, then it may be too embedded to c-command the NPI in the subject position. On the other hand, he suggests that, following Roberts' reformulation of head movement as a special case of Agree, the licensing effects may be due to the Agree relationship between the NPI and a negative feature which is already present in C.[9] If this is the case, T-C movement *per se* does not contribute to successful licensing.

Another case that takes NPI licensing as evidence for scope effects of head movement is from Japanese. The negation *-na(i)* in Japanese can license subjects associated with NPIs such as *sika* 'only'. Different from previous analyses that suggest a low position of the NPI subjects, (e.g., Takahashi 1990; Aoyagi and Ishii

---

9. This suggestion is also discussed in Harizanov and Gribanova (2019, p. 513–517).

1994; Kato 2000), Kishimoto (2007) argues instead that the negation -*na(i)* has undergone movement to T so that it can license the NPI in subject position.[10]

(162) Japanese negation licensing NPI subjects   (Kishimoto 2007, p. 264, modified)
Gakusei-sika hon-o   yoma-**nakat**-ta.   NEG-T movement
student-only book-ACC read-NEG-PST
'Only students read books.'

Importantly, the ability to license NPI subjects disappears if the negation does not undergo movement. Kishimoto (2007) suggests that the negation in the sentence in (163a) does not move to T, as it is separated from T by the causative verb *si* 'make' (and focus particles such as -*sae* 'even' and -*mo* 'also'). In such case, it fails to license subject NPIs, as shown in (163b).[11]

(163) Japanese negation without moving to T   (Kishimoto 2007, p. 270, modified)
a. John-ga   Mary-o   heya-ni haire-**naku**(-sae/mo)   si-ta.
   John-NOM Mary-ACC room-to enter.can-NEG-even/also make-PST
   'John made Mary unable to enter the room.'
b. *John-sika Mary-o   heya-ni haire-**naku**   si-ta.
   John-only Mary-ACC room-to enter.can-NEG make-PST
   'Only John made Mary unable to enter the room.'

However, as will be discussed shortly in sentences like (167), the negation in Japanese cannot outscope objects that are marked by *dake* 'only', for example. The scope behaviors between negation and objects appear to be inconsistent with the negation movement analysis advocated by Kishimoto (2007).

(ii)   *Scope relations with subject quantifiers*
The second type of cases concerns the scope relation between negation and subject quantifiers. Matyiku (2017) argues at length that in some varieties of English, such as West Texas English, African American English, and Appalachian English, the auxiliary-first word order, or negative auxiliary inversion, is derived via a movement of the negated auxiliary to a position higher than the subject. For example, (164b) is derived from (164a), where *don't* moves over *many people.* Since the two sentences convey different scope readings (i.e., *many > not* vs. *not > many*), this constitutes evidence for the scope effects of head movement.[12]

---

10. It is assumed that the whole TP, instead of the complement of the T head, is the licensing domain of negation if negation occupies the T head (cf. the *m-command* domain of the T head).

11. There are other contexts where the negation does not move to T, which likewise correlate with the inability to license NPI subjects. For further discussions, see Kishimoto (2007, 2013).

12. Landau (2020) discusses similar cases in standard English, where the movement of a negative auxiliary in question formation outscopes subject quantifier, as in (i).

108 The Unity of Movement

(164) West Texas English and negative auxiliary inversion (Matyiku 2017, p. 37–38)
    a.   Many people **don't** like you.
    b.   **Don't** <u>many people</u> like you.

However, the two concerns posited in Hall (2015) for arguments drawing on NPI licensing also apply to these cases. More importantly, Blanchette and Collins (2019) propose an alternative analysis to Matyiku's head movement approach, where the negation is based generated in the subject NP/DP (e.g., [$_{Subj}$ **not** many people]). As such, the fact that the negation scopes over *many people* in (164b) is not because of negation movement, it is argued, but because of different base generated positions of negation.[13]

(iii) *Scope relations with object quantifiers*

The third type of cases concerns the scope of negation and object quantifiers in languages like Korean and Japanese. Han, Lidz, and Musolino (2007) report that the sentence in (165) is scopally ambiguous for a population of Korean speakers. In particular, the 'NEG > every' reading is available for some Korean speakers they tested, indicated by the % symbol.

(165) Korean short negation and object quantifiers
    John-i   <u>motun chayk-ul</u> **an**   'every' > NEG; %NEG > 'every'
    John-NOM   every book-ACC NEG
    ilk-ess ta.
    read-PAST-DECL
    a.   'every' > NEG: 'John read no book.'
    b.   NEG > 'every': 'John didn't read every book.'
                    (Han, Lidz, and Musolino 2007, p. 24)

Importantly, they argue that the availability of such a reading indicates the movement of negation over the object quantifier 'every book'. This argument relies on three assumptions in the derivation of (165).[14]

(166) Assumptions on the derivation of the sentence in (165)
    a.   The (short) negation *an* is adjoined to VP.
        [$_{VP}$ *an* [$_{VP}$ V Obj.]]

    (i)   Negative auxiliary movement enhances scope
        a.   Everybody didn't see the fight.   not > every; every > not
        b.   Didn't everybody see the fight?   not > every; *every > not

13. Blanchette and Collins (2019) suggests that the negation undergoes negative raising from the subject position to a higher position, and the auxiliary appearing in the high position is a result of *do*-support for the contracted negation.

14. For justifications, see Han, Lidz, and Musolino (2007, p. 12–22).

b. The object moves from its base position to a VP-external position.
[$_{FP}$ Obj. [$_{VP}$ *an* [$_{VP}$ V t$_{Obj.}$]]]
c. Korean is a scope-rigid language (i.e., the scope of a quantificational element is determined by its surface position).

For the negation to scope over the object quantifier, it must move (together with the main verb) to a position higher than the object quantifier (presumably a T position). This constitutes an instance of head movement with scope effects.

However, Zeijlstra (2017) challenges the generality of the assumption in (166c): while it may be true of scope relations *between* nominal quantifiers, it does not necessarily hold true of negation and nominal quantifiers. Object reconstruction below the negation is a possible option.[15] On the other hand, Harizanov and Gribanova (2019) raise concerns over (166a). They suggest that the speakers allowing the 'NEG > every' reading may permit flexible positions of *an*, i.e., one below the object and one above the object. If so, no negation movement is needed.

Another case taken as evidence for scope effects of negation is verb-echo answers in Japanese. In Japanese, negation cannot take scope over objects associated with focus-sensitive particles such as *-dake* 'only', as shown in (167).

(167) Japanese *-dake* 'only' and negation   (Shibata 2015, p. 73)
Taroo-wa <u>pan-dake</u>   kaw-**anak**-atta.   only > NEG; *NEG > only
Taro-TOP bread-only buy-NEG-PST
'Taro didn't buy only bread.'

Crucially, Sato and Maeda (2021) observe that the negation may scope over the *dake*-marked object in verb-echo answers to polarity questions, illustrated in the question-answer pair in (168).

(168) Japanese verb-echo answers with negation   (Sato and Maeda 2021, p. 9)
a. Q: Taroo-wa   pan-dake   kat-ta-no?
Taro-TOP   bread-only buy-PST-Q
'Did Taro buy only bread?'
b. A: Kawa-**nakat**-ta-yo.   ?? 'only' > NEG; NEG > 'only'
buy-NEG-PST-SFP
Lit.: 'Didn't buy.'

Following the clausal ellipsis theory of verb-echo answers proposed in Holmberg (2015), Sato and Maeda (2021) argue that the derivation of verb-echo answers in Japanese involves V-T-C movement, followed by TP-ellipsis. The wide scope reading of the negation over the *dake*-marked object is a direct consequence of negation moving together with the verb in the V-T-C movement.

---

15. A similar challenge is presented in Harizanov and Gribanova (2019) as well.

110   The Unity of Movement

4.2.3.3 *Movement of modal verbs*

Turning to cases of movement of modal verbs, Lechner (2007) presents an argument for scope effects with head movement based on the scope relations between modal verbs and negative (universal) quantifiers. The primary observation concerns the interpretation of sentences like (169).

(169)   English modal verbs and the scope splitting constructions (Lechner 2007, p.3)
Not <u>every boy</u> **can** make the team.   not > every > can ; not > can > every

The reading of interest is the one where the possibility modal verb *can* is interpreted within the scope of negation but above the universal quantifier, i.e., not > can > every. This reading conveys that there is no possible world in which all of the boys makes the team. Setting aside many details of the argument,[16] Lechner (2007) suggests that this (scope-splitting) reading results from the covert movement of the modal verb *can* into a position between the negation and the universal quantifier, as shown in (170). Note the obligatory nature of this modal movement. The surface scope reading (i.e., 'not > every > can') is available when the modal verb *can* reconstructs. Thus, scope ambiguity is due to the optionality of modal reconstruction.

(170)   The assumed LF of (169), where *can* undergoes movement to a higher position[17]
$[_{\text{NegP}}$ Not $[$**can** $[_{\text{TP}}$ <u>every boy</u> $[_{\text{T'}}$ t_{can} $[_{\text{VP}}$ $t_{\text{every boy}}$ make the team$]$ $]$ $]$ $]$

For this argument to go through, it is crucial that the subject does not reconstruct back to the base, VP-internal position, as illustrated in (171); otherwise, there is no need to posit modal movement to derive the relevant scope reading. To justify this, Lechner assumes that strong (universal) quantifier DPs cannot reconstruct below raising verbs (i.e., below the modal verbs).

(171)   The LF of (169), where *every boy* reconstructs[18]
$[_{\text{NegP}}$ Not $[$ $[_{\text{TP}}$ ⟨every boy⟩ $[_{\text{T'}}$ **can** $[_{\text{VP}}$ <u>every boy</u> make the team$]$ $]$ $]$ $]$

However, it is precisely this assumption on strong quantifier DPs that arouses controversies. Hall (2015) and McCloskey (2016) specifically argue against this assumption (among other assumptions).[19]

---

16. See Hall (2015) for a detailed evaluation.

17. Negative quantifiers are assumed to be licensed by an abstract negation operator in the clause. For simplicity, I indicate the negation scope by putting *not* in a high NegP. It is not meant to indicate negation movement.

18. Angle brackets < ... > indicate the surface position.

Another reported case of the scope effects of modal movement concerns the interpretation of modal verbs and negation in English. It is observed that a group of deontic modals across languages consistently resist being interpreted within the scope of negation, i.e., they are Positive Polarity Items, or PPI modals (Israel 1996; Iatridou and Zeijlstra 2013; Homer 2015). Assuming that deontic modals are base-generated below negation, Iatridou and Zeijlstra (2013) suggests that the □ > NEG reading in the sentences in (172) is due to head movement of the modal over negation.[20] The difference in the surface word order is due to the fact that modal movement is overt in English, but covert in Greek and Spanish. As such, this modal movement shifts the scope between deontic modals and negation.[21]

(172) PPI modals must be interpreted above negation

(Iatridou and Zeijlstra 2013, p. 530, 550)

    a.   John **must/ should** <u>not</u> leave.   English, □ > NEG

    b.   O Yanis <u>dhen</u> **prepi** na figi.   Greek, □ > NEG
          the Yanis NEG must NA leave
          'Yanis must not leave.'

    c.   Juan <u>no</u> **debe** ir.   Spanish, □ > NEG
          Juan NEG must go
          'Juan must not go.'

Citing the analysis proposed in Homer (2015), McCloskey (2016) argues that an "alternative analysis ... depends not on head movement ... but rather on scope-enhancing covert movement of the relevant modals." (p. 9) and that "appeal to head-raising is futile and they propose covert scope-expanding movement, of the kind that Homer appeals to also for English" (p. 9). In other words, the movement involved in (172) is not head movement *per se*, but some scope-expanding movement (e.g., Quantifier Raising). According to McCloskey, this movement does not constitute a case for head movement with scope effects.[22]

---

19. However, Lechner (2017) argues that the validity of the argument need not hinge on the validity of the assumption on strong quantifiers. He also presents further evidence from comparatives in support of modal movement with scope effects.

20. The square symbol □ indicates the (deontic) necessity modals.

21. See also Matushansky (2006) for relevant discussions.

22. It seems that the argument here relies on a distinction between the notion of *Head Movement* as a distinct syntactic operation and the notion of *head movement* as a descriptive term for all instances of movement of a head. My understanding of McCloskey's suggestion is that the case of modal movement is not an instance of *Head Movement*, but, some other movement operation such as Quantifier Raising. However, the case of modal movement still constitutes an instance of *head movement* with scope effects.

4.2.3.4 *Movement of aspectual verbs*

The last case concerns the interpretation of aspectual verbs. Szabolcsi (2010, 2011) reports that in Shupamem (Bantu, SVO), aspecctual verbs can be optionally be fronted over a (quantificational) subject and take scope in the derived position.[23] The sentence in (173a) is the baseline example where *yeshe* 'begin' is in the low position. Crucially, it raises over the subject in (173b) and scopes over the subject 'only Maria'. Both sentences convey an unambiguous surface scope reading.

(173) Aspectual verbs in Shupamem (Szabolcsi 2010, p. 38)
    a. <u>Ndùù</u> Maria ka **yeshe** inget   ndàà li?.   'only' > 'begin'
        only   Maria past begin have.INF good roles
        'Only Mary is such that she began to get good roles'
    b. A   ka **yeshe** <u>ndùù</u> Maria inget   ndàà li?.   'begin' > 'only'
        it-FOC past begin only Maria INF.have good roles
        'It began to be the case that only Mary is getting good roles'

McCloskey (2016) suggests that if, following Szabolcsi, aspectual verbs are quantifiers over time variables, then it is expected to see the same scope effects with heads that involve quantification over world variables, e.g., modals, which, he suggests, has not been documented so far.[24] This represents a concern on the generality of head movement with scope effects. It applies to proposals on modal movement which consistently exclude a comparison with aspectual verbs.

4.2.4 Interim summary

To sum up, I have reviewed cases of head movement that do not seem to have any semantic effects, and they are taken to be evidence that this is a general empirical property of head movement. However, many instances of head movement beyond the core inflectional system are argued to impose semantic effects such as discourse effects or scope effects. These suggestions are not uncontroversial, either because there may be alternative analyses to a head movement approach, or because the proposed head movement lacks generality.

Against this background, I now turn to the core empirical foundations of this chapter, where aspectual verbs and (a subset set of) modals in Cantonese, I argue, can undergo scope-shifting head movement.

---

23. Szabolcsi (2010, 2011) reports similar scope effects in verb/V2 movement in Dutch. See discussions in § 4.7.3.

24. In fact, Szabolcsi (2011, p. 21) gives one example of the modal counterpart in Shupamem.

4.3 The distribution of aspectual verbs and modal verbs

This section presents basic data concerning the distribution of aspectual verbs and modal verbs in Cantonese. §4.3.1 focuses on the availability of a pre-subject (high) position for these elements and corresponding interpretive effects. §4.3.2 examines the types of verbs that can appear in the high position. §4.3.3 and §4.3.4 discuss, respectively, two licensing conditions of the high position of aspectual verbs and modal verbs. It is revealed that the presence of quantificational elements or focused elements is crucial in licensing the high position. I establish a distributional correlation between quantificational/focused elements and the verbs in the high position, given in (174).

(174) Generalization on the high position of aspectual verbs and deontic/future modals
A high position of aspectual verbs and deontic/future modals is licensed iff the constituent that immediately follows this position (i) is quantificational or (ii) receives a focus interpretation.

4.3.1 The (restricted) high position

The canonical position of aspectual verbs and modal verbs is a post-subject one. As already seen in (152), the aspectual verb *hoici* 'begin', for example, can appear after the subject (i.e., the low position), not before it (i.e., the high position), repeated below as (175).

(175) The canonical low position of *houci* 'begin'   = (152)
     a.   Aaming **hoici** haau-dou hou   singzik.
         Aaming begin get-able   good result
         'Aaming begins to get good results.'
     b.   ***Hoici** Aaming haau-dou hou   singzik.
         begin Aaming get-able   good result
         Int: 'Aaming begins to get good results.'

However, the high position for *hoici* 'begin' is possible under certain circumstances. For example, if the subject is marked with *dak* 'only', then *hoici* 'begin' can appear in either the high or low position.

(176) The low and high positions of *houci* 'begin'   = (151)
     a.   <u>Dak</u>   Aaming **hoici** haau-dou hou   'only' > 'begin' / *'begin' > 'only'
         only   Aaming begin get-able   good
         singzik.
         result
         'Only Aaming is such that he begins to get good results.'

b. **Hoici** <u>dak</u> Aaming haau-dou hou   *'only' > 'begin' / 'begin' > 'only'
begin   only Aaming get-able   good
singzik.
result
'It begins to be the case that only Aaming is getting good results.'

Notably, the position of *hoici* 'begin' indicates different scope relations with *dak* 'only'. In (176a), *hoici* 'begin' unambiguously takes scope below 'only', whereas in (176b) it unambiguously scopes above 'only'. Here, it is instructive to see how these scope readings are truth-conditionally independent of each other. Consider the following two scenarios in Table 4.2, which concern the exam results in a class of three student (building on the scenario first discussed in Szabolcsi (2010, 2011)).

Table 4.2 Two scenarios of exam results in a class of three

Who is getting good results...			
Scenario 1		Scenario 2	
Test 1	Test 2	Test 1	Test 2
Aaming: 40	Aaming: 100	Aaming: 100	Aaming: 100
Bill: 40	Bill: 40	Bill: 40	Bill: 40
Chris: 100	Chris: 100	Chris: 100	Chris: 40
→ (176a) only Aaming > begin		→ (176b) begin > only Aaming	

In Scenario 1, among all students, Aaming is the only student who obtains an improved result in Test 2, while other students are doing as good/bad as before. This scenario is true of (176a), i.e., only Aaming is such that he begins to get good results. This is not true of (176b). In Scenario 2, Aaming performs as good as before in Test 2. However, Chris, who was doing great in Test 1, performs not so well in Test 2. This renders Aaming being the only person who obtain good results in the class. This scenario is true of (176b), i.e., it begins to be the case that only Aaming is getting good results. This is not true of (176a). The sentences in (176) are thus not only unambiguous but also truth-conditionally distinct.

In other words, the high position, if available, enables a verb to take scope there over other structurally lower elements. In all following relevant cases, unless otherwise specified, I will only indicate the surface scope reading in the English translation.

4.3.2 Verbs that can appear in the high position

This subsection focuses on the types of verbs that can appear in the high position. The core observation is that only raising predicates can occupy the high position. In all cases, I will contrast sentences with and without *dak* 'only'. However, it should be noted that *dak* 'only' is not the only element that can license the high position. I postpone further discussions on the licensing conditions to § 4.3.3 and § 4.3.4.

4.3.2.1 *Aspectual verbs*

In addition to *hoici* 'begin', the same pattern is observed with *gaizuk* 'continue' in (177). In (177) (and all the subsequent examples in this subsection), the (a) sentences serve as the baseline, where the low position is insensitive to the presence/absence of *dak* 'only'. Crucially, the (b) sentences indicate that the high position is available if the subject is marked by *dak* 'only'. Note that some examples are given in embedded contexts to show that the high position is insensitive to root/embedded environments.

(177) The aspectual verb *gaizuk* 'continue' and the high position
  a. Ngo tenggong [(dak) Hoenggong **gaizuk** paai tau sapwai].
     I hear only Hong.Kong continue rank initial tenth
     'I heard that (only) HK is such that she continues to rank among the top ten.'
  b. Ngo tenggon [**gaizuk** *(dak) Hoenggong paai tau sapwai].
     I hear continue only Hong.Kong rank initial tenth
     'I heard that it continues to be the case that (only) HK ranks among the top ten.'

Additionally, a less discussed aspectual predicate, *si-gwo* 'tried', shows the same pattern. In morphological terms, *si-gwo* consists of the verb *si* 'try' and the experiential suffix *-gwo*, but it has arguably undergone lexicalization and become a predicate (Shi, Wang, and Zhu 2002; Wu 2020). Meaning-wise, it acquires the meaning of 'have a certain experience'/'once', in addition to the original meaning of 'try'.[25]

(178) The lexicalized aspectual predicate *si-gwo* 'tried' and the high position
  a. (Dak) ni-dou **si-gwo** linzuk lok sap-jat jyu.
     only this-place try-EXP consecutively fall ten-day rain
     '(Only) this place once rained for ten consecutive days.'

---

25. One of the signature properties of such aspectual usage is its compatibility with inanimate subjects (for further discussions, see Wu 2020).

b. **Si-gwo** *(dak) ni-dou   linzuk   lok sap-jat jyu.
try-EXP only   this-place consecutively fall ten-day rain
'It was once the case that only this place rained for ten consecutive days.'

A common property shared by *hoici* 'begin', *gaizuk* 'continue' and *si-gwo* 'tried' is that all of them can be used as raising predicates, i.e., predicates that do not select an external argument.[26] This is in contrast with control predicates such as *soengsi* 'try' and *kyutding* 'decide'. The high position is disallowed, no matter whether the subject is associated with *dak* 'only' or not.

(179) Control predicates cannot occupy the high position
a. (dak) Aaming {**soengsi**/ **kyutding**} tai   ni-bun syu.
only Aaming try   decide   read this-CL book
'(Only) Aaming tries to/ decides to read this book.'
b. {*****Soengsi**/ *****Kyutding**} (dak) Aaming tai   ni-bun syu.
try   decide   only Aaming read this-CL book
Int.: '(Only) Aaming tries to/ decides to read this book.'

4.3.2.2 *Modal verbs*

For the deontic modal verb *hoji* 'may' and the futurity modal verb *wui* 'will' in (180), the high position is available in the presence of *dak* 'only'. Note that the high position can be embedded in the complement clause of the preposition *deoi* 'to'.

(180) The deontic modal *hoji* 'may' and the future modal *wui* 'will'
a. Ngo deoi [gamjat (dak) Aaming { **hoji**/ **wui** } zou fan] mou   jigin.
I   to   today   only Aaming may/ will   early sleep not.have opinion
'I have no opinion on (the claim that) (only) Aaming may/will sleep early today.'
b. Ngo deoi [gamjat { **hoji**/ **wui** } *(dak) Aaming zou   fan] mou
I   to   today   may/ will   only   Aaming early sleep not.have
jigin.
opinion
'I have no opinion on (the claim that) it is allowed/it will be the case that (only) Aaming sleeps early today.'

In contrast, modal verbs relating to ability, such as *sik* 'be.able', and volition, such as *gaam* 'dare', fail to occupy the high position, no matter whether the presence of *dak* 'only' is present or not, as shown in (181).

---

26. For discussions on the Mandarin counterparts of 'begin' and 'continue', see Y.-H. A. Li (1990). I assume the same applies to Cantonese.

Chapter 4. Scope effects **117**

(181) Modal verbs concerning ability and volition fail to occupy the high position
  a. (Dak) Aaming { **sik**/ **gaam**} tai ni-bun syu.
     only Aaming be.able/ dare   read this-CL book
     '(Only) Aaming is able/ dare to read this book.'
  b. { *Sik/ *Gaam} (dak) Aaming tai ni-bun syu.
     be.able dare   only Aaming read this-CL book
     Int.: '(Only) Aaming is able dare to read this book.'

Note that the split between deontic/future modal verbs and modal verbs relating to ability/volition is not one between root and non-root modals. Following Lin and Tang (1995), Bhatt (1998), and Wurmbrand (1999), deontic/future modals can be regarded as raising predicates, as opposed to modal verbs relating to ability/volition (which are regarded as control predicates). This shows that raising predicates, but not control predicates, can occupy the high position.

A complication arises if epistemic modals such as *honang* 'possible' and *jing-goi* 'should' are taken into consideration. While *honang* can occupy the pre-subject position, it does not require the presence of *dak* 'only'. This is different from the previous cases of the high position for aspectual verbs and deontic/future modals.

(182) The epistemic modal *honang* and the pre-subject position   (Lin 2011, p. 51)
  a. Aaming **honang** zyu-gan   faan.
     Aaming be.possible cook-PROG rice
     'Aaming may be cooking.'
  b. **Honang** Aaming zyu-gan   faan.
     be.possible Aaming cook-PROG rice
     'It is possible that Aaming is cooking.'

The same can be said to the modal *jinggoi* 'should' on its epistemic reading.[27]

(183) Epistemic *jinggoi* 'should' and the pre-subject position
  a. (Dak) Aaming camjat **jinggoi** lai-gwo ngo ukkei.
     only Aaming yesterday should come-EXP my home
     '(Only) Aaming should have come to my home yesterday.'

---

27. The modal verb *jinggoi* 'should' is ambiguous between an epistemic reading and a deontic reading. If it is interpreted deontically, it is predicted that it requires the presence of *dak* 'only' to occur in the high position. For example, a deontic reading should be lacking in (i) due to the absence of *dak*.

  (i) **Jinggoi** Aaming lai.
      should Aaming come
      ?Deontic reading: 'Aaming should come.'
      OKEpistemic reading: 'It is probable that Aaming comes.'

b. **Jinggoi** (<u>dak</u>) Aaming camjat   lai-gwo   ngo ukkei.
  should only Aaming yesterday come-EXP my home
  'It should be the case that (only) Aaming case to my home yesterday'

4.3.2.3 *Interim summary*

To sum up, it is observed that the (restricted) high position is available for raising predicates including aspectual verbs and (some) modal verbs, when the subject is associated with *dak* 'only'. However, epistemic modals can occupy the same position freely, in an unrestricted way. Note that I distinguish the restricted high position from the unrestricted one (with epistemic modals), even though both of them are descriptively a pre-subject position.

(184) The types of verbs in the high position
   a. Only raising predicates can occur in the (restricted) high position.
   b. Epistemic modals can freely occupy the pre-subject position.

Anticipating the discussions in §4.3.4, focused elements also license the high position. The deontic *jinggoi* may occupy the high positin by virtue of the focus interpretation of the subject *Aaming*. To avoid potential complications due to the polysemy of *jinggoi*, I focus on the unambiguous deontic modal *hoji* 'may', as discussed in (180).

4.3.3 Quantificational elements

This subsection and the next examine the licensing conditions of the high position. The upshot is that the availability of the high position depends on the nature of the constituent that immediately follow this position. In this subsection, I show that the high position is licensed if the relevant constituent is *quantificational*. This is consistent with the data in §4.3.2, where the presence/absence of the quantificational element *dak* 'only' is crucial to licensing the high position.

In what follows, it is further shown that (i) the licensing elements can be quantificational elements other than *dak* 'only'; and (ii) the relevant constituent is not confined to subjects, but may take various forms, ranging from topics to adverbials and clauses. The general pattern is schematized below, where XP ranges over different constituents.

(185) The high position is licensed by the (immediately) following quantificational element
   a. ^{OK}**Asp./Mod.** $[_{TP/CP} XP_{[+quantificational]} \cdots$
   b. *$^{}$**Asp./Mod.** $[_{TP/CP} XP_{[-quantificational]} \cdots$

First, I start with different quantificational elements in the subject position. For example, the high position of *gaizuk* 'continue' is licensed if the subject is an (existential) quantifier (186a), as opposed to a pronoun (186b). Recall that a proper name (e.g., *Aaming*) without *dak* 'only' also fails to license the high position.

(186) Group denoting quantifiers vs. pronouns in the subject position[28, 29]
    a. **Gaizuk** {$_{\text{SUBJ}}$ jau jat-go jan   } __ haau-dou hou singzik.
        continue   have one-CL person   get-able   good result
        'It continues to be the case that one person is getting good results.'
    b. *__**Gaizuk** {$_{\text{SUBJ}}$ keoi } __ haau-dou hou singzik.
        continue   he   get-able   good result
        Int.: 'It continues to be the case that he is getting good results.'

The sentences in (187) illustrate the same point with other quantificational elements. The high position is licensed by negative quantifiers, counting quantifiers and *wh*-expressions.

(187) Different quantificational elements in the subject position
    a. **Hoji** {$_{\text{SUBJ}}$ mou   jan   } __ lai   hoiwui.
        may   not.have person   come meeting
        'It is allowed that no one comes to the meeting.'
    b. **Hoji** {$_{\text{SUBJ}}$ zuido   saam-go jan   } __ lai   hoiwui.
        may   at.most three-CL person   come meeting
        'It is allowed that at most three people come to the meeting.'
    c. **Hoji** {$_{\text{SUBJ}}$ geido   jan   } __ lai   hoiwui?
        may   how.many person   come meeting
        'How many people are allowed to come to the meeting?'

Second, a similar contrast is observed in the topic position. Aspectual verbs and modals are allowed to occupy the position higher than the topic if the topic is quantificational, but not if the topic is a (non-quantificational) definite expression.[30]

(188) Universal quantifiers vs. definite NPs in the topic position
    a. **Hoici** {$_{\text{TOP}}$ cyunbou jan   } Aaming dou __ hou jansoeng.
        begin   every   person Aaming all   very praise
        'It begins to be the case that Aaming praises everyone.'

---

28. The underline in the examples indicates the canonical position of the aspectual verbs or modals in the high position. The same applies to all subsequent examples.

29. For convenience, I have bracketed *jau* 'have' and *jat-go jan* 'one person' to show its status as a subject. Indeed, it is more common to treat them as parts of an existential construction (Huang 1987; Paul 2021). This also applies to the sentence in (187a).

30. The adverb *dou* 'all' is strongly preferred in the presence of universal quantifiers.

b. *Hoici {$_{TOP}$ ni-go jan } Aaming __ hou jansoeng.
begin   this-CL person Aaming   very praise
Int.: 'It begins to be the case that Aaming praises this person.'

Third, locative or frame-setting adverbials can occur above the subject. The high position of *hoici* 'begin' (i.e. the position above the locative/frame-setting adverbial) is allowed if the adverbial is quantificational.

(189) Quantificational vs. non-quantificational adverbs
     a. **Hoici** {$_{ADV}$ hai mui-gaan hokhaau } Aaming dou __ haau-dou hou
        begin   at every-CL school   Aaming all   get-able good
        singzik.
        result
        'It begins to be the case that at every school, Aaming is getting good results.'
     b. ??**Hoici** {$_{ADV}$ hai ngodei hokhaau } Aaming __ haau-dou hou singzik.
        begin   at our   school   Aaming   get-able good result
        'It begins to be the case that at our school Aaming is getting good results.'

If there is more than one quantificational element in the sentence, there are multiple possible positions for *hoici*, and they deliver different scope readings.

(190) Quantificational adverbs and subjects and multiple high positions
     a. {$_{ADV}$ Hai mui-gaan hokhaau } **hoici** {$_{SUBJ}$ 'every' > 'begin' > 'most'
        at every-CL school   begin
        daaiboufan jan   } dou __ haau-dou hou singzik.
        most   person all   get-able good result
        'At every school, it begins to be the case that most people are getting good results.'
     b. **Hoici** {$_{ADV}$ hai mui-gaan hokhaau } {$_{SUBJ}$ 'begin' > 'every' > 'most'
        begin   at every-CL school
        daaiboufan jan   } dou __ haau-dou hou singzik.
        most   person all   get-able good result
        'It begins to be the case that, at every school, most people are getting good results.'

Additionally, a similar contrast between quantificational and non-quantificational elements can be illustrated with subordinate clauses. The sentences in (191) contain an *if*-clause and a *whenever*-clause. They can be regarded as quantificational elements since they quantify over possible worlds. Crucially, they license the high position of *hoici* 'begin'. To facilitate comprehension, I provide a relevant context for each sentence.

Chapter 4. Scope effects **121**

(191) *If*-clauses and *whenever*-clauses licensing the high position

    a. *Context: the speaker is reporting a recent mutational change on trees: decrease in temperature leads to their leaves turning red. Previously, decrease in temperature did not necessarily lead to this result.*

    Hoici [$_{CP}$ jyugwo zyun   laang], syujip __ zau wui bin hung.
    begin   if   become cold   leaves   then will turn red
    'It begins to be the case that, if it becomes cold, the leaves will turn red.'

    b. *Context: the speaker is reporting a recent climate change: it now becomes a certain fact that an approaching typhoon is associated with the appearance of big waves on the sea. Previously, this association is only a matter of chance.*

    Hoici [$_{CP}$ faanhai   daa-fung],   hoimin dou __ wui jau
    begin   whenever approach-typhoon sea   all   will have
    daailong.
    big.waves
    'It begins to be the case that, whenever typhoons approach, there will be big waves on the sea.'

Crucially, these subordinate clauses are in contrast with with the non-quantificational *although*-clauses and *because*-clauses. Neither of them license the high position of *hoici* 'begin'.

(192) *because*-clauses and *although*-clauses fail to license the high position

    a. *****Hoici** [$_{CP}$ jaujyu   di linggin loufaa], bou dinnou   __ waaiwaaidei.
    begin   because CL part   aging   CL computer   out.of.order
    Int.: 'It begins to be the case that, because the parts are aging, the computer is out of order.'

    b. *****Hoici** [$_{CP}$ seoijin   mou daa-fung],   hoimin dou __ jau
    begin   although not approach-typhoon sea   all   have
    daailong.
    big.waves
    Int.: 'It begins to be the case that, although no typhoon is approaching, there are big waves on the sea.'

Based on these observations, the distribution of aspectual verbs and deontic/future modals in Cantonese can be stated as follows in (193).

(193) Licensing conditions of the high position, part 1
A high position of aspectual verbs and deontic/future modals is licensed if the constituent that immediately follows this position is quantificational.

4.3.4 Focused elements

Another licensing condition of the high position concerns focused elements. In additional to quantificational elements, a high position is also licensed by a focused element that immediately follow the high position. I substantiate this claim by adopting different focus marking devices and show that all of them may license the high position. The general pattern shows the schema in (194).

(194)   The high position licensed by the (immediately) following focused element
    a. ^{OK}**Asp./Mod.** $[_{TP/CP} XP_{[+focus]}$ ⋯
    b.   *****Asp./Mod.** $[_{TP/CP} XP_{[-focus]}$ ⋯

Note that part of the observations in this subsection were first discussed in Yip and Lee (2020) for Mandarin. I provide the Cantonese counterparts below, which pattern with the Mandarin data.

First of all, a focus reading can be contributed by the copula *hai*. The high position is licensed if *hai* is associated with the subject as in (195a). It is not, however, licensed by object focus, as in (195b).

(195)   Copula focus and the high position
    a.   **Hoji** hai <u>Aaming</u> heoi Hoenggong.
        may cop Aaming go   Hong.Kong
        'It may be the case that Aaming (but not others) goes to Hong Kong.'
    b.   *****Hoji** Aaming hai   heoi <u>Hoenggong</u>.
        may Aaming cop go   Hong.Kong
        Int.: 'It may be the case that Aaming goes to Hong Kong (but not other places).'

Second, a contrastive focus reading can be forced by the following continuation. In (196a), a contrastive focus reading is forced on the subject, where *Aaming* is contrasted with *Aafan*. However, if the contrastive focus falls in elements in the VP, the high position is no longer licensed. The sentence in (196b) is degraded.

(196)   Contrastive/ corrective focus and the high position
    a.   **Si-gwo** (hai) <u>Aaming</u> haau-dou daijat, m-hai   Aafan.
        try-EXP cop   Aaming get-able   first,   not-cop Aafan
        'It was once the case that Aaming got first place, not Aafan.'
    b. $^{??}$**Si-gwo** <u>Aaming</u> (hai) haau-dou daijat, m-hai   daiji.
        try-EXP Aaming cop get-able   first,   not-cop second
        Int.: 'It was once the case that Aaming got the first place, not the second.'

Also, other focusing devices such as the 'even'-focus constructions can also license the high position, as long as the focused element occupies a position higher than the verb. In (197a), the subject receives focus reading, but in (197b), a fronted object is focused and, in (197c), the verb *zou* 'do' is focused. All these focused elements license the high position.

(197) 'Even'-focus constructions and the high position
    a. **Si-gwo** lin <u>Aaming</u> dou haau-m-dou hou singzik.
        try-EXP even Aaming also get-not-able good result
        'It was once the case that even Aaming failed to get good results.'
    b. Ngo gokdak [**wui** lin <u>ni-bun</u> <u>syu</u> Aaming dou mou tai].
        I   think will even this-CL book Aaming also not read
        'I think that it could be the case that Aaming didn't read even this book.'
    c. **Hoici** lin <u>zou</u> Aaming dou zou-cou-saai.
        begin even do Aaming also do-wrong-all
        'It begins to be the case that Aaming even did it all wrong.'

One more example concerns *wh*-expressions, whose presence also licenses the high position. This is in line with the suggestion in Rochemont (1986) that *wh*-expressions bear inherent focus reading.

(198) *Wh*-expressions and the high position
    Hoji <u>bin-go</u> haa-nin heoi Hoenggong?
    may who   next-year go Hong.Kong
    Lit.: 'It is allowed that who goes to Hong Kong next year?'

It should be noted that other information structural notions, such as topics, do not license the high position. The sentence in (199a) involves a topicalized object and the one in (199) involves a base generated topic. Neither of them licenses the high position of the aspectual verb or the modal verbs.

(199) Topics do not license the high position
    a. *****Hoici** ni-bun   syu, Aaming jau tau   tai-hei.
        begin this-BOOK   Aaming from beginning read-up
        Int.: 'It begins to be that case that Aaming reads this book from the beginning.'
    b. *****Hoji** seoigwo, Aaming m-sik pinggwo.
        may fruit   Aaming not-eat apple
        Int.: 'It may be the case that, as for fruits, Aaming doesn't eat apples.'

The observations in this subsection can be summarized in (200).

(200) Licensing conditions of the high position, part 2
    A high position of aspectual verbs and deontic/future modals is licensed if the constituent that immediately follows this position receives a focus interpretation.

4.3.5 Interim summary

Taking stock, the empirical observations reported in this subsection are repeated and summarized below. In §4.3.1, I established that there is a high position in the clause that allows certain verbs to take scope from there. In §4.3.2, I show that only raising predicates may occur in the (restricted) high position. Epistemic modals can also occupy the pre-subject position, but this patterning is unconstrained.

(201) The types of verbs in the high position
    a.   Only raising predicates can occur in the (restricted) high position.
    b.   Epistemic modals can freely occupy the pre-subject position.

In §4.3.3 and §4.3.4, two licensing conditions of the high position, were brought to light, combined in (202) and schematically represented in (203).

(202) Licensing conditions of the high position (part 1 + part 2)
A high position of aspectual verbs and deontic/future modals is licensed iff the constituent that immediately follows this position (i) is quantificational or (ii) receives a focus interpretation.

(203) The high position licensed by the (immediately) following quantificational/focused element
    a. ^{OK}**Asp./Mod.** $[_{TP/CP} XP_{[+quantificational/+focus]} \cdots$
    b.   *****Asp./Mod.** $[_{TP/CP} XP_{[-quantificational/-focus]} \cdots$

4.4 Proposal: Scope-shifting head movement

To capture the empirical observations on aspectual verbs and modal verbs in §4.3, I propose that the high position of aspectual verbs and deontic/future modals is derived via head movement. I further propose that the application of this head movement is constrained by Scope Economy (Fox 2000), which dictates that scope-shifting operations must have a semantic effect.

4.4.1 Two components of the proposal

Before I detail the proposal, I assume that aspectual verbs and deontic/future modals are *raising* predicates (Y.-H. A. Li 1990; Lin and Tang 1995; Bhatt 1998; Wurmbrand 1999), and that the embedded subject has to move to Spec TP for Case (Y.-H. A. Li 1990), as shown in the clausal structure in (204).

(204) The basic structure of sentences with aspectual verbs and deontic/future modals

[$_{TP}$ Subj$_i$ [$_{AspP/ModP}$ **Asp./Mod.** [$_{vP}$ t_i V (Obj)]]]

As raising predicates, the base position of these verbs is vP-external. I will assume for illustrative purposes that an aspectual verb heads an Aspect Phrase and a modal verb a Modal Phrase. These verbs may alternatively head a verbal projection above the main verb (i.e., another vP).

4.4.1.1 *Overt scope-shifting head movement*

I propose that aspectual verbs and modal verbs can undergo overt head movement to the high position, and take scope from there.

(205) The proposed overt head movement

[$_{TP}$ **Asp./Mod.** [$_{TP}$ Subj$_i$ __ [$_{vP}$ t_i V (Obj)]]]

Scope-shifting head movement

Regarding the implementation of this head movement, I tentatively assume that (i) the moving head adjoins to the root structure right above the quantificational or the focused element, and that (ii) this head movement is not driven by a syntactic feature, but by interpretation/ scope considerations, in a way similar to other scope-shifting operations such as Quantifier Raising (May 1977, 1985; Fox 2000; Bobaljik and Wurmbrand 2012). However, this is not the only way to implement the proposed head movement. I return to other possibilities in §4.4.3.

I illustrate the proposal with the examples in (176), repeated in (206).

(206) The low and high positions of *hoici* 'begin'
  a. Dak Aaming **hoici** haau-dou hou singzik.
     only Aaming begin get-able good result
     'Only Aaming is such that he begins to ('only' > 'begin' / *'begin' > only)
     get good results.'
  b. **Hoici** dak Aaming haau-dou hou singzik.
     begin only Aaming get-able good result
     'It begins to be the case that only Aam- (*'only' > 'begin' / 'begin' > 'only')
     ing is getting good results.'

Under the current proposal, the sentence in (206b) is derived from the sentence in (206a), where *hoici* 'begin' moves to the high position and takes scope over *dak* 'only'. The derivation is illustrated with English glosses in (207).

(207) Deriving (206b) from (206a) under a head movement approach
[TP **begin** [TP only Aaming_i ___ [vP t_i get-good-result]]]
⬆_____|
Scope-shifting head movement

scope enrichment

It should be noted that the proposed head movement can move over different elements, as long as the element is quantificational or focused. The flexibility of the landing site can be schematically illustrated in (208). Note that, for illustrative purposes, the notation [+Q/+F] is added to indicate the quantificational or focus nature of the relevant constituent. I am not committed to the presence of any [+Q/+F] feature in these elements.

(208) A schematic representation of the proposed head movement

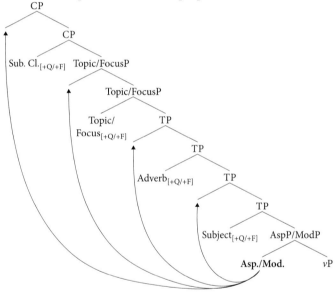

A potential concern of the proposal is that the proposed head movement as illustrated in (208) appears to violate the Head Movement Constraint (the HMC, Travis 1984), since the moving head, as proposed, moves in one fell swoop and potentially crosses other heads such as the T/C head or the Topic/Focus head.[31] I suggest that violation to the HMC does not preclude a head movement analysis, since the status of the HMC as a general syntactic constraint is not uncontroversial. Many instances of head movement have been reported in the literature to show a clear violation to the HMC, including (but not limited to) Long Head

---

31. For a clear violation of the HMC, see (232).

Movement (Lema and Rivero 1990; Rivero 1991; Borsley, Rivero, and Stephens 1996, i.a.), and predicate clefts/verbal reported in various languages (Vicente 2007; Hein 2018; Harizanov 2019, i.a.) fronting. I suggest that the proposed head movement falls into the family of head movement that does not obey the HMC.[32]

A remaining question is how this head movement is constrained in a way such it only allows certain verbs to occupy the high position under certain circumstances. I discuss this issue in the next subsection.

4.4.1.2 *Scope Economy*

To account for the constraints on the proposed head movement, I suggest that only *quantificational heads*, or heads that are generalized quantifiers (i.e., functions from properties to truth values, cf. Barwise and Cooper (1981)), can be targeted for the proposed head movement. Substantially, I propose a parallel quantificational analysis of aspectual verbs and modals. On one hand, aspectual verbs are generalized quantifiers over *times* (of semantic type $\langle\langle i,t\rangle,t\rangle$, i.e., functions from sets of time intervals to truth values) (cf. Szabolcsi 2010, 2011).[33] On the other hand, deontic/future modals are generalized quantifiers over *worlds* (of semantic type $\langle\langle s,t\rangle,t\rangle$, i.e., from sets of worlds to truth values) (cf. Matushansky 2006; von Fintel and Heim 2011; Iatridou and Zeijlstra 2013).

Table 4.3 A parallel quantificational analysis of aspectual verbs and modal verbs

	Aspectual verbs	Deontic/Future modal verbs
Core meaning	generalized quantifiers over times	generalized quantifiers over worlds
Semantic type	<<i,t>,t>	<<s,t>,t>

Importantly, I suggest that their movement is subject to a constraint on (scope-shifting) movement of generalized quantifiers, Scope Economy (Fox 2000).[34] Fox's original discussion of Scope Economy focuses on nominal/phrasal

---

32. This is not to say that the HMC should be abandoned, but that the HMC appears to be too strong as a general constraint on *all* instances of head movement. Reformulation of the HMC is much desired, but would go beyond the scope of this chapter. See Roberts (2001), Matushansky (2006), and Harizanov and Gribanova (2019), and Chapter 3 for discussions.

33. This is not meant to unify different usages of aspectual verbs – they can also be used as transitive predicates, for example. The claim here is that at least the usage of aspectual verbs under discussion *can* receive a quantificational analysis.

34. While the original version of Scope Economy is a constraint on covert operations, Takahashi (2002) and Matyiku (2017) report cases where overt head movement is constrained by Scope Economy, suggesting that Scope Economy is not a constraint specific to covert syntax. See also Bobaljik and Wurmbrand (2012) for a similar suggestion.

quantifiers, but if Scope Economy is a constraint on scope-shifting operations in general, there is no *a priori* reason to rule out its application to scope-shifting operations of verbal/non-phrasal quantifiers.

(209) Scope Economy (Fox 2000, p. 23, modified)
Scope-shifting operations must have a semantic effect.

This constraint is crucial in explaining the generalization in (202). This is because, in the absence of a quantificational or a focused element (i.e., the unacceptable cases), applying the proposed movement would not shift/affect the relative (quantificational or focus) scope relations. Before I detail how the relative scope is shifted/affected in § 4.4.2, the idea can be illustrated in (210).

(210) The high position licensed by the (immediately) following quantificational/focused element

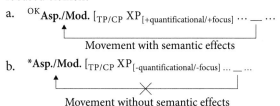

To see an example, in the sentences in (175), repeated in (211), where the subject is non-quantificational (because it is a proper name). In such case, the movement of *hoici* 'begin' fails to shift scope relations, and thus violates Scope Economy. The diagram in (212) illustrates this idea with English glosses.

(211) The canonical low position of *houci* 'begin'   = (175)
    a. Aaming **hoici** haau-dou hou singzik.
       Aaming begin get-able good result
       'Aaming begins to get good results.'
    b. ***Hoici** Aaming haau-dou hou singzik.
       begin Aaming get-able good result
       Int: 'Aaming begins to get good results.'

(212) An attempted derivation of (175b) from (175a) under a head movement approach
[$_{TP}$ **begin** [$_{TP}$ Aaming$_i$ __ [$_{vP}$ t_i get-good-result]]]

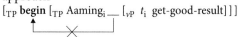

no scope-shifting

As such, a head movement analysis, coupled with Scope Economy, derives the basic paradigm discussed in (151)/(176) and (152)/(175).

Some qualifications are in order. I assume with Fox (2000) that Scope Economy can be implemented as a syntactic, derivational constraint on movement (cf. Bobaljik and Wurmbrand 2012, for a similar stance). In other words, it is a condition that applies in a local manner during a syntactic derivation. In effect, at each step of a derivation, it determines whether a quantificational element can undergo movement, by checking whether the movement would potentially have a semantic effect. For example, when the non-quantificational subject *Aaming* is merged in Spec TP in (212), Scope Economy determines that the movement of 'begin' would not have a semantic effect, hence blocking its movement. In contrast, when the quantificational subject *dak Aaming* 'only Aaming' is merged in Spec TP in (207), Scope Economy sanctions the movement of 'begin' for its potential scope effects (it does not force the movement, however).[35]

One immediate question relating to the mechanics of Scope Economy is how such determination is possible in syntax, provided that semantic/scope effects are commonly assumed to be properties read off in the Logical Form (LF). I again assume with Fox (2000, p. 66–74) in that a subset of formal logical properties are accessible to syntax, and Scope Economy is calculated based on these properties. In principle, it might be suggested that these formal logical properties are syntactically represented, e.g., as a (null) syntactic feature on certain constituents.

4.4.2 Deriving the properties of movement of quantificational heads

In this subsection, I illustrate how the semantic effects of the proposed head movement are achieved, which are crucial in licensing the proposed head movement. I first illustrate in §4.4.2.1 the *quantificational scope effects* with aspectual verbs, with special focus on compositionality. Then I illustrate in §4.4.2.2 the *focus scope effects* with modal verbs, emphasizing the subtle but detectable effects on the calculation of focus sets. Lastly, in §4.4.2.3, I show how the current proposal derives the restriction on verbs based on considerations of semantic types.

4.4.2.1 *Deriving the quantificational scope effects*

Before I proceed, I assume basic compositional rules from Heim and Kratzer (1998) and a framework where time and world variables are explicitly introduced in the syntax (by the Aspect head and the Modal head, respectively), suggested in Beck and Stechow (2015).

Following Szabolcsi (2010, 2011), the lexical semantics of *hoici* 'begin' can be given in (213). It indicates that there exist two time intervals t′ and t″ such that

---

35. It should be noted that Scope Economy may be suggested to be a representational constraint, which, for example, applies at each Spell-Out.

t' precedes a contextually determined time variable, presumably the speech time, which precedes t". A proposition P is false at (the earlier) time t' but it is true at (the later) time t".

(213) The lexical semantics of *hoici* 'begin' (largely based on Szabolcsi 2010, 2011)
⟦*hoici*⟧ = λP_{⟨i,t⟩}. ∃t' ∃t" [t' < t* ≤ t" ∧ P(t') = 0 ∧ P(t") = 1]
(where t* is a time variable whose value is contextually determined)

With all these ingredients, the quantificational scope effects of movement of *hoici* 'begin' in sentences like (176b), repeated in (214), can be illustrated in (215). After undergoing the proposed head movement, *hoici* 'begin' takes scope in the high position over *dak* 'only' in the subject position. Note that subject movement from the specifier of *v*P to the specifier of TP is due to Case reasons (cf. Y.-H. A. Li 1990). For simplicity, I assume that *dak Aaming* 'only Aaming' forms one constituent as a DP.

(214) *Hoici* 'begin' in the high position
Hoici dak Aaming haau-dou hou singzik. =(176b)
begin only Aaming get-able good result
'It begins to be the case that only Aaming is getting good results.'

(215) A compositional analysis and the semantics of (176b)
a.

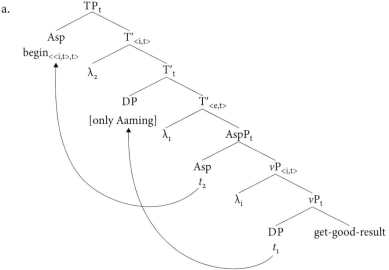

b. ⟦(215a)⟧ = ∃t' ∃t" [t' < t* ≤ t" ∧ [only Aaming λx. get-good-result(x)(t') = 0] ∧ [only Aaming λx. get-good-result(x)(t") = 1]]

As proposed here, aspectual verbs (and deontic/future modals) are (verbal) generalized quantifiers. Following the analysis on nominal generalized quantifiers (Heim and Kratzer 1998), I suggest that their movement leaves a trace of a lower type (i.e., a time/world variable) in a similar way as phrasal quantifiers (of type $\langle\langle e,t\rangle,t\rangle$) they leave behind an individual type trace in instances of movement. When *hoici* moves, crucially, it leaves behind a trace (i.e., t_2 in (215a)), which is a time variable of type i.[36] *Hoici* lands at a position right above the subject and takes scope there, delivering the meaning in (215b).[37] Similar can be said about deontic/future modals, with the only difference being the semantic types. The world variables would replace the time variables. In the absence of a quantificational element, the movement would not be licensed as it would not impose any scope effects.

As a remark, Szabolcsi (2011) proposes an alternative semantic type for aspectual verbs, where they are of modifier type $\langle\langle i,t\rangle,\langle i,t\rangle\rangle$. This is a possible option, but it must also come with additional assumptions on the movement trace. Under the current approach, the trace cannot be a low type trace (a time variable), as it would lead to a potential type mismatch issue when the modifier type *hoici* 'begin' takes scope in the derived position: it returns a function $\langle i,t\rangle$ instead of a truth value. Different solutions have been suggested in the literature. For example, the movement may be an instance of trace-less movement or the trace might be deleted at LF (Cable 2010; Stepanov 2012; Matyiku 2017). Alternatively, employing flexible types, aspectual verbs may be type-lifted in case of movement (Matyiku 2017) or they may undergo function composition with a type-lifted tense operator (Szabolcsi 2011). To the extent that modals are more commonly identified as generalized quantifiers than as modifiers, I adopt a uniform analysis of both aspectual verbs and modals. But the precise choice between generalized quantifier types and modifier types does not bear on the proposal. In principle, the proposed head movement can target heads that are of either type (see further discussions in §4.7.2).

4.4.2.2 *Deriving the focus scope effects*

I now turn to the scope effects when modal verbs (and aspectual verbs) move over a focused element.[38] It should be stressed that the proposed head movement does not affect the focus scope, but the *calculation of the focus set*, or the *focus alterna-*

---

36. If *hoici* does not move, it takes scope at the position above vP but below the subject in Spec TP.

37. One concern on meaning in (215b) is that the first conjunct in the scope of 'begin' *presupposes* that Aaming got good results as well at t', since *dak* 'only' presupposes its prejacent to be true (similar to English *only*). This is however not the intended reading of (214). I acknowledge that this is a non-trivial issue for an accurate formulation of the lexical semantics of *hoici* 'begin', but I have to leave this issue to future research.

38. The discussions in this subsection is based on Yip and Lee (2020, 2022).

tives.[39] Focus scope is determined independently by the marking of the copula *hai* or *lin* 'even', for example. The proposed head movement does not impose an effect on what is marked as focus. Instead, it affects the size of the focus set, whose calculation rests on the structural position of the modal verbs and the focus operator.

To illustrate this idea, two assumptions are needed. I assume an alternative semantic framework on focus interpretation (Rooth 1985, 1992). Alternative semantics keep track of both the *ordinary semantic values* and the *focus semantic values* (or, equivalently, the alternative set) during the syntactic derivation. The focus semantic values consist of the set of all ordinary semantic values obtained by replacing alternatives for any focus-marked sub-parts. Take (216) as an example, which is the baseline sentence for (195a), i.e., the modal is in the base position. The sentence may receive a subject focus reading or a sentential focus reading.

(216)   Copula focus marking on the subject
Hai <u>Aaming</u> **hoji** heoi Hoenggong.   baseline of (195a)
COP Aaming may go   Hong.Kong
'It may be the case that Aaming (but not others) goes to Hong Kong.'

The ordinary semantic value is the proposition in (216). On a subject focus reading, the alternative semantic value is the set of propositions obtained by replacing the focus-marked *Aaming* with other entities, such as *Aafan, John, Mary,* etc. Similarly, on a sentential focus reading, the alternative semantic value is obtained by replacing the whole proposition with other propositions.

(217)   The ordinary and alternative semantic values of (216)[40]
a. $[\![(216)]\!]^O$ = Aaming may go to Hong Kong.
b.
$$[\![(216)]\!]^{alt} = \left\{ \begin{array}{l} \text{Aafan may go to Hong Kong.} \\ \text{John may go to Hong Kong.} \\ \text{Mary may go to Hong Kong.} \\ \cdots \end{array} \right\}$$ subject focus

c.
$$[\![(216)]\!]^{alt} = \left\{ \begin{array}{l} \text{Aafan should come to US.} \\ \text{John must stay in Japan.} \\ \text{Mary wants to leave Taiwan.} \\ \cdots \end{array} \right\}$$ sentential focus

The second assumption concerns the role of focus operators/focus particles. Following Beck (2006), I suggest that a focus operator can look at the focus semantic

---

39. Y.-y. Hsu (2019) suggests that the movement of modal verbs to the high position gives rise to a propositional focus reading, but this is not necessarily the case. For example, the sentence in (195a) retains a subject focus reading.

40. $[\![\alpha]\!]^O$ is the interpretation function for an ordinary semantic value, whereas $[\![\alpha]\!]^{alt}$ is for a focus semantic value.

values and "reset" the focus semantic values of its complement by replacing the focus semantic values with the ordinary semantic values (cf. Rooth's ~ operator; see also discussions in Kotek (2016, 2019) and Erlewine (2020a)).

With these ingredients, the scope effects of the movement of the modal verb in (216) can be illustrated in (218). For simplicity, I focus on the subject focus reading, but the same applies to the sentential focus reading.

(218) Focus scope effects of the proposed head movement
    a. **Hoji** hai Aaming heoi Hoenggong.   =(195a)
       may COP <u>Aaming</u> go   Hong.Kong
       'It may be the case that Aaming (but not others) goes to Hong Kong.'
    b. $[\![(218a)]\!]^{O}$ = Aaming may go to Hong Kong.
    c.

$$[\![(218a)]\!]^{alt} = \text{It is allowed that} \left\{ \begin{array}{l} \text{Aafan goes to Hong Kong.} \\ \text{John goes to Hong Kong.} \\ \text{Mary goes to Hong Kong.} \\ \qquad\qquad \dots \end{array} \right\} \quad \text{subject focus}$$

Crucially, the size of the alternative set in (218c) is different from that in (216b). The modal verb *hoji* 'may' escapes the scope of the focus operator *hai* by moving to the high position. As a result, the structural relation between the modal verbs and the focus operators changes, and so does as the size of the focus set.

A straightforward prediction along this line of reasoning is that what can serve as a felicitous continuation differs in cases with and without movement. This is borne out in the contrast revealed in (219). In (219a), the modal verb moves to the high position, and the continuation cannot felicitously contain the same modal verb *hoji* 'may', as it is no longer within the scope of the focus operator. This is in contrast with the sentence in (219b), where the modal verb does not undergo movement, and the same continuation becomes felicitous.

(219) Differences in felicitous continuation with and without movement of the modal verb
    a. #**Hoji** hai <u>Aaming</u> heoi Hoenggong, m-hai   Aafan hoji heoi.
       may COP Aaming go   Hong.Kong not-COP Aafan may go
       Int.: 'It may be the case that Aaming goes to Hong Kong, but not that Aafan may go (to Hong Kong).'
    b. Hai <u>Aaming</u> **hoji** heoi Hoenggong, m-hai   Aafan hoji heoi.
       COP Aaming may go   Hong.Kong not-COP Aafan may go
       'Aaming may go to Hong Kong, but not Aafan may go (to Hong Kong).'

It is obvious that *hai* is not the only focus operator in Cantonese. Cases with *lin* 'even' show the same pattern, as discussed in (197). For cases without overt focus operators such as (196), I assume that there is a null focus operator. Since the presence of focus operators is crucial in licensing the proposed head movement, it follows that topic structures discussed in (199) do not license the movement.

One remaining issue is that, if the high position hinges on whether the movement alters scope relations with the focus operator, then the unacceptability of (195b) might at first glance be surprising. This is because if the modal verb is base generated below the focus operator (= (220)) and undergoes movement, it crosses the focus operator. However, (195b) is unacceptable. I suggest that the movement is disallowed not because it violates Scope Economy, but because it violates another locality constraint on movement, Shortest Move. I postpone the discussion of these cases to § 4.5.2.

(220) A puzzle on the unacceptability of (195b)
    a. *__Hoji__ Aaming hai heoi Hoenggong.   =(195b)
        may Aaming COP go Hong.Kong
        Int.: 'It may be the case that Aaming goes to Hong Kong (but not other places).'
    b. Aaming hai __hoji__ heoi Hoenggong.   baseline of (195b)
        Aaming COP may go Hong.Kong
        'Aaming may go to Hong Kong (but not other places).'

4.4.2.3 Deriving the restriction on verbs

Recall the restriction on the types of verbs that can appear in the high position, repeated below in (221).

(221) The types of verbs in the high position
    a. Only raising predicates can occur in the (restricted) high position.
    b. Epistemic modals can freely occupy the pre-subject position.

It is observed that the high position is not available for control verbs and ability/volition modal verbs. In other words, these verbs fail to undergo the same head movement proposed for aspectual verbs and deontic/future modals. I suggest that it is the *semantic types* of these verbs that differentiate the two groups.

Under the current proposal, aspectual verbs and deontic/future modal verbs are generalized quantifiers and are of type $\langle\langle a,t\rangle,t\rangle$. This semantic type is possible for raising predicates, as they do not take any external argument but one clausal argument, i.e., they are functions from sets of properties to truth values. In contrast, control verbs and ability/volition modals take two arguments, namely, a clausal argument and an external argument. As such, they are functions from sets of propositions to functions from entity to truth value, for example, of type $\langle\langle s,t\rangle,\langle e,t\rangle\rangle$. I suggest that the reason why they cannot undergo the proposed head movement is that there is no possible type of their trace that would render successful composition. For example, if their corresponding trace is of individual type (e.g., a time variable or a world variable), a type mismatch is unavoidable. Other higher type traces (if possible) could not avoid the type mismatch either.

In order to guarantee successful composition, the only possible type of the trace would be the same type as the moving head, i.e., $\langle\langle s,t\rangle,\langle e,t\rangle\rangle$. If this is the case, the moving head, however, would fail to take scope in its derived position; it is (semantically) reconstructed back to its base position. Its movement would then fail to shift scope and violate Scope Economy.[41] Therefore, control verbs and ability/volition modal verbs fail to undergo the proposed head movement because they have a semantic type substantially different from aspectual verbs and deontic/future modals, and their movement would either lead to compositional conflicts or a violation of Scope Economy.

Interestingly, this explanation points to a predication on possible movement of control verbs and ability/volition modals. If the movement of these heads is triggered not by interpretation/scope considerations, but by some syntactic feature, their movement should be allowed. This is because their trace can be of the same type, i.e., the movement can reconstruct without violating Scope Economy. This prediction is borne out. In Cantonese, it is argued that a verb can be fronted (with doubling) to deliver a topic reading (222a) or it can move on its own to the end of the sentence to escape a focus interpretation (222b) (Cheng and Vicente 2013; Lee 2017; Lai 2019).[42]

(222) a. Topic constructions of verbs
          Soengsi, Aaming hai soeng **soengsi** tai   ni-bun syu.   control verbs
          try   Aaming FOC want try   read this-CL book
          'As for trying, Aaming wants to try to read this book.'
       b. Right dislocation of verbs
          Aaming __ tai   ni-bun syu gaa3 **sik.**   ability modals
          Aaming   read this-CL book SFP be.able
          'Aaming is able to read this book.'

These observations suggest that it is not that control verbs and ability/volition modal verbs can never move. They can move, if reconstruction does not lead to any violation of the grammar. However, they cannot undergo the proposed movement because reconstructing the movement would violate Scope Economy.

---

41. Unlike modifier types, it appears to be technically impossible to ensure a wide scope reading of control verbs and ability/volition modal verbs and successful composition at the same time. For example, type-lifting the moving heads would lead to a higher type $\langle\langle\langle s,t\rangle,\langle e,t\rangle\rangle$, $\langle\langle s,t\rangle,\langle e,t\rangle\rangle\rangle$ in the high position, but then it would lack the relevant arguments for further composition. Assuming trace-less movement or LF deletion of traces would not help either since the composition would crash at the base position.

42. For extensive disccussions on these structures, see Chapter 3.

The Unity of Movement

Turning to the unrestricted pre-subject position of epistemic modal verbs, recall that they can freely appear before or after the subject, regardless of whether the subject is quantificational or focused. At first glance, the distribution of epistemic modals appears to speak against the current proposal as the pre-subject position is not regulated by Scope Economy, i.e., epistemic modals appear to be immune from Scope Economy. I suggest that this is because epistemic modals have a different syntax compared to aspectual verbs and deontic/future modals, and that the pre-subject position is not derived via movement. Following a recent proposal by Lin (2011, 2012), epistemic modals take a finite TP complement, as opposed to deontic/future modals, which take a non-finite TP complement (i.e., the latter are raising predicates). Under this view, epistemic modals occurring in the pre-subject position have the base structure in (223a).

(223) The difference between epistemic and deontic modals under the proposal in Lin (2011, 2012)
    a. ... [$_{ModP}$ epistemic modals [$_{finite\ TP}$ **Subj. V Obj.**]]
    b. ... [$_{ModP}$ deontic/future modals [$_{non\text{-}finite\ TP}$ **Subj. V Obj.**]]

Assuming that Chinese has Case and finite clauses can assign nominative Case in Chinese (Y.-H. A. Li 1990), the (post-modal) subject in (223a) is in a Case position, and it can stay there without further movement. This is different from deontic modals (or other raising predicates), where the subject is in a non-finite clause in (223b). It needs to move for Case (i.e., the sentence is a raising structure). For cases where the epistemic modals follow the subject, this can be derived via an optional movement of the subject over the epistemic modal,e.g., triggered by an EPP feature (Lin 2011), or a topic feature (Chou 2013; Tsai 2015).[43] In other words, epistemic modals have a non-raising structures, and this explains why their pre-subject position is less restricted (because they are base-generated there), as opposed to other raising predicates.

This explanation of the less restricted epistemic modals is corroborated by the distribution of sentential negation, which shows a similar pattern to epistemic modals. The high position of the sentential negation *m-hai* 'not' is unrestricted.

(224) Sentential negation and the pre-subject position
    a. (<u>Dak</u>) Aaming **m-hai**   haau-dou hou singzik.
            only   Aaming not-COP get-able good results
            '(Only) Aaming didn't get good results.'

---

43. This amounts to a hyperraising construction (i.e., A-dependencies across finite boundaries). Its existence is defended in Lee and Yip (Accepted).

b. **M-hai** (<u>dak</u>) Aaming haau-dou hou singzik.
   not-COP only Aaming get-able good result
   'It is not the case that (only) Aaming gets good results.'

The facts for both epistemic modals and sentential negation follow if both of them can take a finite complement clause, where the subject can stay in-situ. If these analyses are on the right track, their unrestricted distribution is irrelevant to Scope Economy, since there is no movement of epistemic modals (or sentential negation) in the first place.

4.4.3 Remarks on the landing site and the trigger

In the proposal, I have assumed that the proposed head movement is achieved by adjunction to the root structure and that the movement is triggered by interpretation/ scope considerations. It should be acknowledged that this is not the only way to implement the proposed head movement. I discuss a number of possibilities, which rely on different assumptions. However, the ultimate choice among these options does not affect the central claim that head movement can induce scope effects.

4.4.3.1 *The landing site*

Within the rich literature on head movement, almost all logically possible landing sites have been proposed. (225) illustrates (with *hoici* 'begin') four possible landing site, namely, (a) a head-adjoined position, (b) a specifier position, (c) a derived head position and, (d) a phrase-adjoined position, illustrated with *hoici* as follows, respectively. (225a) is achieved via head-to-head adjunction (Baker 1988, *et seq.*) and (225b) is achieved via head-to-specifier movement (Matushansky 2006; Vicente 2007; Harizanov 2019). (225c) is achieved via reprojection of heads (Fanselow 2003; Donati 2006; Surányi 2005, 2008; Georgi and Müller 2010). Lastly, (225d) represents a less conventional but logically possible option, where the head is adjoined to a phrase (cf. *Internal Pair-Merge,* M. Richards 2009).

(225) a. A head-adjoined position

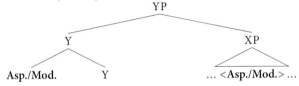

b. A specifier position

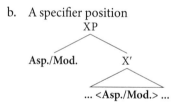

c. A derived head position

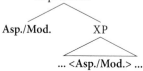

d. A phrase-adjoined position

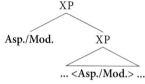

One crucial criteria of the landing site is that it must allow the moving head to take scope over the structurally lower quantificational elements or focused elements. This criterion raises a concern to the head-to-head adjunction approach in (225a). If the moving head is adjoined to another head, then it cannot c-command the quantificational element in the XP. It must be assumed that, for example, the scope property of the moving head may "percolate" to the higher segment of Y such that it can take scope there.

The other three options do not differ in structural terms and all of them allow the moving head to c-command the complement X'/XP. Distinguishing between them may be a theory-internal issue. I briefly discuss some potential concerns or required assumptions in these options.

One concern for the specifier approach in (225b) is that, since the moving heads can land above quantificational or focused elements of different types, it does not seem to target a specifier position of a particular (functional) projection (e.g. FocusP or TopicP). More importantly, the example in (190), repeated below in (226), shows that the moving heads can target multiple positions, if there is more than one quantificational/focused element in the same sentence.

(226) Quantificational adverbs and subjects and multiple high positions

    a.   {$_{ADV}$ Hai mui-gaan hokhaau } **hoici** {$_{SUBJ}$ daaiboufan jan   } dou __
       at   every-CL school   begin   most   person all
       haau-dou hou singzik.   'every' > 'begin' > 'most'
       get-able   good result
       'At every school, it begins to be the case that most people are getting good results.'

    b.   **Hoici** {$_{ADV}$ hai mui-gaan hokhaau } {$_{SUBJ}$ daaiboufan jan   } dou __
       begin   at   every-CL school   most   person all
       haau-dou hou singzik.   'begin' > 'every' > 'most'
       get-able   good result
       'It begins to be the case that, at every school, most people are getting good results.'

While it is possible that there may be multiple relevant projections in the CP domain, one may actually need to posit one such projection above *each* quantificational/focused element that is present in the sentence. In other words, there is a correlation between the number of functional projections (that host the moving heads) in the CP and the number of quantificational/focused elements. Also, movement to a specifier position into the CP domain typically involves discourse effects, but it is unclear what these effects would be when the aspectual verbs and modal verbs occupy the high position.[44]

As for the reprojection approach in (225c), it is common to assume that a category feature is the trigger of the reprojecting movement (Fanselow 2003; Surányi 2005, 2008)). Similar to the head-to-specifier movement approach, one would be forced to posit different categorial projections in the CP, e.g., different AspectPs or ModalPs.

The last option, i.e., the head-to-phrase adjunction approach in (225d), seems to be less problematic. It takes advantage of the flexible nature of adjunction and allows different landing sites for the proposed head movement. As long as the output of the derivation is interpretable, aspectual verbs and modal verbs can adjoin freely adjoin to any syntactic category (cf. Heim and Kratzer 1998). I acknowledge that the notion of adjunction as a syntactic operation is still an unsettled issue in the literature, but such an approach is analogous to other scope-shifting operation

---

44. Indeed, Y.-y. Hsu (2016, 2019) argues that modals move into FocusP, but she also agrees that it is *not* the case that the moving head receives a focus interpretation. This differs from proposals that adopt a head-to-specifier analysis, where the head in the specifier position receives a focus/topic interpretation. See § 4.4.3.2 for discussions and further arguments against a discourse-feature-driven approach.

140   The Unity of Movement

such as English Quantifier Raising (May 1977, 1985; Fox 2000), both of which are able to shift scope and are subject to Scope Economy.

4.4.3.2   *The trigger*

As for the trigger of the proposed head movement, it is not immediately clear what the trigger of the movement is. I first discuss what the trigger is unlikely to be, and then return to other possible options.

While discourse features or A'-feature are often held responsible for predicate fronting (Vicente 2007; Cheng and Vicente 2013; Hein 2018; Harizanov 2019, among many others), it is unlikely that this is the case for the proposed head movement. First of all, the aspectual verbs and the modal verbs in the high position do not seem to receive any focus or topic interpretation. This is in sharp contrast with the verb doubling constructions discussed in Chapter 3.[45] Additionally, sentences with an aspectual verb or a modal verb in the high position are felicitous in out-of-the-blue contexts or the 'what happened?' contexts, as illustrated in (227).

(227)   An out-of-the-blue/ A 'what happened' context
    a.   Faatsaang me si   aa3?
        happen   what event sfp
        'What happened?'
    b.   **Hoici** <u>dak</u> Aaming haau-dou hou singzik.   =(206b)
        begin only Aaming get-able   good result
        'It begins to be the case that only Aaming is getting good results.'

It should be noted that Y.-y. Hsu (2016, 2019) argues that modal movement is an instance of focus movement, where the modal serves as a propositional focus operator and marks the whole proposition/TP as focus. She argues for this claim based on the unacceptability of (228) (which is the Cantonese counterpart of the original Mandarin example). She suggests that the sentence is ruled out because *hoji*, as an focus operator, intervenes between the (null) question operator (higher in the clause) and the *wh*-expressions, as an instance of (semantic) intervention effects (Beck 1996, 2006).

(228)   *Wh*-objects and the high position
    ***Hoji** Aaming zungji <u>bin-go</u>?
    may Aaming like   who
    Lit. 'It is allowed that Aaming likes who?'

---

45. Recall also that modal verbs resist a focus or topic reading, as they cannot be targeted in verb doubling constructions.

However, such an analysis incorrectly predicts the unacceptability of (198), repeated below in (229), where the *wh*-expression in the subject position.

(229)   *Wh*-subjects and the high position
        Hoji <u>bin-go</u> haa-nin   heoi Hoenggong?   = (198)
        may who   next-year go   Hong.Kong
        Lit.: 'It is allowed that who goes to Hong Kong next year?'

The subject-object asymmetry follows from the current proposal that the high position is only licensed if the immediately following constituent receives a focus interpretation (or is a quantificational element). Thus, (228) is unacceptable not because *hoji* causes intervention effects, but because *Aaming* does not receive a focus interpretation.[46]

If discourse/A'-features are not responsible for the proposed head movement, there are still two possibilities. The first one is to suggest that the movement is triggered by an EPP feature on a null head, without a prior Probe-Goal Agree relation (Collins 1997; Miyagawa 2001; Nevins and Anand 2003). An advantage of this approach is that it allows us to capture the lack of scopal ambiguity of sentences like (227b). Nevins and Anand (2003) suggest that A-movement only for EPP feature does not reconstruct. If this reasoning can be extended to *head* movement only for EPP feature, then the lack of scopal ambiguity follows.

Another possibility is to suggest that the proposed head movement is not feature-driven, but is triggered by interpretation or scope considerations, or is "free," in a sense similar to English Quantifier Raising and Japanese/German A-scrambling. (May 1977; 1985; Fox 2000; Bobaljik and Wurmbrand 2012, i.a.). Under the model proposed by Bobaljik and Wurmbrand (2012), the lack of reconstruction of this movement is due to the "¾ Signature Effects", in a way similar to A-scrambling in Japanese and German, which cannot be reconstructed for scope interpretation. The proposed head movement is compatible with these possibilities.[47]

---

46. The intuition that the sentences with a high modal verb come with propositional focus or TP focus is not implausible. However, instead of suggesting that such an interpretation is directly contributed by the modal movement *per se*, I suggest that it is a result of the change of the calculation of the focus sets/ focus alternatives, as suggested in § 4.2.3. Modal movement allows the modal verbs to escape from the focus scope of the focus operator, leaving the rest of the sentence, usually a TP, to be within the focus set. This may give rise to the intuition that the TP as a whole is focused.

47. The discussion in the subsection has greatly benefited from discussions with Stefan Keine and Roumyana Pancheva.

4.5 Further evidence for the proposal

In this section, I discuss further evidence for the proposed movement. In § 4.5.1, I examine cases where multiple quantificational heads are stacked in the high position. In § 4.5.2, I show that it is constrained by a locality constraint on movement, Shortest Move. In 4.5.3, I report cases where the quantificational heads can undergo Across-the-Board (ATB) movement. All these cases fall out naturally from the proposed movement analyses. Lastly, in § 4.5.4, I examine whether the proposed movement exhibits island effects, which are typical properties of syntactic movement. I suggest that there is no conclusive evidence for the presence or absence of island effects.

4.5.1 Stacking of quantificational heads in the high position

It is suggested that a quantificational element can license the proposed head movement, as moving across it potentially leads to scope effects (hence obeying Scope Economy). It is also suggested that the moving head is quantificational by nature (i.e., a generalized quantifier). These combine to predict that the movement of a quantificational head to the high position would license the movement of another quantificational head to the high position. In other words, it is predicted that quantificational heads can be "stacked" in the high position, if the proposed movement applies more than once.

This prediction is borne out. Observe that *hoici* 'begin' and *hoji* 'may' can co-occur in the (post-subject) low positions in (230a). Since the subject is quantificational, the movement of *hoici* 'begin' to a higher position is possible, as it obeys Scope Economy (as in (230b). Furthermore, the movement of *hoji* 'may' to a position higher than *hoici* 'begin' is also allowed, as illustrated in (230c). *Hoji* 'may' takes scope over both *hoici* 'begin' and *dak* 'only'.

(230) Stacking of aspectual verbs and deontic modals
    a. <u>Dak</u> Aaming **hoici hoji** zou fan.   'only' > 'begin' > 'may'
        only Aaming begin may early sleep
        'Aaming begins to be allowed to sleep early.'
    b. **Hoici** <u>dak</u> Aaming __ **hoji** zou fan.   'begin' > 'only' > 'may'
        begin only Aaming   may early sleep
        'It begins to be the case that it is allowed that only Aaming sleeps early.'
    c. **Hoji hoici** <u>dak</u> Aaming __ __ zou fan.   'may' > 'begin' > 'only'
        may begin only Aaming   early sleep
        'It is allowed that it begins to be the case that only Aaming sleeps early.'

To see an additional examples with different quantificational heads, consider the sentences in (231). The modal verb *wui* 'will' and the aspectual verb *gaizuk* 'continue' can be stacked in the high position (in the embedded clause), as shown in (231c).

(231) Stacking of future modals and aspectual verbs
    a. Ngo gokdak [<u>dak</u> gupiu **wui gaizuk** sing].   'only' > 'will' > 'continue'
        I   think only stock will continue rise
        'I think that only stock (prices) will continue to rise.'
    b. Ngo gokdak [**gaizuk** <u>dak</u> gupiu **wui** __ sing]. 'continue' > 'only' > 'will'
        I   think continue only stock will   rise
        'I think that it will continue to be the case that only stock (prices) rise.'
    c. Ngo gokdak [**wui gaizuk** <u>dak</u> gupiu __ __ 'will'> 'continue'> 'only'
        I   think will continue only stock
        sing].
        rise
        'I think that it will continue to be the case that only stock (prices) rise.'

Under the current proposal, the derivation of (230c), for instance, involves two steps, namely, the movement of *hoji* 'may', followed by the movement of *hoici* 'begin'. Note that the two movement steps are independent of each other (i.e., they need not occur together), and both observe Scope Economy.

(232) A two-step derivation of (230c)
    may begin [$_{TP}$ only Aaming$_i$ __ __ [$_{vP}$ t_i sleep-early]]

4.5.2 Shortest Move

In addition to Scope Economy, the proposed head movement is also subject to a locality constraint on movement, *Shortest Move*. Consider the configuration in (233) where there are a quantificational subject and a non-quantificational adverbial in a sentence.

(233) A configuration showing possible landing sites under Scope Economy
    ❷ [$_{TP}$ Adverbial$_{[-Q]}$ ❶ [$_{TP}$ Subject$_{[+Q]}$ **Asp./Mod.** [$_{vP}$ ...]]]

It has been shown that the position right above the quantificational subject (=❶) is a possible landing site in adherence to Scope Economy. The position right above the non-quantificational adverbial (=❷), at least in principle, should be another possible landing site, since the moving heads can take wide scope from there over the quantificational subject. This movement step does not violate Scope Economy and should be allowed. This, however, is not the case, as illustrated in (234).[48]

(234) A non-quantificational adverbial and a quantificational subject
     ❷ [??]**Hoici** [$_{ADV}$ hai ngodei hokhaau] ❶ **hoici** [$_{SUBJ}$ daaiboufan jan   ] dou __
        begin   at our   school   begin   most   person   all
     haau-dou hou   singzik.
     get-able   good result
     'At our school, it begins to be the case that, most people are getting good results.'

The unavailability of the high position in ❷ suggests that the movement of *hoici* cannot be longer/higher than it needs to shift scope. It must land *right above* the quantificational subject. Such a restriction does not fall out from Scope Economy.

   I suggest that this follows from a version of Shortest Move, given in (235). Recall that I have suggested that Scope Economy is a syntactic, derivational constraint on movement, and that certain formal logical properties are accessible in syntax. I suggest that the proposed Shortest Move in (235) bears a similar character in the sense that it applies right after the evaluation of Scope Economy, and dictates that the time when a scope-shifting operation is sanctioned by Scope Economy is the only possible time that the scope-shifting operation can apply.[49]

(235) Shortest (scope-shifting) Move
     A scope-shifting operation must move a quantifier to the closest position in which *it shifts scope*.

As such, (235) dictates that the position ❶ in (234) is the only possible landing site that delivers the wide 'begin'-scope, as it is the *closest* position. This explains why the landing site of the moving quantificational heads must be *immediately* followed by a quantificational/focused element (as stated in (202)), as it is the closest position. I take this as further evidence for a movement approach to the high position of quantificational heads.

   Shortest Move as formulated in (235) provides an explanation of the unacceptable cases discussed at the end of § 4.4.2.2, repeated below as (236).

---

48. The high position in ❷ is available if the adverbial is quantificational, as shown in (190).

49. This is reminiscent of the "Adjoin-as-soon-as-possible" condition proposed in Erlewine (2015, 2017), which is originally proposed to regulate adjunction of Externally-Merged elements. If this can be extended to Internally-Merged elements, and if the the proposed movement is achieved via adjunction (as one of the four possibilities discussed in § 4.4.3.2), then the proposed Shortest Move may be subsumed under the "Adjoin-as-soon-as-possible" condition.

Chapter 4. Scope effects **145**

(236) A puzzle on the unacceptability of (195b)
    a. *__Hoji__ Aaming hai heoi Hoenggong.   =(195b)
        may Aaming COP go Hong.Kong
        Int.: 'It may be the case that Aaming goes to Hong Kong.'
    b. Aaming hai **hoji** heoi Hoenggong.   baseline of (195b)
        Aaming COP may go Hong.Kong
        'Aaming may go to Hong Kong.'

The sentence in (236a) appears to be problematic: if it has the base structure in (236b), then the movement of *hoji* 'may' to the high position should not violate Scope Economy, since it crosses the focus operator (and affects the calculation of the focus sets). This suggests that (236a) is disallowed for reasons other than Scope Economy. With (235), the unacceptability of (236a) can be attributed to reasons similar to why (234) is ruled out: it does not land *right* above the focus operator, i.e., its movement is too "long". If the movement does not cross the subject, it is allowed, as shown in (237).

(237) Movement of *hoji* 'modal' in compliance to Shortest Move and Scope Economy
    Aaming **hoji** hai heoi Hoenggong.
    Aaming may COP go Hong.Kong
    'Aaming may go to Hong Kong.'

The spirit behind (235) is similar but not identical to Fox's version suggested in Fox (2000, p. 23).

(238) Shortest (interpretable) Move (Fox's version)
    [Quantifier Raising] must move a [quantifier phrase] to the closest position in which *it is interpretable*. In other words, a [quantifier phrase] must always move to the closest clause-denoting element that dominates it.

The crucial difference with (235) lies in what is relevant in the calculation of "closest position". Fox's version suggests that it is the clause-denoting elements (i.e., the nodes that are of proposition type *t*). Importantly, movement to all these positions is constrained by Scope Economy, i.e., moving to each of these positions must shift scope relations. On the other hand, the version proposed here is less restricted in that it suggests that only scope-taking elements count when calculating "the closest position". Effectively, the two versions make different predictions on whether the moving quantifier element can skip a clause-denoting non-quantificational node.

146   The Unity of Movement

(239) Different predictions on the movement of α (where XP/YP/ZP are all clause-
denoting)

    a.   Fox's Shortest Move: *α [$_{XP}$ [+Q] ... [$_{YP}$ [-Q] ... [$_{ZP}$ $\langle\alpha\rangle$...]]]

                                          YP = non-skippable

    b.   The proposed Shortest Move: $^{OK}\alpha$ [$_{XP}$ [+Q] ... [$_{YP}$ [-Q] ... [$_{ZP}$ $\langle\alpha\rangle$...]]]

                                          YP = skippable

The prediction made by the proposed version is borne out, at least in Cantonese, since the movement of *hoici* 'begin' can skip the TP.[50]

(240) The proposed movement may skip intervening nodes that denote clauses

Hoici [$_{TopP}$ [cyunbou jan]   [$_{TP}$ Aaming dou __ hou jansoeng]].   = (188a)

begin   every   person   Aaming all   very praise

'It begins to be the case that Aaming praises everyone.'

Concerning the status of Shortest Move in (235), it might be subsumed under Scope Economy since both make reference specifically to scope and are evaluated locally. Evidence for this claim would rely on overt scope-shifting operations that are subject to Scope Economy. As far as I am aware, there are two such cases: determiner raising in Japanese (Takahashi 2002) and negative auxiliary inversion in some varieties of English (Matyiku 2017). Shortest Move in (235) is compatible with their data, where the moving heads land right above the element that they scope over. Alternatively, Shortest Move in (235) might be subsumed under Minimal Link Condition (Chomsky 1995b), Shortest Attract/Move (N. Richards 2001), or the featural Relativized Minimality (Rizzi 2001, 2004), if the relevant formal logical properties are realized as syntactic features (as discussed in § 4.4.1.2),

---

50. The motivation for Fox's version comes from the contrast in (i), discussed in Fox (2000), p. 64, fn.52. Fox's version derives the contrast without relying on the assumption that QR is clause-bounded (*contra* Moltmann and Szabolcsi 1994). This is because in (ia) the CP is the closest clause-denoting node for the universal quantifier, but it is non-quantificational, and the position is thus ruled out by Scope Economy. In contrast, in (ib) the CP is quantificational (due to the *wh*-expression) and thus the position is sanctioned. Together with the assumption that *know* is quantificational, the universal quantifier moves further to the matrix v/VP and then to TP over the existential subject, delivering the wide scope reading.

  (i) a. *Wide universal scope: One girl knows [$_{CP}$ **that**$_{[-Q]}$ <u>every</u> boy bought a present for Mary].

       b. ^{OK}Wide universal scope: One girl knows [$_{CP}$ **what**$_{[+Q]}$ <u>every</u> boy bought for Mary].

However, as Fox admits, the unavailability of wide universal scope in (ii) (discussed in Moltmann and Szabolcsi 1994) is unexplained. I leave open the precise formulation of the locality constraint on English QR.

  (ii) * Wide universal scope: One girl wonder [$_{CP}$ **what**$_{[+Q]}$ <u>every</u> boy bought for Mary].

such that the notion of "shortest" is calculated based on the distance between the movement trigger and the corresponding syntactic features. However, additional assumptions are needed to constrain the *landing* site of the movement, rather than the *launching* site (i.e., the base position of the moving element). I leave the precise formulation open.

4.5.3 Movement out of coordinate structures

One further piece of evidence for the proposed movement comes from Across-the-Board (ATB) movement out of coordinate structures. In Cantonese, disjunctive scope can be marked by *m-hai ... zauhai ...* 'either ... or ...'. In (241), the two disjuncts are sentential and both contain the aspectual verb *hoici* 'begin'.

(241)   A coordinate structure containing *hoici* 'begin' in each clause
        Context: It is heard that either Aaming or Aafan has studied very hard recently. The speaker guesses:
        M-<u>hai</u>   Aaming **hoici** haau-dak   hou,   <u>zau-hai</u>   Aafan **hoici** haau-dak
        not-COP Aaming begin get-RESULT good, then-COP Aafan begin get-RESULT
        hou.
        good
        'Either Aaming begins to perform well, or Aafan begins to perform well.'

Importantly, it is possible for *hoici* 'begin' to occupy the high position above the disjunctive scope, as in (242). The scope of *hoici* 'begin' is extended and now it scopes over the disjunctive scope. The sentence is true under a different scenario. Note that it is not true under the scenario in (241).

(242)   ATB movement out of coordinate structures
        Context: In past exams, either Aaming or Aafan or Chris got good results. Recently, Chris is distracted from study, and now either Aaming is getting good results, or Aafan is getting good results.
        Hoici <u>m-hai</u>   Aaming __ haau-dak hou,   <u>zauhai</u>   Aafan __ haau-dak hou.
        begin not-COP Aaming   get-RES   good, then-COP Aafan   get-RES   good
        'It begins to be the case that either Aaming performs well, or Aafan performs well.'

The high position can be derived by applying the proposed head movement in an across-the-board (ATB) fashion (Ross 1967; Williams 1978). Specifically, the aspectual verb *hoici* 'begin' in each disjunct undergoes head movement to a clause-external, high position, in a way depicted in (243).[51]

---

51. ATB movement is attested elsewhere in Chinese, such as in gapping-like constructions (Tang 2001) and *wh*-movement (Pan 2011).

(243) A simplified representation of the derivation of (242), in English glosses
begin [[$_{CP1}$ either Aaming __ ...][$_{CP2}$ or Aafan __ ...]]

ATB movement

Note that such movement is impossible if only one instance of *hoici* 'begin' moves out. This is because the movement would violate the Coordinate Structure Constraint, which precludes movement out of coordinate structure (Ross 1967).[52]

(244) Illicit non-ATB movement out of coordinate structures
Hoici <u>m-hai</u>   Aaming hoici haau-dak hou, <u>zauhai</u>   Aafan __ haau-dak
begin not-COP Aaming begin get-RES   good then-COP Aafan   get-RES
hou.
good
Int.: 'It begins to be the case that either Aaming begins to perform well, or Aafan performs well.'

4.5.4 A remark on the indeterminacy of island sensitivity

In this last subsection, I examine whether the proposed head movement exhibits island effects, since island sensitivity is commonly taken to support syntactic movement.[53] However, it is shown, for independent reasons, that there is no clear evidence from syntactic islands for or against a movement approach. This is because it is difficult, if not impossible, to fix the base position of the aspectual verbs and modal verbs in bi-clausal structures.

In order to determine whether the proposed head movement is sensitive to syntactic islands, the configuration containing a complex NP island in (245b) is of interest.

(245) Complex NP Island intervention
a. Baseline: S V [$_{Complex NP}$ [S **Asp./Mod.** VP] NP]
b. Target: **Asp./Mod.** S V [$_{Complex NP}$ [S VP] NP]

---

52. The sentence in (244) without the initial *hoici* 'begin' is acceptable under the following context: if Aaming is a younger brother and Aafan is his sister, and Dad bought just one present, saying, "if Aaming is doing better than last time, then he gets the present. If Aaming didn't and Aafan is doing as good as last time, then Aafan gets the present." One day, the present was gone, and the speaker inferred from this by saying (244) without the initial *hoici*.

53. I thank Colin Davis for critical and constructive comments on this issue.

The following sentences illustrate these configurations with *hoici* 'begin'. Note that the subjects in both matrix and embedded must be quantificational in order to license the proposed head movement.

(246)   Two positions of *hoici* 'begin' in sentences with a complex NP island
   a.   Dak Aaming zung soengseon [$_{NP}$ [go-go dou **hoici** haau-dak hou] ge
        only Aaming still   believe   CL-CL all   begin get-able   good GE
        siusik].
        rumor
        'Only Aaming still believes the rumor that everyone begins to perform well.'
   b.   **Hoici** dak Aaming zung soengseon [$_{NP}$ [go-go dou haau-dak hou] ge
        begin only Aaming still   believe   CL-CL all   get-able   good GE
        siusik].
        rumor
        'It begins that only Aaming still believes the rumor that everyone performs well.'

The high position of *hoici* 'begin' in (246b) suggests that movement occurs and its acceptability indicates that there is no island violation. One may then suggest that the proposed head movement is *insensitive* to syntactic islands, but this is based on the assumption that (246b) is derived from (246a), where *hoici* originates from the embedded clause.

(247)   A possible derivation for (246b), movement across a complex NP island
        begin SV [$_{Complex NP}$ [S__VP] NP]

However, there could be another possible derivation for (246b), where *hoici* is base generated in the matrix clause.

(248)   An alternative derivation for (246b), no movement across a complex NP island
        begin S__V [$_{Complex NP}$ [SVP] NP]

Since the target configuration may have either one of the possible base structures, it is crucial to determine the base position of *hoici* 'begin'. However, there are at least two reasons that the base positions cannot be easily determined. On one hand, since aspectual verbs and modal verbs are raising predicates as suggested (Y.-H. A. Li 1990; Lin and Tang 1995, i.a.), they do not impose selectional requirement on the subject (i.e., they only select a clausal complement). Therefore, both the matrix and the embedded positions are possible base position of these verbs. On the other hand, reconstruction is unavailable for independent reasons (i.e.,

150 The Unity of Movement

arguably due to Scope Economy; see § 4.4.3.2). It is thus not possible to detect the base positions of these verbs based on interpretations either. Similar issues arise in other island configurations. As such, I conclude that standard island diagnostics do not provide evidence for or against a movement approach to the high position.[54]

It should be acknowledged that the proposed head movement does not exhibit typical movement properties such as reconstruction, scope ambiguity and island effects. The evidence for movement must rely on other less standard (but not necessarily less convincing) evidence discussed in previous subsections.

4.6 Alternative analyses to a head movement approach

In this section, I argue against four alternative analyses to the proposed head movement account. I first discuss two non-movement approaches to the positional alternation of aspectual verbs and modal verbs in § 4.6.1 and § 4.6.2. I then discuss two variants of a phrasal movement approach in § 4.6.3 and in § 4.6.4, where movement is involved, but it is phrasal movement instead of head movement.

4.6.1 Multiple base positions of aspectual verbs and modal verbs

Under a non-movement approach, it might be suggested that the high and low positions of aspectual verbs and modal verbs are not derivationally related by movement. Instead, they would be merged directly in the high or low positions (i.e., they are adjunct-like elements). Recall the paradigm discussed in § 4.3.1, simplified in (249).

(249) A simplified representation of the sentences in (175) and (176)
    a. Aaming > **begin** > VP   cf. (175a)
    b. *****Begin** > Aaming > VP   cf. (175b)
    c. Only Aaming > **begin** > VP   cf. (176a)
    d. **Begin** > Only Aaming > VP   cf. (176b)

---

54. Similar issues arise when determining whether the proposed head movement is clause-bounded or not, i.e., whether a head can exit an embedded clause (and result in a long-distance dependency). The relevant configuration is schematically illustrated in (i) below. Therefore, there is no clear evidence for or against the clause boundedness of the proposed head movement either.

(i) CP intervention
    a. Target: **Asp./Mod.** S V [$_{CP}$ S VP]
    b. Possible base structure 1: S V [$_{CP}$ S **Asp./Mod.** VP]
    c. Possible base structure 2: S **Asp./Mod.** V [$_{CP}$ S VP]

Such a multiple base position approach could capture the admissible cases in (249a, c, d). In order to rule out cases like (249b), this approach would have to employ an additional constraint which dictates that the high base position is only available when the following constituent is quantificational or receives a focus interpretation.

At least two issues arise with such an approach. First, this approach must *look ahead* to determine the timing of adjunction of the relevant heads. This is because if there is a quantificational element that is going to be merged, these heads must "wait" until then. In other words, the timing of adjunction of these heads must be based on the the result of this look-ahead operation. In contrast to this, a head movement account coupled with Scope Economy does not give rise to similar look-ahead issues.

Second, the constraint on the high position appears to be a re-statement of the generalization in (202), or we must stipulate a base-position version of Scope Economy, which dictates "do not merge high unless you take wider scope there". Such a constraint on base position is, as far as I know, rarely heard of. It is unclear why merging at a low position would be more preferred to merging at a high one.

One possibility is to suggest that the high position of aspectual verbs and modal verbs may impose a selectional requirement on the adjacent XP. For example, the unacceptability of (249b) follows if we assume that *hoici* (semantically) selects a quantificational element and thus a proper name in the subject position fails this requirement. Such a requirement, at least superficially, bears similarity to English *almost*, illustrated below.

(250) The selectional requirement of *almost* in English
    a.   John/Ten people **almost** died.   cf. (249a,c)
    b.   *[**Almost** John] died.   cf. (249b)
    c.   OK[**Almost** ten people] died.   cf. (249d)

However, there are two issues concerning this suggestion. First, if it is assumed that *hoici* 'begin' imposes a selectional requirement on the adjacent element, it must be also assumed that the complement clause selected by *hoici* 'begin' (such as the VP in (307a, c)) is also quantificational, but it is unclear why this is so.

Second, a selectional requirement presupposes constituency between the selecting element and the selected element. The sentence in (251) shows that the universal quantifiers do not form a constituent with *hoici* 'begin'. Note that the coverb *tung* 'with' takes nominal structures as its complement.

(251) *Hoici* 'begin' does not form a constituent with the nominal quantifiers
    *Ngo tung **hoici** [mui-go jan]   dou gong-zo je.
    I   with begin every-CL person all talked thing
    Int.: 'It begins to be the case that I have talked to everyone.'

152 The Unity of Movement

Notably, this is in contrast to *caa-m-do* 'almost' in Cantonese which shows similar distributional properties to English *almost*. It forms a constituent with the adjacent nominal.

(252) Ngo tung **caa-m-do** [mui-go jan]   dou gong-zo je.
     I   with almost   every-CL person all talked thing
     'I have talked to almost everyone.'

I therefore suggest that the unavailability of the high position of aspectual verbs and modal verbs cannot be attributed to selectional requirements. I conclude further that the base position approach does not adequately capture the paradigm in (307).

4.6.2   An in-situ approach to aspectual verbs and modal verbs

Another variant of a non-movement approach is to suggest that the quantificational heads under discussion are indeed in-situ, and the word order alternation is due to the optional movement of XPs surrounding them (e.g., subjects, topics, adverbials, etc.), as illustrated in (253). A conceivable possibility of this XP movement in Cantonese might be topic movement, which can target different types of constituents. Under this approach, no head movement is needed.

(253)   A hypothetical approach that employs optional XP movements
     (XP) [$_{\text{AspectP/ModalP}}$ **Asp./Mod.** [(XP) …]]

       Optional XP movement

There are, however, two reasons not to adopt such an analysis. First, recall the paradigm in (307), repeated in (254). While this approach would be able to capture the word order alternation in (254c–d), it wrongly predicts that (254b) to be acceptable.

(254)   A simplified representation of the sentences in (175) and (176)   = (307)
     a.   Aaming > **begin** > VP   cf. (175a)
     b. ***Begin** > Aaming > VP   cf. (175b)
     c.   Only Aaming > **begin** > VP   cf. (176a)
     d. **Begin** > Only Aaming > VP   cf. (176b)

In other words, this approach does not capture the sensitivity to the quantificational/focus nature of XP. In order to rule out examples like (254b), it must be assumed that non-quantificational elements must move across the aspectual verbs and modal verbs (when embedded under them), whereas quantificational elements optionally do so. However, this assumption would also require all non-quantificational objects (e.g., *hou singzik* 'good result'), to move, contrary to facts.

Reasoning along this line would also need to account for why non-quantificational/non-focused elements are special in that they must undergo movement in the relevant configurations, or why quantificational/focused elements are exceptionally allowed to resist movement. Such an account is not impossible to formulate, but would be less plausible when compared to a head movement account, since the latter can resort to Scope Economy to capture the sensitivity to quantificational/focused elements, and Scope Economy receives independent support from different phenomena in different languages (Fox 2000; Takahashi 2002; Matyiku 2017, i.a.).

4.6.3 A remnant movement approach

Another alternative analysis to a head movement approach is a remnant movement approach. It shares the idea that movement of aspectual verbs and modal verbs is involved, but differs from the current proposal in that the moving element is not a head, but a phrase. Such an approach would suggest that what surfaces as head movement could indeed be remnant VP movement in disguise (den Besten and Webelhuth 1990; Koopman and Szabolcsi 2000; Mahajan 2003, among many others). Specifically, it might be suggested that, before VP movement, all other elements except the verb are extracted from the VP. As a result, the remnant VP would contain just a verb, and when the VP moves, it appears that the verb is moving on its own, but in fact this is an instance of phrasal movement.

Implementing this idea on (176b/206b), illustrated with English glosses below, the vP complement of *hoici* 'begin' is first extracted to a higher position, as indicated in the step in (255b). Subsequently, AspectP containing only the aspectual verb is fronted, as in (255c).

(255) Deriving (176b from (176a) under a remnant movement approach
    a. *Base structure:*
       [$_{TP}$ only Aaming [$_{vP_1}$ begin [$_{vP_2}$ get-good-result]]]
    b. *Fronting of the complement of 'begin', i.e. vP:*
       [$_{TP}$ only Aaming [$_{vP}$ get-good-result] [$_{AspectP}$ begin t_{vP}]]

                    vP movement

    c. *Remnant phrasal movement of AspectP:*
       [$_{AspectP}$ begin t_{vP}] [$_{TP}$ only Aaming [$_{vP}$ get-good-result] $t_{AspectP}$]

               (remnant) AspectP movement

There are, however, two issues with this approach. First, the legitimacy of fronting vP in (255b) must be stipulated, since this intermediate step by itself does not form an acceptable sentence, as shown in (256). In other words, its application is dependent on the subsequent AspectP movement, i.e., vP movement is construction-specific.

(256)   Fronting of vP above AspectP is disallowed
  *Dak Aaming [$_{vP}$ haau-dou hou singzik] **hoici.**
  only Aaming get-able good result begin
  'Only Aaming is such that he begins to get good results.'

Secondly, and crucially, while this approach derives the desirable word order, it does not deliver the relevant scope facts. According to the structure in (255c), 'begin' is "buried" in the AspectP, and it does not c-command *dak* 'only'. A surface scope reading would require some non-standard scope-taking mechanism or redefinition of the notion of c-command. Additionally, even if *hoici* 'begin' could take scope from within the AspectP, the sentence would be expected to be ambiguous, since vP fronting reconstructs (cf. Huang 1993; assuming the same for AspectP fronting). However, *hoici* 'begin' unambiguously takes wide scope in the high position. As such, it is unlikely that phrasal movement is at play here; instead, a head movement account straightforwardly accounts for both the surface word order and the wide scope reading of 'begin'.

4.6.4   Movement of aspectual verbs and modal verbs as phrasal movement

Another variant of the phrasal movement approach is to suggest that aspectual verbs and deontic/future modals are phrases, instead of heads (i.e., they are not minimal elements). If so, the proposed movement should be regarded as phrasal movement, instead of head movement.

It should be noted that the head vs. phrase distinction is not always clear in languages like Chinese which lack verbal inflection. The phrase-structural status of an element can only be diagnosed indirectly. Here, I first offer an argument from VP ellipsis for the head status of deontic/future modals (and I will return to aspectual verbs below). It has been observed that a VP can be elided in Mandarin when it follows modal auxiliaries (Tsai 2015; Law and Ndayiragije 2017), similar to English (Sag 1976, i.a.). The same applies to Cantonese, illustrated below (Δ marks the elided site).

(257)   Modals that license VP ellipsis
  Aaming **hoji/wui** [lai], Aafan dou **hoji/wui** Δ.
  Aaming may/will come Aafan also may/will
  'Aaming may/will come, and Aafan may/will, too.'

Chapter 4. Scope effects **155**

This is in contrast with other phrasal/adverbial modal elements, which do not license VP ellipsis.

(258) Modals that do not license VP ellipsis
??Aaming **bitseoi**　　[lai], Aafan dou **bitseoi**　　Δ.
Aaming necessarily come Aafan also necessarily
'Aaming must come, Aafan must, too.'

The contrast follows if we make the common assumption that VP ellipsis requires head licensing (or head government, Huang 1993; Tsai 2015). Crucially, the modals that can license VP ellipsis are those that can undergo the proposed movement, suggesting their head status.

The situation concerning aspectual verbs is different, however. For example, *hoici* 'begin' does not license VP ellipsis.

(259) Aspectual verbs do not license VP ellipsis
??Ni-po faa　　**hoici** [maanmaan bin hung] laa3, go-po faa　　dou **hoici** Δ
this-CL flower begin slowly　　　turn red　SFP that-CL flower also begin
laa3.
SFP
Int.: 'The flower begins to turn red slowly. That flower begins, too'

This might be taken to suggest that aspectual verbs are indeed adverbs (hence phrasal elements). Anticipating the discussions in § 4.7.2, the proposed movement also applies to phrases, which can be extended to capture distribution of a subset of adverbs. The phrasal/adverb status of aspectual verbs would not be a concern to the proposal, but this would mean that the evidence for head movement with semantic effects come exclusively from modal verbs.

It might also be that the unacceptability of (259) is due to the fact that VP ellipsis is additionally constrained by other principles, and being a head is only a *necessary* but not *sufficient* condition in licensing VP ellipsis. In other words, VP ellipsis is a unidirectional diagnostic: if an element can license VP ellipsis, then it is a head. But it is agnostic on elements that fail to license VP ellipsis. If this is the case, (259) does not necessarily speak against the head status of aspectual verbs. Indeed, the possibility that VP ellipsis requires something more than head licensing is recently explored in Lee and Pan (to appear).

4.7 Discussions and implications

4.7.1 Semantic effects of head movement

The proposed movement of aspectual verbs and (a subset of) modal verbs in Cantonese constitute new evidence for head movement with scope effects, alongside the cases discussed in § 4.2. Here it can be noted that the case in Cantonese avoids certain concerns facing head movement with scope effects.

The first of these concerns generality. Among the four types of quantificational heads, namely, determiners, negation, modal verbs, and aspectual verbs (as discussed in § 4.2.3), the proposed movement applies to the last two types. These two types form a natural (semantic) class, as they can be regarded as generalized quantifiers over times/worlds. Movement of the other two types are not observed in Cantonese. This is because Cantonese lacks determiner (at least in the sense of English or Japanese) in the first place. Also, the pre-verbal negation *m-* is prefixal, i.e., it is a bound morpheme (M. Yip 1988), its failure to move is expected.

Additionally, the proposed movement may shift scope relations between aspectual verbs and modal verbs on one hand and various quantificational elements on the other. These elements include quantificational subjects and topics, as well as quantificational adverbials and subordinate clauses. This differs from the cases discussed in § 4.2.3, which usually involve only one type of quantificational element in the discussion (e.g., a quantificational head moves over a subject/object quantifier or the negation).

In addition to scope effects with regard to quantificational elements, it has been argued that the proposed movement may affect focus scope, or precisely, the calculation of the focus set. This is achieved by a quantificational head escaping the scope of the focus operator. This type of scope effect has received little attention in the literature, but it nevertheless increases the range of possible scope effects induced by head movement.

Furthermore, the proposed movement is argued to be constrained by an economy condition on interpretation, Scope Economy (as proposed in § 4.4.1.2), and also by a locality condition, Shortest Move (as discussed in § 4.5.2). This lends important support to a movement analysis, in addition to the effects of scope enrichment/enhancement.

4.7.2 A parallel observation with phrasal elements

While the discussions so far focus on heads that occupy the high position, a natural question is whether the proposed movement applies exclusively to heads. In other words, the question is whether phrasal elements can undergo the proposed scope-shifting movement. In what follows, I argue for a positive answer with evidence from adverbs that have a fixed base position.

Li and Thompson (1981) observe that adverbs in Mandarin can be divided into two groups, *movable* adverbs and *non-movable* adverbs. The descriptive term "(non-)movable" is used to indicate whether adverbs can appear in different positions (such that on the surface they seem to be able to move around). It is the non-movable ones that are relevant to the discussion here, as non-movability suggest that such elements have a fixed position in the sentence. This observation in Mandarin applies to Cantonese as well. For example, the adverb *jau* 'again' canonically appears after the subject.

(260) "Non-movable" post-subject adverbs
   a. Aaming **jau**   haau-dou hou singzik
       Aaming again get-able   good result
       'Aaming gets good results again.'
   b. ??**Jau**   Aaming haau-dou hou singzik.
       again Aaming get-able   good result
       'Aaming gets good results again.'

Importantly, *jau* 'again' can occupy the pre-subject position if the subject is quantificational. Notably, it takes wide scope over 'only one person' in the derived position in (261b).

(261) The adverb *jau* 'again' and the high position
   a. <u>Dak</u> jat-go jan   **jau**   haau-dou hou singzik.
       only one-CL person again get-able   good result
       'Only one person got good results again.'
   b. **Jau**   <u>dak</u> jat-go jan   haau-dou hou singzik.
       again only one-CL person get-able   good result
       'It is again the case that only one person got good results.'

Note that the unacceptability of (260) is not because *jau* cannot modify a noun (provided that *dak* 'only' is verbal by nature), as shown in (262).

(262) The adverb *jau* 'again' followed by nominal quantifiers
       Jau   <u>cyunbou</u> jan   haau-dou hou singzik laa3.
       again every   person get-able   good result   SFP
       'It is again the case that everyone got good results.'

The distribution of *jau* 'again' follows immediately from the proposed movement account, and the high position is constrained by Scope Economy.

To see more examples, the high position of adverbs like *jatzik* 'straight/always' and *batdyun* 'continuously' is constrained in a similar way. The (b) sentences in

(263) and (264) show that the presence of quantificational elements (i.e., the subjects) is crucial to the high position.

(263) The adverb *jatzik* 'straight' and the high position
    a. {Zisiu saam-go jan/   Aaming} **jatzik**   haau-dou hou singzik.
        at.least three-CL person Aaming   straight get-able   good result
        'At least three people/ Aaming always got good results.'
    b. **Jatzik** {zisiu   saam-go jan/   ??Aaming} haau-dou hou singzik.
        straight at.least three-CL person Aaming   get-able   good result
        'It is always that at least three people/ Aaming got good results.'

(264) The adverb *batdyun* 'continuously' and the high position
    a. {Zisiu saam-go jan/   Aaming} **batdyun**   haau-dou hou singzik.
        at.least three-CL person Aaming   continuously get-able   good result
        'At least three people/ Aaming always got good results.'
    b. **Batdyun**   {zisiu   saam-go jan/   *Aaming} haau-dou hou singzik.
        continuously at.least three-CL person Aaming   get-able   good result
        'It is always that at least three people/ Aaming got good results.'

The above cases of adverbs show that the high position is constrained in a similar way to aspectual verbs and modal verbs. Their distribution follows from the proposed movement approach, which is also constrained by Scope Economy. If adverbs are phrases (as commonly assumed), then the proposed movement can be generalized to apply to both heads and phrases. Also, Scope Economy, as an interface condition on interpretation, does not seem to discriminate head movement from phrasal movement.

4.7.3 The trigger of head movement

In § 4.4.3.2, I suggested that the proposed HM may be triggered by an EPP feature (without a prior Agree relation) or by interpretation/ scope considerations. Either way, the scope effects brought along with this HM are obligatory (i.e., the lack of reconstruction effects). This leads us to the predict that the close tie between HM and obligatory scope-shifting ceases to exist if the HM has a different syntactic trigger. This subsection discusses (i) HM triggered by categorial feature and (ii) HM triggered by discourse feature, and I show that the prediction is borne out.

Let us first consider cases where HM is triggered by categorial features. I assume with Szabolcsi (2010, 2011) and Harizanov and Gribanova (2019), among others, that the verb second (V2) word order in German and Dutch involves syntactic verb movement triggered by categorial features (on the C head). In German, verb movement to C does not bring along scope effects. (265a) serves as the baseline, where the verb moves to C and the subject to Spec CP. The sentence

Chapter 4. Scope effects

unambiguously delivers the surface scope reading. In (265b), instead of the subject, the adverbial moves to Spec CP. The verb then occupies a position higher than the subject because of verb movement. Crucially, the sentence conveys the same scope reading as in (265a), suggesting that the HM of 'begin' does not shift scope (i.e. it must reconstruct).

(265) German V2 movement (p.c. Stefan Keine)
    a. [$_{CP}$ <u>Nur</u> die Aktienkurse [$_{C'}$ **begannen**$_i$ im Mai t$_i$ zu steigen]]
          only the stock.prices   began   in May to rise
          'In May, only stock prices begins to   ('only' > 'begin' / *'begin' > 'only')
          rise.'
    b. [$_{CP}$ Im Mai [$_{C'}$ **begannen**$_i$ <u>nur</u> die Aktienkurse t$_i$ zu steigen]]
          in May   began   only the stock.prices to rise
          'In May, only stock prices begins to   ('only' > 'begin' / *'begin' > 'only')
          rise.'

On the other hand, head movement in Dutch shows a slightly different picture. Szabolcsi (2010, 2011) reports that verb movement to C in Dutch optionally induces scope effects. (266a) is similar to German (265a), and only surface scope is available. However, different from the German counterpart (265b), Dutch (266b) is ambiguous between a wide and low scope reading of 'begin', suggesting that the verb optionally reconstructs.

(266) Dutch V2 movement (Szabolcsi 2010, p.38, adapted)
    a. [$_{CP}$ Alleen Marie [$_{C'}$ **begon**$_i$ goede rollen t$_i$ te krijgen]]
          only   Mary   began.3sg good roles   to get.INF
          'Only Mary is such that she began to   ('only' > 'begin' / *'begin' > 'only')
          get good roles.'
    b. [$_{CP}$ In mei [$_{C'}$ **begon**$_i$ alleen Marie goede rollen t$_i$ te krijgen]]
          in May   began.3SG only Mary good roles   to get.INF
                                 ('only' > 'begin' / 'begin' > 'only')
        i.   'Only Mary is such that she began to get good roles.'
        ii. 'It began to be the case that only Mary is getting good roles.'

The cases in German and Dutch illustrate that scope effects of HM is *not* obligatory if it is triggered by categorial features.[55]

Let us turn to cases of head movement that are triggered by discourse features. As discussed in Chapter 3, a verb can be right dislocated to the end of the sentence in Cantonese (with or without doubling). Arguably, the movement is triggered by some discourse feature (e.g., a defocus feature) and the verb lands at the CP

---

55. I do not have an answer to the difference between German and Dutch with regard to the reconstruction facts.

periphery (Lee 2017). The prediction on quantificational heads in Cantonese is that, if they move for discourse effects, such movement need not alter scope relations. This is borne out in (267), where the right dislocation of *hoici* 'begin' gives rise to a scopally ambiguous sentence, suggesting that reconstruction is optional.[56]

(267)   Cantonese Right dislocation of quantificational heads
        Dak Aaming __ haau-dou hou   singzik aa3 **hoici**.
        only Aaming   get-able   good result   SFP begin
        'Only Aaming begins to get good results.'   'only' > 'begin' / 'begin' > 'only'

This is, however, not to say that discourse-feature-driven head movement can never come with obligatory scope effects. Consider again the case in Shupamem (Bantu), where a verb arguably undergoes movement and obligatorily takes wide scope over the subject in (268b).

(268)   Shupamem fronting of aspectual verbs (Szabolcsi 2010, p. 38)   = (173)
        a.   <u>Ndùù</u> Maria ka   **yeshe** inget   ndàà li?.   'only' > 'begin'
             only   Maria past begin have.INF good roles
             'Only Mary is such that she began to get good roles'
        b.   A   ka   **yeshe** <u>ndùù</u> Maria inget   ndàà li?.   'begin' > 'only'
             it-FOCUS past begin only   Maria have.INF good roles
             'It began to be the case that only Mary is getting good roles'

While the nature of the movement is not explicitly stated in Szabolcsi (2010, 2011), this movement is accompanied with a participle/expletive-like element *a* before the verb, a construction said to involve subject focus (Nchare 2012). It thus seems plausible to treat this movement as being triggered by a focus feature.

Summing up, the above cases in German, Dutch, Cantonese and Shupamem suggest that, while head movement triggered by pure EPP features/ scope considerations entails obligatory scope effects, other instances of head movement show different possibilities with regard to scope effects. The reconstruction effects of head movement are not uniform (even for cases with similar syntactic triggers) and appears to be regulated by some independent mechanism.

It should be remarked that one implication of the discussion in this subsection is that the empirical properties of head movement hinge on the relevant triggers, which could be a categorial feature, a discourse feature or pure EPP features/ scope considerations. This patterns nicely with phrasal movement, whose properties of movement also depend on the relevant triggers. While further comparison

---

56. The precise derivation of right dislocation should not concern us here (for discussions, see Chapter 3, and also L. Y.-L. Cheung (2009), Lee (2017), and Lai (2019), i.a.). The crucial observation here is that the aspectual verb finds a way to scope below *dak* 'only', which is unavailable in the absence of a discourse-featural trigger.

has to await future research, syntactic triggers, rather than the phrase structural status, appear to be the most reliable basis for the classification of movement dependencies.

4.8   Conclusions

This chapter has focused on the semantic effects of head movement, which are often said to be absent from such movement. I presented a novel piece of evidence for head movement with semantic effects from Cantonese.

An in-depth investigation into the distribution of quantificational heads such as aspectual verbs and modal verbs in Cantonese shows that these heads can occupy a non-canonical, high position in the sentence, if they are immediately followed by a quantificational element or a focused element.

I proposed that these quantificational heads can undergo overt head movement to a higher position and take scope in the landing site (i.e, scope-shifting head movement). Additionally, the proposed movement of quantificational heads is constrained by an independently motivated condition on interpretation, Scope Economy, which precludes semantically vacuous scope-shifting operations.

The findings lend support to the claim that head movement can induce semantic effects. Importantly, head movement can shift scope relations, in a way similar to Quantifier Raising proposed for nominal quantifiers. Furthermore, Scope Economy is shown to be a general constraint on both phrasal movement and head movement.

The conclusion of this chapter challenges the view that head movement does not result in any semantic effects – a view which has been used to claim that head movement is non-syntactic and occurs at PF. It is shown that head movement is no different from phrasal movement in its potential to induce semantic effects. This motivates a unified theory of movement of head movement and phrasal movement.

CHAPTER 5

Linearization
Doubling effects of heads and phrases[*]

This chapter investigates asymmetries in doubling among verbs, objects and subjects in Cantonese. It is shown that each of these elements has a distinct doubling profile in topic constructions and right dislocation: doubling is sometimes prohibited, required or optional. Couched in terms of the copy theory of movement, I suggest that that the operation responsible for erasing copies in a movement chain is regulated by phonological requirements that follow from a version of cyclic linearization. Particularly, I propose that the copy-erasing operation can be suspended as a last resort in cases where its application would otherwise violate phonological requirements imposed by cyclic linearization. The differences in doubling possibility among verbs, objects and subjects follow from the availability of the edge position of a phase to these elements. The proposal derives the Cantonese doubling pattern without recourse to the phrase-structural status of the (non-)doubling elements and maintains that the mechanism that determines copy pronunciation is the same for heads and phrases. I take this as a further piece evidence for the unification of head and phrasal movement, resonating with much recent work on this topic.

5.1 Introduction

The goal of this chapter is two-fold. First, while I have suggested a parallel analysis on verb doubling constructions and their phrasal counterparts in Chapter 3, a crucial difference between them concerns the doubling effects: doubling effects in verb doubling constructions are *mostly* obligatory, whereas doubling effects of their phrasal counterparts are *mostly* forbidden. This chapter examines the pattern of doubling effects of these constructions in greater details and develop an analysis to account for the asymmetries in doubling.[1]

---

[*]. With slight modification, this chapter is reproduced with permission from Lee, Tommy-Tsz Ming, "Asymmetries in doubling and Cyclic Linearization," *Journal of East Asian Linguistics 30*: 109–139, 2022, Springer Nature.

[1]. Specifically, I will focus on topic constructions and right dislocation, but the analysis can be extended to 'even'-focus constructions and copula focus constructions.

Second, with the emergence of the copy theory of movement (Chomsky 1995b, *et seq.*), an interesting line of research has focusd on how the copies in a movement chain are phonetically realized (see Bošković and Nunes 2007; Nunes 2011, and references therein). In connection with this, the doubling phenomenon formed in verb/predicate fronting constructions in certain languages have led to various proposals which attempt to derive overt doubling effects, with reference to different components of the grammar (Landau 2006; Aboh and Dyakonova 2009; Trinh 2009; Cheng and Vicente 2013; Hein 2018). The current chapter aims to contribute to this discussion by investigating the doubling patterns of not only verbs, but also subject and objects in Cantonese, which each have a distinct doubling profile. The diverse patterns call for an analysis not only on how doubling is made possible, but also, more importantly, on how patterns of doubling are regulated by the grammar.

As has been noticed in the literature on Chinese (and briefly in Chapter 3), there is a doubling-related asymmetry between verb and objects in topic constructions. For example, when the verb *soeng* 'want' in (269) undergoes topicalization, it is (and must be) doubled.[2]

(269) Verb topicalization in Cantonese
soeng, Aaming hai　*(**soeng**) sik jyu ge2.
want　Aaming COP want　　eat fish SFP
'As for (whether he) wants, Aaming wants to eat fish (but...)'
(Cheng and Vicente 2013)

This doubling requirement seems to be specific to verbs. As noted in Cheng and Vicente (2013) for Mandarin (which also applies to Cantonese), when an object is topicalized, doubling is not required (and indeed dispreferred), as in (270).

(270) Object topicalization in Cantonese
ni-tiu jyu, Aaming soeng sik (??**ni-tiu jyu**).
this-CL fish, Aaming want eat this-CL　fish
'This fish, Aaming wants to eat.'

The contrast between (269) and (270) might appear to suggest a difference between head and phrasal displacement, where, for example, displaced heads must be doubled while displaced phrases must not. This suggestion, however, is empirically challenged by the observation that a verb can be displaced to the end of the sentence with or without doubling as in (271). Associating the doubling

---

2. The phenomenon is called *verb doubling clefts* in Cheng and Vicente (2013) in Mandarin, which involves both a topic reading of the verb and a verum focus reading. Since the precise discourse interpretive effect does not bear on the arguments in the discussion in this chapter, I use the term "verb topicalization" as a convenient label. See Chapter 3 for discussions.

possibility with the head/phrase distinction thus overgeneralizes and would disallow the non-doubling case of verbs in right dislocation.

(271) Right dislocation of verbs in Cantonese
Aaming (**sik**) ni-di   je   aa4 **sik?**
Aaming eat   this-CL thing Q   eat
'Aaming eats this thing?'   (Lee 2017; Lai 2019)

Another empirical challenge to such a head vs. phrase-based approach is that it is possible to double a phrase in right dislocation (also called *Dislocation Copying* in L. Y.-L. Cheung 2015). If phrases are inherently incompatible with doubling, right dislocation of subjects should never allow two occurrences of dislocated subjects. These two initial observations suggest that an element's phrasal structural status is not sufficient to explain the (non-)doubling patterns in Cantonese.

(272) Right dislocation of subjects
(**Aaming**) soeng sik ni-tiu   jyu aa3 **Aaming.**
Aaming   want eat this-CL fish SFP Aaming
'Aaming wants to eat this fish.'   (L. Y.-L. Cheung 2009, 2015)

Against such a background, this chapter pursues an account on how and why doubling is *prohibited*, *required*, or *optional* in different cases. Specifically, I propose that the operation responsible for erasing copies in a movement chain (i.e. Copy Deletion) is regulated by phonological requirements that follow from, with some qualifications, the version of phase theory advocated in Fox and Pesetsky (2005), namely, Cyclic Linearization (CL). The core idea will be that Copy Deletion can be *suspended* as a last resort in cases where its application would otherwise violate a phonological requirement relating to Cyclic Linearization. Doubling occurs as a result of the suspension of Copy Deletion. The differences in doubling possibility among verbs, objects and subjects are derivable from the availability of the edge position of a phase to such elements.

The implications of the proposal are two-fold. First, it lends further support to Cyclic Linearization, an alternative to Chomsky's version of phase theory (Chomsky 2000, 2001) in the study of syntactic locality. Second, the proposal derives the Cantonese doubling pattern without resource to the phrase-structural status of the (non-)doubling elements and maintains that the mechanism that determines copy pronunciation is the same for heads and phrases. This provides a further argument for the limited role of the phrase structural status of constituents in movement theories, resonating with recent efforts to unify head and phrasal movement (Hartman 2011; Funakoshi 2012, 2014; Harizanov 2019; Harizanov and Gribanova 2019; Pesetsky 2020).

This rest of the chapter is organized as follows: §5.2 describes the pattern of doubling in Cantonese with regard to two constructions: topic constructions and right dislocation. §5.3 introduces the framework and details the proposal. §5.4 illustrates how the proposal derives the doubling asymmetries in topic constructions and right dislocation. §5.5 discusses three existing accounts of doubling, which fall short of explaining the fine-grained doubling patterns in Cantonese. §5.6 serves as an extension of the proposal and addresses the question as to why verb doubling is not always required or allowed across languages. §5.7 concludes the chapter.

5.2 Asymmetries in doubling in Cantonese

The pattern of doubling in Cantonese is considerably intricate. In what follows, I discuss the pattern of subjects, verbs and objects in topic constructions and right dislocation, where each of the former elements has its own doubling profile. As will be seen, contrasts between the doubling possibilities in topicalization and right dislocation suggest that the directionality of displacement plays an important role in determining whether doubling is possible or not.

A first asymmetry in doubling has already been noted in the introduction. The relevant examples (269) and (270) are repeated below in (273). The crucial observation is that, while both verbs and objects can be topicalized, verbs must be doubled,[3] but objects cannot be doubled.

(273) Topic constructions
   a. **Soeng**, Aaming hai *(**soeng**) sik jyu ge2.   verbs, =(269)
       want   Aaming COP want   eat fish SFP
       'As for (whether he) wants, Aaming wants to eat fish (but...)'
   b. **Ni-tiu jyu**, Aaming soeng sik (??**ni-tiu jyu**).   objects, =(270)
       this-CL fish, Aaming want   eat this-CL   fish
       'This fish, Aaming wants to eat.'

Two remarks are in order. First, verb topicalization is different from object topicalization in that when a verb is topicalized, the presence of the copula *hai* is strongly preferred. No such preference is observed in object topicalization. While it is clear that the copula contributes to a verum focus reading (Cheng and Vicente

---

3. It is also possible to topicalize the lower verb *sik* 'eat', where doubling is obligatory.

(i) **Sik**, Aaming hai soeng *(**sik**) jyu ge2.
     eat Aaming FOC want   eat   fish SFP
     'As for (whether he wants to) eat, Aaming wants to eat fish (but...)'

2013), it is less clear why it is associated with verb topicalization, but not object topicalization. I will not pursue an explanation of this difference, however.

Second, there is a difference in terms of acceptability with regard to the absence of doubling in verb topicalization (i.e. (273a) without the second occurrence of *soeng* 'want') and the presence of doubling in object topicalization (i.e. (273b) with the second occurrence of *ni-tiu jyu* 'this fish'). While both are judged as deviant, the latter is judged as redundant and is slightly more acceptable than the former.[4] I mark sentences with a reported sense of redundancy with ??, instead of *, to indicate the difference in acceptability. The difference seems to suggest a violation of different grammatical principles. I will return to this point in §5.4.3.

To see a second asymmetry of a similar kind, let us turn to right dislocation. It has been reported that both verbs and objects can be dislocated to the right of sentence-final particles (Lee 2017; Lai 2019). However, we observe that verbs are *optionally* doubled, whereas objects can hardly be doubled (as it gives rise to a heavy sense of redundancy).

(274) Right dislocation
    a. Aaming (**sik**) ni-di je   aa4 **sik**?   verbs, =(271)
        Aaming eat this-CL thing Q   eat
        'Aaming eats this thing?'
    b. Aaming sik (**??ni-di je**) aa4 **ni-di** **je**?   objects
        Aaming eat this-CL thing Q   this-CL thing
        'Aaming EATS this thing?'

Note that for (274a), the sentences with and without a doubled verb show different focus interpretations. When the verb is doubled, the verb receives a focus interpretation. In contrast, when the verb is right dislocated without doubling, the object receives a focus interpretation. I will return to this observation in §5.4.2.

Finally, let us take the pattern of subjects into consideration, where we observe yet another asymmetry: topicalized subjects do not go well with doubling (as it similarly gives rise to an air of redundancy), whereas right-dislocated subjects are *optionally* doubled. Note that doubling of the subjects in (275b) is *not* judged as redundant, unlike the doubling of objects in (273b) and (274b). Again, there is an interpretive difference associated with doubling: the subject is focused when doubled. When the subject is not doubled, the whole verb phrase is focused.

(275) a. Topic constructions
        Aaming (ne), (**??Aaming**) soeng sik ni-tiu jyu.   subjects
        Aaming TOP Aaming   want eat this-CL fish
        'As for Aaming, (he) wants to eat this fish.'

---

4. I thank Audrey Li for pointing out this difference to me.

b. Right dislocation
(**Aaming**) soeng sik ni-tiu jyu aa3 **Aaming.**   subjects, =(272)
Aaming want eat this-CL fish SFP Aaming
'Aaming wants to eat this fish.'

Table 5.1 below provides a summary of the doubling profile of verbs, subjects and objects. The patterns can be described as follows: (i) *object* doubling is generally prohibited (in both topic constructions and right dislocation); (ii) *verb* doubling is obligatory in topic constructions, but optional in right dislocation; (iii) *subject* doubling is prohibited in topic constructions, but optional in right dislocation.

Table 5.1 Doubling asymmetries in Cantonese

	Subject	Verb	Object
Topic constructions	prohibited	obligatory	prohibited
Right dislocation	optional	optional	prohibited

Capturing such diverse patterns of doubling in Cantonese in a non-trivial way presents a significant challenge. One thing that seems clear, however, is that the possibility for an element to be doubled does not immediately follow from any head/phrase distinction, because it is not the case that heads always require doubling (e.g. (274a)) or that phrases can never be doubled (e.g. (275b)).

5.3 Proposal: Cyclic Linearization and Copy Deletion suspension

Under the copy theory of movement, while it is generally agreed that some operation is responsible for deleting redundant copies in the process of linearization (e.g. Copy Deletion, see Chomsky 1995b; Nunes 1995, 2004), opinions vary as to what in the grammar allows or even requires the survival of a second copy. I propose that the deletion of a (lower) copy may be suspended if it violates linearization requirements imposed by Cyclic Linearization (Fox and Pesetsky 2005). I first overview the proposal of Cyclic Linearization, CL, and then go into the details of my proposal.

5.3.1 Cyclic Linearization

Fox and Pesetsky (2005) propose that syntactic structure is linearized cyclically. Particularly, in each domain where all (necessary) syntactic operations are applied and the structure is ready to be linearized (e.g. *v*P and CP), it is *Spelled-*

Out. Upon Spell-Out, Ordering Statements (OS), the ordering information among overt elements, is established. Crucially, OS must be preserved by overt elements in the final output. OS can thus be considered as phonological requirements derived along the syntactic derivation. Also, OS are cumulative and cannot be overwritten.

I implement the idea of CL under the copy theory of movement.[5] I suggest that two operations take place at each instance of Spell-Out:

(276) A copy-theoretic implementation of CL
    At each Spell-Out domain, two independent operations apply one after the other:
    (i) **Copy Deletion** (CD, typically deleting the low copies), followed by
    (ii) **Linearization** (LIN, establishing Ordering Statements).

Let us consider the two scenarios in (277) and (278) below. In both scenarios, LIN occurs at domain D, establishing the OS_D: $X < Y < Z$. In the next domain D', some element α is merged. The two scenarios diverge from here. In Scenario 1, movement of X to D' and the deletion of its lower copy (marked in gray color) would not violate the previously established OS, i.e. X still precedes both Y and Z. However, in Scenario 2, movement of Y to D' poses a linearization problem. This is because when CD applies to the low copy of Y at the Spell-Out of D', the requirement that X precedes Y is no longer obeyed.

(277) Scenario 1 ($LIN_D \to Move_X \to CD \to LIN_{D'}$)
$$[_{D'} \ldots X \, \alpha \, [_D X \, YZ]]$$

$$OS_D\text{'}: X < \alpha < D_{(X < Y < Z)}$$

(278) Scenario 2 ($LIN_D \to Move_Y \to CD \to LIN_{D'}$)
$$*[_{D'} \ldots Y \, \alpha \, [_D X \, Y \, Z]]$$

$$*OS_D\text{'}: Y < \alpha < D_{(X < Y < Z)}$$

Importantly, it is not the case that movement of non-edge elements is never possible. It is possible if a non-edge element moves successive cyclically out of a Spell-Out domain. For example, if Y moves to the edge of D before it moves out to D', then the OS established at D would be different from Scenario 1 and 2: $Y < X < Z$. Subsequent movement of Y to a higher domain as depicted in Scenario 3 is possible, as applying CD to the low copies of Y would not violate any OS, i.e. Y still precedes X and Z when Spelled-Out at D'.

---

5. In Fox and Pesetsky (2005), movement is construed as an operation of *remerge*, which establishes multi-dominance relations among the elements.

Chapter 5. Linearization · **169**

(279) Scenario 3 (**Move$_Y$ within D** → CD → LIN$_D$ → Move$_Y$ → CD → LIN$_{D'}$)
  [$_{D'}$ ... Y α [$_D$ Y X Y Z]]

  OS$_D$': Y < α < D$_{(Y < X < Z)}$

Differing from standard assumptions about phases (particularly the version in Chomsky 2000, 2001), CL opens certain other possibilities for movement of non-edge elements. In Scenario 4, non-edge elements can move across edge elements if the movement of the former is followed by some "compensating movement" of the latter that preserves the ordering relations. For example, the movement of Y is allowed if X also moves to a position higher than Y. Consequently, the order between X and Y is preserved and there is no violation of any OS.[6]

(280) Scenario 4 (LIN$_D$ → Move$_Y$ & **Move$_X$** → CD → LIN$_{D'}$)
  [$_{D'}$ ... X ... Y α [$_D$ X Y Z]]

  OS$_D$': X < Y < α < D$_{(X < Y < Z)}$

5.3.2 Copy Deletion suspension

Against this background, I propose that the application of Copy Deletion is constrained by linearization requirements imposed by CL.

(281) Copy Deletion suspension
  Copy Deletion is suspended *as a last resort* if its application violates linearization requirements imposed by CL.

Crucially, the doubling phenomenon arises as a result of the suspension of CD. Recall that when a non-edge element exits a domain D to another domain D', the OS established at D is violated. However, the violation is avoided if the non-edge element is pronounced (i.e. doubled). Schematically, consider Scenario 5 below:

(282) Scenario 5 (LIN$_D$ → Move$_{non-edge}$ → **CD suspension** → LIN)
  [$_{D'}$ ... **Y** α [$_D$ XYZ]]

  OS$_D$': Y < α < D$_{(X < Y < Z)}$

When D is Spelled-Out, the OS: X > Y is satisfied by the pronunciation of the lower copy of Y. At the later Spell-Out of D', the OS: Y > X is also satisfied by virtue of the higher copy of Y. As such, the movement of Y does not violate any OS.

---

6. This is arguably the case for object shift in Scandinavian languages, see Fox and Pesetsky (2005) for extensive discussion.

A potential concern, however, is that the two OS above require that Y must precede X and X must precede Y, and crucially, by transitivity, Y must precede Y. Under a multi-dominance or remerge approach to movement as originally assumed in Fox and Pesetsky (2005), this requirement constitutes a linearization contradiction since a precedence relation cannot be reflexive, i.e. there is no way for Y to precede or to be preceded by itself. With the adaptation of CL to the copy theory of movement, the conclusion that Y must precede Y need not be a contradiction. While the two copies are identical to each other (in terms of featural makeup), they are two separate elements in a chain of movement. A precedence relation between two copies should therefore, in principle, be possible. The question is that how the computational system differentiates the two copies if they are indeed identical. One way is to introduce indices to copies, but this would violate the Inclusiveness Condition (Chomsky 1995b); another is suggested in Nunes (2004, p. 165 fn. 15): if a new term is introduced into the computation *without* reducing the numeration, the computational system "knows" that a copy of some syntactic object has been created. The current proposal does not hinge on which choice is adopted here. Relevant to us is that the requirement "Y must precede Y" can be satisfied, provided that the computational system is capable of differentiating copies and establishing a precedence relation among them.

Before discussing the consequences of the proposal, I will make a few assumptions in the upcoming discussion. First, I assume that right dislocation in Cantonese involves syntactic movement within a mono-clausal structure, a position defended in L. Y.-L. Cheung (2009), Lee (2017), and Lai (2019).

Second, following Cheng and Vicente (2013), Lee (2017), and Lai (2019), I assume that verb movements are involved in both verb topicalization and the right dislocation of verbs, i.e. the displaced verbs are not base generated.[7] The arguments for a movement analysis comes from the observation that the displaced verbs show connectivity effects with the other copy. These include island effects and lexical identity effects. The former is illustrated with the sentences in (283), where the doubled verbs cannot be separated by an island boundary.

(283) a. Verb topicalization (based on Cheng and Vicente (2013, p. 8))
            ***Tai**, ngo tongji [$_{NP}$ go-go   keoi hai **tai**-gwo ge jigin],   batgwo...
            see   I   agree   that-CL s/he COP see-EXP GE opinion but
            'As for seeing, I agree with the opinion that s/he has indeed seen it, but...'

---

7. See Chapter 3 for a detailed proposal of a head movement analysis on these constructions.

b. Right dislocation of verbs (based on Lee (2017, p. 65))
*Aaming zipsau-m-dou [NP Aafan (**sik**) gong sap-zung jyujin   ge
Aaming accept-not-able   Aafan know speak ten-CL   language GE
sisat] aa3 **sik**.
fact   SFP know
'Aaming cannot accept the fact that Aafan can speak ten languages.'

Additionally, the two verbs must be lexically identical to each other, an observation taken to be evidence for movement (Cable 2004; Vicente 2007; Cheng and Vicente 2013). I illustrate the idea with the verb *caa* 'check' and *cek* 'check' (an English loanword). The identity effect is observed in spite of the semantic identity of the two verbs.

(284) a. Verb topicalization
{**Caa/*Cek**}, ngo hai **caa**-gwo   ni-go jan,   batgwo…
check/check I   COP check-EXP this-CL person but
As for checking, I have checked this person, but…'
b. Right dislocation of verbs
Nei soeng **cek**   ni-go jan   aa4 {**cek/*caa**?}
you want check this-CL person Q   check/check
'Do you want CHECK this person?'

Lastly, I assume that a head cannot move into its own specifier. This assumption may follow from a version of anti-locality constraint which prohibits movement operations that are too "local" (Abels 2003, i.a.); or it may be due to the lack of motivation: a head need not move to its own specifier to check features (if there is any). Either assumption would rule out the movement step illustrated below, using the *v* head as an example.

(285)   Illicit *v*-movement

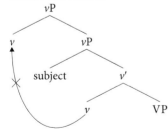

172   The Unity of Movement

5.4   Deriving the asymmetries in doubling

Now, we have all the ingredients we need to account for the doubling asymmetries in Cantonese. §5.4.1 and §5.4.2 illustrate how the proposal derives doubling asymmetries in topics constructions and right dislocation, respectively. §5.4.3 returns to the acceptability issue mentioned in passing in §5.2. §5.4.4 discusses one more asymmetry which also falls out from the current proposal.

5.4.1   Licit and illicit cases in topic constructions

I start with the doubling case in verb topicalization, followed by the obligatory absence of doubling for subjects and objects. Recall that verb doubling in topic constructions is obligatory. The relevant example is repeated below as (286).

(286)   Verb topicalization
Soeng, Aaming hai **soeng** sik jyu ge2.   =(269)
want   Aaming COP want   eat fish SFP
'As for (whether he) wants, Aaming wants to eat fish (but...)'

Under the current proposal, (286) has the derivation given in (287). First, in (287a), the vP headed by *soeng* 'want' is built, with *Aaming* being the subject and *sik jyu* 'eat fish' the (clausal) complement.[8] The copula *hai* is assumed to occupy a vP-internal position sandwiched between the main verb and the subject. Note that *soeng* does not (and cannot) move to the edge of vP. In (287b), the vP is Spelled-Out, and the order between the subject/*hai* and the verb *soeng* 'want' is fixed. (287c) indicates the movement of *soeng* to a Topic position, one that is higher than the subject.[9] In (287b), at the final Spell-Out domain TopicP, crucially, CD of *soeng* 'want' is suspended, because deleting its lower copy would violate the OS established in vP. The whole structure is thus linearized with the presence of two copies of *soeng*.[10, 11]

---

8. The derivation is also compatible with an analysis where *soeng* 'want' is base generated at V and then undergoes head movement to v (Huang 1994, 1997; Tang 1998b), but this step does not bear on the proposal.

9. I abstract over the standard subject movement to Spec TP for its irrelevance.

10. For simplicity, the sentence-final particle *ge2* which is external to the vP is not shown in the derivation.

11. An anonymous JEAL reviewer points out that modal verbs such as *wui* 'will' can be doubled as well, as in (i).

(i)   Keoi **wui** lai   hoiwui   gaa3 **wui**.
s/he will come join.meeting SFP   will
'S/he will come to the meeting.'

Chapter 5. Linearization 173

(287) Derivation of (286)
    a. Building of *v*P (headed by *soeng* 'want')
      [$_{v\text{P}}$ Aaming hai soeng sik jyu]
    b. Spell-Out of *v*P (CD does not apply or applies vacuously)
      (CD) → LIN$_{v\text{P}}$; OS$_{v\text{P}}$: **Aaming < hai < <u>soeng</u> < sik < jyu**
    c. Verb movement for topicalization
      [$_{\text{TopicP}}$ <u>soeng</u> … [$_{v\text{P}}$ Aaming hai soeng sik jyu]]
    d. Spell-Out of TopicP
      CD suspension → LIN$_{\text{TopP}}$;
      OS$_{\text{TopP}}$: **<u>soeng</u> < Aaming < hai < <u>soeng</u> < sik < jyu**

On the other hand, objects behave different from verbs in topic constructions. Doubling of objects is disallowed. Recall (270), repeated below as (288).

(288) Object topicalization
    Ni-tiu jyu, Aaming soeng sik (??**ni-tiu jyu**).   = (270)
    this-CL fish, Aaming want eat this-CL fish
    'This fish, Aaming wants to eat.'

I suggest that the crucial difference between verbs and objects does not lie in their phrase structural status, but in their possibility of movement to Spec *v*P. While a verb cannot move to its own specifier, the Spec position is available to objects.[12] In cases where the object moves to Spec *v*P, the OS at the Spell-Out of *v*P becomes: **O < S < V**. Movement of the object to a higher domain would not suspend CD at Spell-Out. Lower copies are deleted by CD, resulting in the absence of doubling (cf. Scenario 3). The derivation is schematically represented in (289).

One potential concern is that modal verbs might occupy a position beyond *v*P such that their relative position with the *v*P-internal elements is not fixed upon the Spell-Out of *v*P and hence doubling is expected not to be necessitated. It should be noted, however, that the modal verbs have been argued to be lexical predicates, heading a V/*v* position (Lin and Tang 1995). In such case, modal verbs double in the same way as *soeng* 'want'. Alternatively, it is possible that modal verbs are also phase heads. If we follow a contextual approach to phasehood as advocated by Bošković (2014) where the highest position of an extended projection constitutes a phase. In such case, doubling is as expected.

12. This difference between head movement and phrasal movement is not due to some inherent properties of head movement; rather, as suggested in the discussion around (285), this might be attributed to a general anti-locality constraint on movement or to the lack of motivation.

(289) The schematic derivation of object topicalization
$[_{\text{TopP}}\ O\ ...\ [_{vP}\ O\ S\ V\ O\ ]]$

Object movement → $\underline{CD}$ → LIN_{TopP}; OS_{TopP}: O < S < V

The same line of reasoning applies to subjects in topic constructions where doubling is not allowed. The only difference is that subjects do not move into Spec vP; instead, they are base generated there. Independently of their derivational histories, movement of neither subjects nor objects would trigger suspension of CD.

(290) The schematic derivation of subject topicalization
$[_{\text{TopP}}\ S\ ...\ [_{vP}\ S\ V\ O\ ]]$

Subject movement → $\underline{CD}$ → LIN_{TopP}; OS_{TopP}: S < V < O

Two remarks are in order. First, while the availability of a successive cyclic movement path of objects renders doubling unnecessary, one may wonder why doubling is disallowed. Concretely, if the object does not stop at Spec vP, it would be linearized to the right of the subject and the verb at the Spell-Out of vP: **S < V < O**. When the object subsequently moves out of vP, this should result in CD suspension in the same way as verb topicalization. I suggest that doubling of objects is disallowed because CD can only be suspended *as a last resort*. If successive cyclic movement is available to objects, it must apply (hence no suspension of CD). The last resort nature of CD suspension is probably related to an economy principle that prefers a structure with minimal number of copies, which in turn prefers the application of CD wherever possible.

In sum, under the current proposal, the asymmetry between verbs on one hand and objects and subjects on the other in topic constructions is derivable from the structural position (i.e. the launching site). It hinges on the possibility to occupy Spec vP. Verbs are "special" not because they are heads, but because they fail to move to Spec vP. In contrast, the Spec vP position is available to objects and subjects, hence the absence of doubling. The approach to the doubling phenomenon makes no reference to the head-phrase distinction, which in turn avoids the overgeneralization problem mentioned in the introduction.

5.4.2 Licit, illicit and optional cases in right dislocation

5.4.2.1 *Licit cases*

The situations in right dislocation are more complicated since doubling is optional in some cases. Let us start with the licit and illicit cases. The line of reasoning will be largely similar to what we have seen for topic constructions, with the only difference being the direction of movement. We have seen that doubling

of a *leftward-moving* verb is licit because it is *preceded* by some *v*P-internal elements. We now also have the opposite case, where a *rightward-moving* verb is
doubled because it is *followed* by some *v*P-internal elements. Doubling of moving
verbs are possible in the presence of objects or embedded verbs (as in (291a) and
(292a), respectively), which is otherwise degraded (as in (291b) and (292b)).

(291)   Verb doubling allowed in the presence of objects
    a.   Keoi **sik** ni-di je   aa4 **sik?**
           he   eat this-CL thing Q   eat
    b. ??Keoi **sik** aa4 **sik?**
           he   eat Q   eat
           'He EATS this thing?' Intended: 'He EATS?'

(292)   Verb doubling allowed in the presence of embedded verbs
    a.   Keoi **soeng** heoi gaa3 **soeng.**
           he   want go   SFP want
           'He WANTS to go.'
    b. ??Keoi soeng **heoi** gaa3 **heoi.**
           he   want go   SFP go
           'He wants to GO.'

The contrast follows from the current proposal: when the *v*P headed by the moving verb is Spelled-Out, the order of the verb with regard to the object and the
embedded verb is fixed. The verb must precede them in the final word order.
Accordingly, at the final Spell-Out, CD on the lower copy of the moving verb has
to be suspended (hence doubling occurs), or it would violate the OS. The deriva-
tions of these cases are schematically represented in (293) and (294), respectively.
In what follows, for simplicity, I only detail the operations within *v*P (if any) and
the OS established at the Spell-Out of *v*P. Since OS cannot be overwritten, the final
word order must obey this OS.[13, 14]

(293)   The schematic derivation of (291)
      [$_{vP}$ S V O] SFP V

                                  OS$_{vP}$: S < V < O

---

13. For illustrative purposes, I assume a rightward movement approach of right dislocation,
but the analysis is compatible with whatever mechanism that renders the verb ending up in the
rightmost position (e.g. a Kaynean-style multiple leftward movement).

14. The precise position of the sentence-final particles is immaterial here, as long as they
occupy some position in the CP periphery (L. L.-S. Cheng 1991, i.a.). It may be head-initial (plus
TP movement) or head-final. For discussions on this issue, see L. Y.-L. Cheung (2009).

176   The Unity of Movement

(294)   The schematic derivation of (292)
  [$_{vP}$ S V1 [$_{TP}$ ... V2 ...]] SFP {V1/??V2}   OS$_{vP}$: S <V1 <V2

In a similar vein, subjects are doubled in right dislocation for the same reason that verbs are doubled in right dislocation: subjects are at least followed by a verb (and potentially also an object). This gives rise to the OS$_{vP}$ which dictates **S < V < O**. Right dislocating the subject to the right of the verb triggers CD suspension at a later point of Spell-Out, resulting in doubling. The relevant example and its derivation are given below.

(295)   Subject doubling in right dislocation
  Aaming soeng sik ni-tiu jyu aa3 **Aaming**.
  Aaming want eat this-CL fish SFP Aaming
  'AAMING wants to eat this fish.'

(296)   The schematic derivation of (295)
  [$_{vP}$ S V O] SFP S

                                    OS$_{vP}$: S <V < O

It is noteworthy that the right dislocated elements may contain both a subject and an adverb, as in (297). Since the subject and the adverb do not form one constituent, (297) may involve multiple operations of right dislocation, i.e. they are right dislocated separately, illustrated in (298).

(297)   **Ngo jau**   sihaa sin1 **ngo jau**.
  I   again try SFP I   again
  'Let me try as well.'   (Lai 2019, p. 254)

(298)   The schematic derivation of (297)
  [$_{vP}$ S again V] SFP S again

                                    OS$_{vP}$: S < again <V

Importantly, the relative order between the subject and the adverb are preserved when right dislocated. This follows naturally from the current analysis since their order is fixed when the *v*P is Spelled-Out.

5.4.2.2   *Illicit cases*

Turning to the illicit doubling cases specific to objects, the unavailability of object doubling follows from the fact that an object is typically at the right edge of a *v*P. Right dislocation of the object after the Spell-Out of *v*P would be subject to CD.

Chapter 5. Linearization   177

(299) a.   No doubling in right dislocation of objects
            Aaming sik (??**ni-di je**)   aa4 **ni-di**   **je**?
            Aaming eat this-CL thing Q   this-CL thing
            'Aaming EATS this thing?'   =(274b)
       b.   The schematic structure of (299a)
            [$_{v}$P S V O] SFP O

            OS$_{v}$P: S < V < O

A straightforward prediction is that if there are elements that follow objects, the doubling of objects should be possible. This is indeed the case. Consider the following examples with a duration phrase and an indirect object (in a ditransitive structure), respectively:

(300) a.   Duration phrases
            Aaming tai-zo   **ni-bun syu**   saam-go zong laa3 **ni-bun syu.**
            Aaming read-PERF this-CL book three-CL hour SFP this-CL book
            'Aaming has read THIS BOOK for three hours.'
       b.   Indirect object
            Aaming bei-zo   **ni-bun syu**   Aafan laa3 **ni-bun syu.**
            Aaming give-PERF this-CL book Aafan SFP this-CL book
            'Aaming has given THIS BOOK to Aafan.'

Given sufficient contexts (e.g. one in which the speaker is contrasting the book under discussion with other books), both sentences are acceptable, at least displaying a contrast with (299a). Assuming that both the duration phrase and the indirect object are within the vP, their relative word order is fixed when vP is Spelled-Out. Doubling is possible for the object since it is no longer at the right edge of vP, as illustrated below.

(301) The schematic structure of sentences in (300)
       [$_{v}$P S V O 3-hours/Aafan] SFP O

            OS$_{v}$P: S < V < O < 3-hours/Aafan

It is instructive to note that Lai (2019) argues that object doubling (e.g. the case in (299a)) cannot be ruled out by a pure phonological consideration, such as the avoidance of phonological identity. He supports this claim with the following example. In (302), the object *keoi* 's/he' is phonologically identical to the right dislocated element (which is co-indexed with the subject). Yet, the sentence is acceptable.[15]

---

15. Interestingly enough, Lai (2019) observes that co-indexation between the object and the right dislocated element is disallowed, which is in line with the observation that objects cannot be doubled.

(302) **Keoi**$_i$ zungji keoi$_j$ aa3 **keoi**$_i$.
s/he like   her/him SFP s/he
'S/he likes her/him.'   (Lai 2019, p. 246, with adaptations)

Accordingly, the sentence in (299a) with a doubled object is not ruled out by phonological identity but by an economy consideration in which lower copies have to be deleted in general. The same can be said for the two sentences in (291b) and (292b).[16]

5.4.2.3 Optional cases

The remaining question is why there are cases of optional doubling. More specifically, how can verbs and subjects move without doubling (in a way similar to right dislocating objects)? I propose that this is made possible by independent movement operations that re-arrange the elements in the vP before Spell-Out, as will be described below. As a result of these movements, verbs and subjects may appear on the right edge upon Spell-Out of vP and may move without doubling, like the case of objects.

Let us start with the case of non-doubling verbs. In examples like (303a), I suggest that there is *object movement* before the Spell-Out of vP, establishing a different OS_{vP}: $S < O < V$.[17] Subsequent right dislocation of the verb is followed by CD, which is not suspended, resulting in no doubling.

(303) a.   No doubling in right dislocation of verbs
            Keoi ni-di je   aa4 **sik**?
            he   this-CL thing Q   eat
            'He eats THIS THING?'

---

16. An anonymous JEAL reviewer raises concerns over cases like (i), where the subject and the dislocated element are co-indexed, but they are not identical (referred to as *Imperfect Copying* in L. Y.-L. Cheung (2015)).

 (i) **Aaming**$_i$ soeng sik ni-tiu jyu aa3 **keoi**$_i$.
      Aaming want eat this-CL fish SFP s/he
      'Aaming wants to eat this fish'

Right dislocation involving Imperfect Copying poses a general challenge to existing movement approaches (e.g. L. Y.-L. Cheung 2009; Lee 2017; Lai 2019). The acceptability of these cases is sometimes taken to motivate a bi-clausal analysis of right dislocation, as pursued in L. Y.-L. Cheung (2015). This implies that the right dislocated elements in Cantonese may have different derivational possibilities. Indeed, even within the movement approaches, the status of the dislocated element is not the same: it may be in its base generation position (L. Y.-L. Cheung 2009) or in a derived position (Lee 2017).

17. I assume that the object movement is achieved by some 'tucking-in' operation, landing in a position below the subject (N. Richards 2001).

b. The schematic derivation of (303a)

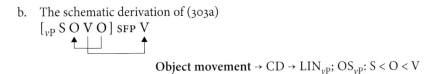

Object movement → CD → LIN$_{vP}$; OS$_{vP}$: S < O < V

There is independent evidence for the proposed object movement. First, it is not parasitic on right dislocation and can be applied independently.

(304) Keoi [**ni-di je**]$_i$ sik t$_i$ gaa4?
he this-CL thing eat Q
'He eats THIS THING?'

Importantly, if the nominal in the object position cannot undergo object movement (e.g. bare noun indefinites) as in (305a), the verb cannot be right dislocated either as in (305b). This suggests that right dislocation of verbs counts on the successful application of object movement.

(305) a. *Aaming **je**$_i$ sik t$_i$ aa4?
Aaming thing eat Q
Int.: 'Aaming eats?'
b. *Aaming je t$_i$ aa4 **sik**$_i$?
Aaming thing Q eat
Int.: 'Aaming eats?'

Further support the the correlation between successful object movement and right dislocation verb without doubling comes from ditransitive structures. Observe that while right dislocation of the verb *bei* 'give' is allowed in (306), it must be doubled.[18]

(306) Aaming *(**bei**) [ni-bun syu]$_{DO}$ ngo$_{IO}$ aa3 **bei**.
Aaming give this-CL book I SFP give
'Aaming gives this book to me.'

The doubling case follows straightforwardly from the proposal (see (300) above). The question is why verb doubling is obligatory. I suggest that doubling is forced because the indirect object *ngo* fails to undergo object movement for independent reasons.[19] Its immobility is evidenced by the following paradigm, independently of right dislocation of verbs.

---

18. I thank an anonymous JEAL reviewer for pointing out this contrast.
19. One possible explanation is that the indirect object is accompanied with a null preposition/ dative marker that forms a larger phrase with the indirect object (Tang 1998a). It may be that the indirect object is too embedded or object fronting cannot target a prepositional phrase. In either case, the indirect object is immobile.

180 The Unity of Movement

(307) a. Aaming bei [ni-bun syu]$_{DO}$ ngo$_{IO}$ aa3. (baseline)
Aaming give this-CL book I SFP
'Aaming gives this book to me.'

b. Aaming **[ni-bun syu]$_{DO}$** bei t_{DO} ngo$_{IO}$ aa3. (fronting of the direct object)

c. *Aaming **ngo$_{IO}$** bei [ni-bun syu]$_{DO}$ t_{IO} aa3. (*fronting of the indirect object)

d. *Aaming **[ni-bun syu]$_{DO}$ ngo$_{IO}$** bei t_{DO} t_{IO}aa3. (*fronting of both objects)

If the indirect object cannot undergo object fronting, there is no way to create an OS_{vP}: S < DO < IO < V (cf. (303) above), where the verb is put at the right edge in the vP. As such, doubling is the only option.[20]

Second, as far as interpretive effects are concerned, it has been suggested that the object movement that creates the (non-canonical) SOV word order renders the object a contrastive focus (Ernst and Wang 1995, i.a.). We observe a similar interpretive effect in case of right dislocation of verbs where there is no doubling. In (303a), *ni-di ye* 'this thing' is contrastively focused. The speaker is clarifying the thing that Aaming eats. Crucially, such as interpretive effect is absent if the verb is doubled, as in (291a), where the verb receives (contrastive) focus interpretation instead. The speaker is clarifying whether Aaming really *eats* the thing or not (see L. Y.-L. Cheung 2015; and also discussions below.).

We are now left with the case of right dislocation of a subject without doubling. Similar to the proposed analysis for verbs above, I suggest that doubling of the subject is not obligatory because the VP can be fronted to the left edge of vP, rendering the subject on the right edge of the vP. The subject, consequently, is right dislocated with its lower copy being deleted by CD. The sentence in (308) has the derivational history given in (309).

(308) No doubling in right dislocation of subjects
Soeng sik ni-tiu jyu aa3 **Aaming.**
want eat this-CL fish SFP Aaming
'Aaming wants to eat this fish.'

---

20. In a similar vein, this line of reasoning also rules out non-doubling cases like (i), where doubling of *ngo* is forced. I thank an anonymous JEAL reviewer for this example.

(i) Aaming gaau *(ngo) jyujinhok gaa3 **ngo.**
Aaming teach I linguistics SFP I
'Aaming teaches me linguistics.'

Specifically, the right dislocation of *ngo* without doubling requires successful fronting of *jyujinhok* 'linguistics'; however, it fails to undergo fronting:

(ii) *Aaming gaau jyujinhok$_i$ **ngo** t_i gaa3.
Aaming teach linguistics I SFP
Int.: 'Aaming teaches me linguistics.'

Chapter 5. Linearization **181**

(309) The schematic derivation of RD of subjects
$[_{vP} \text{VP S VP}]$ SFP S

$$\text{VP movement} \to \text{CD} \to \text{LIN}_{vP}; \text{OS}_{vP}: \text{VP} < \text{S}$$

Arguments for this VP movement come in two forms. First, VPs can move independently of right dislocation.

(310) [Sik ni-tiu   jyu]$_i$, Aaming soeng t$_i$ aa3.
       eat this-CL fish Aaming want   SFP
       (Lit.) 'To eat this fish, Aaming wants.'

Second, the VP in (308) receives focus interpretation, a discourse effect that is extensively discussed in L. Y.-L. Cheung (2009) (referred to as *Dislocation Focus Construction*). If the subject is doubled as in (295), then the it is the subject that receives the (contrastive) focus interpretation, instead of the VP. Such patterns are similar to those found with the doubling/non-doubling cases of right dislocation of verbs, as previously discussed.

Before I leave this subsection, it should be noted that the doubled elements give rise to *contrastive* focus instead of *informational* focus. That it is not the latter can be shown by the following question-answer pair:[21]

(311) a. A: Aaming   wui zou matje aa3?
              Aaming   will do   what SFP
              'What will Aaming do?'
       b. B: **Aaming**   wui tai   dinsi aa3, **Aaming**.
              Aamming   will watch TV SFP
              'Aaming will watch TV.'

In (311), A asks about *what* Aaming will do and thus Aaming cannot be the informational focus of an appropriate answer. Nonetheless, Aaming can be felicitously doubled in the answer given by B. This suggests that the doubled subject does not bear informational focus (i.e. it is the VP 'watch TV' that is informationally focused). In (311b), it is conceivable that B is stressing that the answer only applies to Aaming, but not any other, probably because s/he does not know about others.[22]

To sum up, the current proposal derives the doubling asymmetries in right dislocation in a way largely similar to that in topic constructions. The additional complication comes from the optionality of doubling which is only observed

---

21. I thank an anonymous JEAL reviewer for raising this point.

22. See L. Y.-L. Cheung (2015) for a slightly different scenario and more discussions on the contrastive function of the doubled elements.

in right dislocation. Referencing the occurrence of various independently motivated *v*P-internal movements, I suggest that optionality arises as a consequence of whether these movements occur or not. Crucially, again, the explanation of doubling asymmetries does not resort to the phrase structural status of the moving elements.

5.4.3   A remark on differences in acceptability

As noted in Section 5.2, there is a difference in acceptability between certain of the unacceptable cases described here. On one hand, if an element must be doubled in case of movement (e.g. verb topicalization) but it is not doubled, the sentence is strictly out (as in (269)). On the other hand, if an element strongly prefers not to be doubled (e.g. object topicalization and right dislocation), doubling this elements lead to a less severe unacceptability (relevant examples are marked with ??, such as (270)). In other words, failing to double what should be doubled results in sentences that are more severely degraded than instances of doubling what should not be doubled, i.e. failing to delete what should be deleted. I refer to the former cases as *fail-to-double cases* and the latter as *fail-to-delete cases*. The question is why there is such a difference.

I suggest that the difference indicates that the two cases violate different principles in the grammar. For the *fail-to-double cases*, the absence of the lower copy in verb topicalization directly violates the phonological requirements imposed by CL. For example, in derivation in (287), the step in (287b) dictates that the lower copy of *soeng* 'want' must be preceded by *Aaming* and *hai*. Failing to double (i.e. deleting the lower copy) violates the established OS. Violation of OS requirement leads to a linearization failure and consequently the structure cannot be pronounced.

In contrast, the *fail-to-delete cases* do not constitute such a violation. Consider the schematic derivation in (289), failing to delete the lowest copy of the object (i.e. the most embedded one) would not lead to failures in linearization – nothing restricts the verb from preceding the object. Instead, the structure is degraded due to a failure to apply the operation that is responsible for minimizing copies (e.g. CD). This may violate an economy principle in the grammar such as the one given below:[23]

(312)   Economy condition on identical copies
        Minimize pronunciation of identical copies.

---

23. A similar condition is proposed in Landau (2006, p. 57).

So the *fail-to-delete cases* violate an economy condition, rather than requirements related to linearization. Assuming that economy conditions are more "tolerant", it therefore leads to a less severe level of unacceptability. On a relevant note, I have proposed that the suspension of CD occurs as a last resort to ensure successful linearization, in Section 5.4.1. The last resort nature can be considered as an indication of this economy condition which prefers the application of CD, unless its application leads to ungrammaticality.

5.4.4 Resolving a further asymmetry in doubling

Before I end this section, I discuss a prediction and a further asymmetry in doubling, which also follow from the current proposal. Let us first consider a prediction concerning objects. We have seen that an object cannot be doubled when right dislocated (because it is on the right edge). But if this object also moves for topicalization, then the object movement within *v*P will establish a different OS$_{vP}$: O < S < V. In such case, we expect to see doubling of the object in right dislocation to be possible. This prediction is borne out as seen in (313).

(313) Left-dislocated topics in right dislocation
 Ni-di je Aaming sik aa4 **ni-di je**.
 this-CL thing Aaming eat Q this-CL thing
 'Aaming eats THIS THING?'

The derivation history given in (314) suggests that the object first stops at Spec *v*P, which, after the Spell-Out of *v*P, moves further for topicalization. The object continues to move for right dislocation (indicated by the rightward movement). In order to preserve the OS established in *v*P, the copy in the topic position must not be deleted by CD (such that there is a copy of the object that precedes the subject and the verb). The suspension of CD leads to two copies in the sentence.

(314) The schematic derivation of (313)
 [$_{TopP}$ O … [$_{vP}$ O S V O] SFP O]

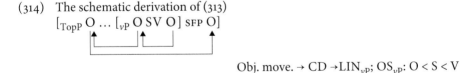

Obj. move. → CD →LIN$_{vP}$; OS$_{vP}$: O < S < V

While (313) shows that a left-dislocated topic can be doubled when it further undergoes right dislocation, it should be noted that not all types of topics can be doubled when right dislocated. For example, a base generated topic (e.g. a hanging topic or an aboutness topic) cannot be doubled when it is right dislocated. An example of this is given in (315) where *seoigwo* is considered as an aboutness topic, as it does not correspond to a gap in the sentence.

(315) Base generated topics in right dislocation
    (^{??} **Seoigwo**) Aaming zungji lei   aa3 **seoigwo**.
      fruit   Aaming like   pear SFP fruit
    'As for fruits, Aaming likes pears.'

The asymmetry between a left dislocated topic and a base generated one follows from the current proposal. Crucially, a base generated topic have a different derivational history to a left-dislocated topic: a base generated topic does not originate within the *v*P, and thus it is not linearized relative to the elements within *v*P. Instead, it is base generated in the topic position in the CP domain. When it is right-dislocated, CD applies upon the Spell-Out of the TopicP and it deletes the copy in the topic position). As a result, a base generated topic is right dislocated without doubling, as schematically shown in (316).

(316) The schematic derivation of (315)
    [$_{\text{TopP}}$ **Topic** ... [$_{v\text{P}}$ S V O] SFP Topic]

$$\text{OS}_{v\text{P}}: \text{S} < \text{V} < \text{O}$$

The current proposal thus not only captures the patterns described in section 5.2, but it also makes a precise prediction on different doubling profiles for different types of topics which follow from their derivational histories.

5.5 Alternative explanations to the doubling effects

In this section, I discuss three alternative explanations to the general analysis of doubling proposed here. For expository purposes, I focus on how these alternatives fail to derive the doubling pattern of verbs in Cantonese, which demonstrate the most complicated pattern found (i.e. obligatory doubling and optional doubling). It should be noted that I am not arguing against the role of these alternatives in potentially deriving doubling patterns in other languages, but that they fall short of explaining the cases we have seen so far.

    The first two alternatives stress the role of the phonological component (similar to the current proposal). Nunes (2004) and Corver and Nunes (2007) take advantage of an independently motivated operation in the phonological component, namely, *morphological fusion*, which applies to two adjacent terminals and leads to the formation of a complex head. This operation is suggested to make a member of a chain to be "invisible" to Copy Deletion, because it is suggested that a morphologically fused element is no longer identical to its other copy. To see how such an idea might work with verb topicalization in Cantonese, it could be the case that the higher copy of a verb is morphologically fused with a null Topic head, forming a complex head #V-top#. Consequently, it would be regarded as distinct from the lower copy, i.e. V. CD does not apply since there are no identical copies. The same might be suggested for the doubling case in right dislocation, except that the null head being a different one, say, a head rd, that hosts right dislocated elements in its specifier. However, the non-doubling case of verbs in right dislocation poses a challenge to such an approach. To maintain a morphological fusion account, one would be forced to say that morphological fusion is optional. Importantly, it would be only optional for the head rd, but not top, because we have seen that doubling in verb topicalization is obligatory. The optionality of the application of morphological fusion, together with the idiosyncratic nature of different functional heads, weakens the explanatory power of such an approach.[24]

Another potential alternative is proposed by Trinh (2009). He proposes a constraint on CD, which suggests that a lower copy can be deleted only if it "ends" an XP.

(317) Constraint on Copy Deletion (CCD, Trinh 2009)
A chain (α, β) is deletable only if β is at the right edge of an XP.

Applying the idea to the Cantonese data, this constraint could capture the asymmetry between verbs and objects in topicalization: the lower copy of an object is deleted because it ends the vP, while that of a verb is not, because it does not end the vP. Schematically,

(318) A schematized illustration of verb and object topicalization in Cantonese

$$\text{V/O} \ldots [_{vP} \text{ S V} \quad \text{O} \quad]$$
*delete ^{OK}delete

This approach, however, would also predict that verb doubling is obligatory when the verb is right dislocated, just like the case of verb topicalization. This is because the verb is not at the right edge. However, as we have seen, verb doubling is optional in right dislocation in Cantonese. Note that object movement within vP

---

24. Further challenges have been discussed in Cheng and Vicente (2013), where they suggest that it is puzzling that morphological fusion does not apply to objects (i.e. no doubling in object topicalization). Citing an example from Brazilian Sign Language (Nunes and Quadros 2006), they note that it is possible to double *wh*-expressions (in addition to heads), which presumably have a complex internal structure (Cable 2007). Words in capital letters indicate the glosses for Brazilian Sign Language.

(i) JOHN SEE **WHO** YESTERDAY **WHO**
'Who exactly is it that John saw yesterday?'

(like the one we have seen in §5.4.2) does not help since covert elements count in the calculation of what "ends" an XP, according to Trinh's proposal (p. 195, fn. 18).

A third possible alternative explanation might be a resort to the notion of parallel chains in Narrow Syntax. Following Chomsky (2008), Kandybowicz (2008), and Aboh and Dyakonova (2009), Lai (2019) proposes that doubling is due to the creation of parallel chains. The idea is that an element moves to two higher positions, creating two independent chains that have the same tail (i.e. the lower copy). When CD applies, only the lower copy is deleted, since both higher copies survive CD and hence there is doubling. While Lai primarily discusses the doubling cases in right dislocation, the same reasoning might be used to apply to verb doubling as follows. In verb topicalization, a verb might be suggested to move independently to both the v head and the Topic head, creating two separate chains. When CD applies, only the V head is deleted, resulting in two occurrences of the verb in the v and Topic heads.

(319)   A schematized illustration of parallel chains in verb topicalization in Cantonese

$[_{\text{TopicP}}$ V-Topic ... $[_{vP}$ SV-v $[_{VP}$ V O$]]$

Analogously, parallel chains might also be able to account for verb doubling in right dislocation, if we assume the verb moves to a counterpart of the Topic head that hosts right dislocation. However, this approach does not predict the optionality of doubling in right dislocation. To account for the absence of doubling in right dislocation, one must suggest that the higher copy of the chain {V-v, V} can sometimes be deleted. Such deletion is technically challenging under a parallel chain approach as we have to stipulate an unconventional deletion operation that targets the whole chain.

In sum, I conclude that existing accounts of doubling primarily focus on how to ensure the second occurrence of a copy, but they are less adaptable to the optional nature of verb doubling in Cantonese. Further challenges to these alternative accounts are posed by the doubling pattern of objects and subjects where doubling is not strictly prohibited or required. The current proposal, by way of contrast, offers a more comprehensive account on the doubling patterns in Cantonese.

5.6   Extension: Verb movement without doubling

Thus far, we have focused exclusively on data in Cantonese. We now turn to some additional crosslinguistic pattern. Given the current explanation of (verb) doubling, the relative position of the verb to the subject is always fixed at the Spell-Out of vP. The proposal seems to predict that the word order of a language is either S-V-O (i.e. the verb does not move across the subject in the vP) or V-S-V-O (i.e. the verb moves across the subject and is doubled). This is too strong in the sense that it (incorrectly) rules out *any* V-S order. For examples, sentences in (320) show two cases of verb movement across the subject without doubling in Swedish and Bulgarian. These non-doubling cases do not immediately follow from the proposal put forth in §5.3.

(320) Verb movement without doubling
- a. Swedish
Hittade han faktist (*hittade) pengarna under sängen?
found he actually found money.the under bed.the
'Did he actually find the money under the bed?'

(Takita 2010, p. 40, with adaptations)

- b. Bulgarian
Razkazvala beše često Marija (*razkazvala) tazi istorija
told was often Maria told this story
'Maria had often told this story.' (Harizanov 2019, p. 8, with adaptations)

These cases, together with the Cantonese data, show that languages vary with regard to whether movement of verbs over the subject require doubling of the verbs or not. Following Takita (2010), I suggest this cross-linguistic difference results from the parameter of Spell-Out domain. Specifically, while Spell-Out invariably applies at vP, languages may differ in the size of the linearization domain.[25] I suggest that languages like Swedish and Bulgarian have *a different linearization domain* from Cantonese. For these languages, upon Spell-Out, only the complement of v but not the whole vP is linearized.

(321) Spell-Out Domain Parameter for vP (Takita 2010)
When Spell-Out applies to vP,
- a. Linearize the whole vP, including the elements on its edge, or
- b. Linearize the complement of v.

If Swedish and Bulgarian take the value of (321b), when Spell-Out applies to the vP, only the VP is linearization (as opposed to the vP in Cantonese). Consequently, the order between S and V is not fixed upon Spell-Out of vP. This is illustrated with the Swedish example in (320a). (322b) only gives the OS upon the the

---

25. The idea that the linearization domain of vP varies across languages has its roots in Ko (2005, 2007), who proposes that the linearization domain of Korean is vP, rather than VP (which is assumed to be the linearization domain for some Scandinavian languages; see also discussions in Fox and Pesetsky (2005, §5).

188 The Unity of Movement

first instance of Spell-Out, where the OS only contains ordering information of V, O and PP, to the exclusion of S. The verb is thus free to move at a later stage of the derivation. The same applies to Bulgarian data as well.

(322) The derivation of (320a)
  a. [$_{CP}$ **Hittade** [$_{TP}$ han faktist [$_{vP}$ **han** [$_{VP}$ **hittade** pengarna under sängen?]]]]

  b. LIN$_{VP}$; OS$_{VP}$: V < O < PP

If this line of reasoning is on the right track, the availability of verb doubling is correlated with the size of Spell-Out domain in the following way:

(323) Verb doubling possibility
  a. Languages that <u>allow</u> verb doubling take the value of (321a);

  e.g. Cantonese
  b. Languages that <u>disallow</u> verb doubling take the value of (321b).

  e.g. Swedish, Bulgarian

Interestingly, the parameter in (321) is originally proposed in Takita (2010) to explain illicit cases of remnant movements in Japanese and licit ones in English and German. Specifically, he proposes that languages that take the value of (321a), i.e. *v*P is linearized upon Spell-Out, would disallow remnant movement. This describes the case of Japanese. Consider the following paradigm (adapted from Takita (2010, p. 11–12)). (324a) is the baseline. (324b) shows that long distance scrambling of PPs is possible. (324c) shows that CP scrambling is also possible. (324d), however, shows that once a PP is scrambled out of an embedded CP, the (remnant) CP cannot be scrambled.

(324) a. Baseline
        Taroo-ga   [$_{CP}$ Hanako-ga   [$_{PP}$ Sooru-ni] i-ru   to] omottei-ru.
        Taroo-NOM   Hanako-NOM   Seoul-in   be-PRES that   think-PRES
        'Taroo thinks [that Hanako lives [in Seoul]].'
    b. (Long distance) PP scrambling
        [$_{PP}$ Sooru-ni]$_i$, Taroo-ga   [$_{CP}$ Hanako-ga   t$_i$ i-ru   to] omottei-ru.
        Seoul-in   Taroo-NOM   Hanako-NOM   be-PRES that   think-PRES
        '(lit.) [In Seoul]$_i$, Taroo thinks [that Hanako lives t$_i$].'
    c. CP scrambling
        [$_{CP}$ Hanako-ga   [$_{PP}$ Sooru-ni] i-ru   to]$_j$, Taroo-ga   t$_j$ omottei-ru.
        Hanako-NOM   Seoul-in   be-PRES that   Taroo-NOM   think-PRES
        '(lit.) [That Hanako lives [in Seoul]]$_j$, Taroo thinks t$_j$.'

Chapter 5. Linearization **189**

d. PP scrambling followed by CP scrambling
$*[_{CP}$ Hanako-ga t_i i-ru to $]_j$ $[_{PP}$ Sooru-ni $]_i$ Taroo-ga t_j
Hanako-NOM be-PRES that Seoul-in Taroo-NOM
omottei-ru.
think-PRES
'(lit.) [That Hanako lives t_i $]_j$, [in Seoul]$_i$, Taroo thinks t_j.'

The unacceptability of (324d) has been attributed to versions of the Proper Binding Condition (PBC, Fiengo 1977; Saito 2003), which states that traces must be bound. Takita (2010) casts doubt on the precise nature of the PBC in the grammar and instead proposes that the PBC-effects observed above follow from some general principle concerning linearization. Adopting the idea of Cyclic Linearization, he proposes that remnant scrambling is ruled out because it leads to conflicts in linearization. To see how, consider first the (long distance) scrambling of the PP in (324d), which requires the PP to move to the edge of the vP. Since Japanese takes the value of (321a), the whole vP is linearized, giving the OS$_{vP}$: **PP < S < V**. The PP is subsequently further scrambled out of the CP. Then, the remnant CP is scrambled to a position higher than the PP. This establishes another OS at the final Spell-Out: **CP < PP**. Note that this CP contains the subject and the verb whose order is relativized to the PP already. So the scrambling of CP would give rise to OS as follows: $\boxed{\text{S < V}}$ CP < PP. This results in linearization conflicts and hence causes the unacceptability of (324d). Remnant movement/scrambling in Japanese is thus systematically ruled out by Cyclic Linearization and the supplementary assumption that the linearization domain of Japanese is vP.

Now consider remnant movement in English and German. In contrast to Japanese, these languages allows remnant movement.

(325) Licit remnant cases
a. *English: A-movement followed by remnant vP movement*
[Criticized t_i by his boss]$_j$, John$_i$ has never been t_j.
b. *German: object scrambling followed by remnant vP/VP topicalization*
[t_i Zu lesen]$_j$ hat keiner [das Buch]$_i$ t_j versucht.
to read has no.one the book tried
'No one has tried to read the book'

Takita (2010) suggests that English and German have a different linearization domain, where only the elements in the VP are linearized upon Spell-Out of vP. Take the English case in (325a) as an example. Assuming that the object *John* can move to the edge of vP due to passivization, its linear order with regard to other elements is not fixed upon the Spell-Out of vP. This is because only the elements in VP are linearized in English, which gives rise to the OS$_{vP}$: **V < PP**. Following

190   The Unity of Movement

this, the object *John* undergoes further movement to Spec TP. Subsequent (remnant) movement of the *v*P would not result in linearization conflicts: no OS forbids V or PP from preceding the object. As a result, remnant movement is allowed in languages with a linearization domain of VP under Cyclic Linearization.

The cases of Japanese and English/German can be summarized as follows: the availability of remnant movement is correlated with the size of the Spell-Out domain in a way specified in (326).

(326)   Remnant movement possibility
    a.   Languages that <u>disallow</u> remnant movement take the value of (321a);
            e.g. Japanese
    b.   Languages that <u>allow</u> remnant movement take the value of (321b).
            e.g. German, English

Returning to our discussion on verb doubling, (326) and (323) combine to predict the distribution of verb doubling and remnant movement, since they require a language to take different values on the Spell-Out domain parameter suggested in (321). The predictions are given in (327):

(327)   Predicted distribution of verb doubling and remnant movement
    a.   Languages that allow verb doubling will disallow remnant movement.
    b.   Languages that allow remnant movement will disallow verb doubling.

(327a) is borne out by the unavailability of remnant *v*P movement in Cantonese. (328a) shows that *v*P-fronting is disallowed if the subject is moved out from the *v*P, i.e. *v*P fronting is disallowed in raising constructions. This follows the same line of reasoning as the explanation of why remnant scrambling is disallowed in Japanese. Note that (328b) is supplied to show that *v*P-fronting is allowed if the subject of the *v*P is not moved out, i.e. *v*P fronting is allowed in control constructions.

(328)   *v*P fronting in Cantonese
    a. *[$_{vP}$ t$_i$ bin   hak]$_j$, go tin$_i$ hoici t$_j$ laa3.   Raising
          become dark   CL sky begin   SFP
          Intended: 'To become dark, the sky begins.'
    b.   [$_{vP}$ PRO pau coengpau]$_i$, keoi soengsi-gwo t$_i$ laa3.   Control
            run long.run   keoi try-EXP   SFP
          'To run long distance, he tried.'

(327b) is borne out in English. While remnant movement is allowed, verb doubling is not, as in (329). With a smaller Spell-Out domain, V occupies the edge position and is thus free to move. Doubling is not required, hence disallowed (due to the last resort nature).[26]

Chapter 5. Linearization 191

(329) Verb doubling in English
*Criticize(d), John criticized his boss.

As a final remark, I briefly discuss what the current proposal does not necessarily predict, listed in (330). The current proposal concerns the *necessary* condition for doubling. If a language disallows verb doubling, it need not allow remnant movement, as there may be independent reasons to rule out verb doubling. Likewise, if a language disallows remnant movement, it need not allow verb doubling either.

(330) Some non-predictions
    a. Languages that disallows verb doubling will allow remnant movement.
    b. Languages that disallows remnant movement will allow verb doubling.

It is, however, interesting to see that if a language disallows verb doubling *precisely* because of its Spell-Out domain being a VP, we do expect to see remnant movement to be possible. This has already been seen in English and we also observe remnant VP topicalization in Swedish, as in (331).

(331) Remnant movement in Swedish (Fox and Pesetsky 2005, p. 25)
    $^?$[Gett henne t$_i$] har jag den$_i$ inte …
    given her   have I it   not
    'I have not given it to her.'

Whether (330b) holds is less clear, however. To the best of my knowledge, the closest Japanese and Korean counterparts of the Cantonese verb doubling constructions are discussed in Nishiyama and Cho (1998), where both languages display some doubling effects in predicate cleft constructions.

(332) Japanese
    John-ga   computer-o   **kai**-wa   **si**-ta
    John-NOM computer-ACC buy-CON do-PST
    'Indeed, John bought a computer, (but…)'

---

26. It should be noted that movement of the verb without doubling is also disallowed:

(i) *Criticized, John t$_i$ his boss.

This should not be regarded as a counterexample to the current proposal, since, the current proposal states the *necessary* condition for doubling, but not the *sufficient* condition for doubling. While verb movement without doubling is allowed in Swedish and Bulgarian, sentences like (i) in English may be ruled out on independent grounds. I do not pursue this further in the current chapter.

(333) Korean
John-i computer-lul **sa-ki-nun** sa-ss-ta
John-NOM computer-ACC buy-KI-CON buy-PAST-DECL
'Indeed, John bought a computer, (but...)'

In the Japanese case, the verb is associated with a dummy verb instead of an identical copy, whereas the Korean case comes closer to a case of verb doubling, but the first verb is marked with the morpheme *-ki*. For reasons of space, I will leave the full investigation of these examples to future research. Table 5.2 summarizes the findings in this section.

Table 5.2 Verb doubling and remnant movement across languages

Parameter	(321a) Linearize *v*P			(321b) Linearize VP		
Language	Cantonese	Japanese	Korean	Swedish	English	German
Verb doubling	Yes	?	?	No	No	No
Remnant movement	No	No	No	Yes	Yes	Yes

Summing up, this section began with cases of verb movement without doubling in languages like Swedish and Bulgarian. Following Takita (2010), I proposed that the difference between languages with/without verb doubling lies in the Spell-Out domain parameter given in (321). I then suggested that such an explanation is further corroborated by a correlation between verb doubling and remnant movement, the availability of which depends on the parametric value for (321) that the language takes.

5.7 Conclusions

In this chapter, I began with a consideration of an asymmetry in verb topicalization and object topicalization. I set up the empirical foundation of this study by giving a description of various patterns of doubling in Cantonese. I discussed the doubling profiles of verbs, subjects and objects with regard to topic constructions and right dislocation. I then proposed an account based on Cyclic Linearization. Specifically, I proposed that doubling is a consequence of the suspension of Copy Deletion. Copy Deletion is suspended as a last resort to avoid violations of linearization requirements imposed by CL. In the final section, I discussed cases where verb movement does not display doubling effects in languages other than Cantonese, and suggested an account based on the parameter of the linearization domain, following ideas in Takita (2010).

The implications of the current proposal are two-fold. First, it lends further support to Cyclic Linearization, which has been argued to capture different phenomena in different languages, e.g. object shift in Scandinavian languages (Fox and Pesetsky 2005), quantifier floating in Korean (Ko 2005, 2007), remnant movement in Japanese (Takita 2010), preposition stranding in English (Drummond, Hornstein, and Lasnik 2010), constraints on the scrambling of genitive-marked arguments in Korean (Simpson and Park 2019) and intermediate stranding in a number of languages (Davis 2020). CL stresses the role of the phonological component in the study of syntactic locality, serving as an alternative direction to Chomsky's version of phase theory (Chomsky 2000, 2001), one that suggests that a syntactic domain is inaccessible both to syntactic and phonological operations.

Second, the proposal derives the Cantonese doubling pattern without linking this to the phrase-structural status of the (non-)doubling elements and maintains that the mechanism that determines copy pronunciation is the same for heads and phrases. This resonates with recent efforts in unifying head and phrasal movement. For example, it is argued that all movement operations leave a trace that feed interpretation (Hartman 2011); substitution, in addition to adjunction, is available to both head and phrasal movement (Funakoshi 2012, 2014); head movement can target specifier positions just like phrasal movement (Harizanov 2019; Harizanov and Gribanova 2019); and dependencies between arguments, non-arguments, and heads may lead to structure reduction in the formation of infinitival clauses (Pesetsky 2020). This findings of this chapter provide a further piece of evidence along such lines.

CHAPTER 6

Conclusions

Based on in-depth investigations into various cases of verb displacement in Cantonese, it is hoped that this volume contributes to our understanding of movement theories of natural language. Following up on the debates of the theoretical status and empirical properties of head movement, I explored the possibility of a unified theory of movement that does not make reference to structural types such as heads and phrases. I discussed three pieces of evidence from Cantonese, showing that movement of heads and phrases are subject to the same set of syntactic principles, which constrain (i) how they move in the syntax, (ii) how they contribute to interpretation, and (iii) how their chains are phonologically realized. To the extent that head movement can be assimilated to phrasal movement, this volume sets the basis of a movement theory that does not discriminate heads from phrases, hence a unified theory of movement.

To restate the theoretical consequences of a unified theory of movement, first, it allows us to maintain the formulation of the structure-building operation, *Merge*, in its simplest form. Internal Merge applies to syntactic constituents without the need to distinguish heads from phrases, in a way comparable to External Merge, which applies equally to both heads and phrases. Second, it opens up questions of whether and how other reported differences between movement of heads and phrases can be attributed to components of the grammar other than the movement mechanism.

References

Abels, Klaus. 2001. "The predicate cleft construction in Russian." In *Proceedings of Formal Approaches to Slavic Linguistics* 9, edited by Steven Franks, Tracy Holloway King, and Michael Yadroff, 1–18. Ann Arbor: Michigan Slavic Publications.

Abels, Klaus. 2003. "Successive Cyclicity, Anti-locality, and Adposition Stranding." PhD diss., University of Connecticut.

Aboh, Enoch Oladé, and Marina Dyakonova. 2009. "Predicate doubling and parallel chains." *Lingua* 119 (7): 1035–1065.

Adger, David. 2013. *A syntax of substance*. Cambridge: MIT Press.

Aelbrecht, Lobke, and Marcel den Dikken. 2013. "Preposition doubling in Flemish and its implications for the syntax of Dutch PPs." *Journal of Comparative Germanic Linguistics* 16 (1): 33–68.

Aissen, Judith. 1974. "Verb raising." *Linguistic Inquiry* 5 (3): 325–366.

Antonenko, Andrei. 2019. "Predicate Doubling in Russian: One process or two?" In *Proceedings of FASL* 27. Michigan Slavic Publications.

Aoun, Joseph, and Yen-Hui Audrey Li. 2003. *Essays on the represetntational and derivational nature of grammar*. Cambridge, MA: The MIT Press.

Aoun, Joseph, and Yen-Hui Audrey Li. 2008. "Ellipsis and missing objects." In *Foundational Issues in Linguistic Theory*, edited by Robert Freidin, Carlos P. Otero, and Maria Luisa Zubizarreta, 251–274. Cambridge, MA: MIT Press.

Aoyagi, Hiroshi, and Toru Ishii. 1994. "On NPI Licensing in Japanese." In *Japanese/Korean Linguistics(4)*, edited by Noriko Akatsuka, 295–312. Stanford: Stanford Linguistics Association.

Arregi, Karlos, and Asia Pietraszko. 2021. "The Ups and Downs of Head Displacement." *Linguistic Inquiry* 52 (2): 241–290.

Badan, Linda. 2007. "High and low periphery: a comparison between Italian and Chinese." PhD diss., Universita' Degli Studi di Padova.

Baker, Mark. 1985. "The Mirror Principle and Morphosyntactic Explanation." *Linguistic Inquiry* 16 (3): 373–416.

Baker, Mark. 1988. *Incorporation*. Chicago, Illinois: University of Chicago Press.

Barrie, Michael, and Eric Mathieu. 2016. "Noun incorporation and phrasal movement." *Natural Language and Linguistic Theory* 34 (1): 1–51.

Barwise, John, and Robin Cooper. 1981. "Generalized Quantifiers and Natural Language." *Linguistics and Philosophy* 4:159–219.

Bastos-Gee, Ana C. 2009. "Topicalization of verbal projections in Brazilian Portuguese." In *Minimalist essays on Brazilian Portuguese Syntax*, edited by Jairo Nunes, 161–190. Amsterdam: John Benjamins.

Beck, Sigrid. 1996. "Wh-constructions and transparent Logical Form." PhD diss., Universität Tübingen.

Beck, Sigrid. 2006. "Intervention Effects Follow From Focus Interpretation." *Natural Language Semantics* 14 (1): 1–56.

Beck, Sigrid, and Shin-Sook Kim. 1997. "On WH- and operator scope in Korean." *Journal of East Asian Linguistics* 6:339–384.

Beck, Sigrid, and Arnim von Stechow. 2015. "Events, Times and Worlds – An LF Architecture." In *Situationsargumente im Nominalbereich*, edited by Fortmann von Christian, 13–46. Berlin: de Gruyter.

Benedicto, Elena. 1998. "Verb Movement and its Effects on Determinerless Plural Subjects." In *Romance Linguistics: Theoretical Perspectives*, edited by Armin Schwegler, Bernard Tranel, and Myriam Uribe-Etxebarria, 25–40. Amsterdam: John Benjamins.

Benincà Paola and Cecilia Poletto. 2004. "The Structure of CP and IP. The Cartography of Syntactic Structures." *Chap. Topic, Foc*, edited by Luigi Rizzi, 2:52–75. New York & Oxford: Oxford University Press.

Bhatt, Rajesh. 1998. "Obligation and Possession." In *Papers from the UPenn/MIT Roundtable on Argument Structure and Aspect*, edited by Heidi Harley, 21–40. Cambridge, MA: MITWPL.

Blanchette, Frances, and Chris Collins. 2019. "On the subject of negative auxiliary inversion." *Canadian Journal of Linguistics* 64 (1): 32–61.

Bobaljik, Jonathan. 2002. "A-chains at the PF-interface: copies and 'covert' movement." *Natural Language and Linguistic Theory* 20 (2): 197–267.

Bobaljik, Jonathan David, and Samuel Brown. 1997. "Interarboreal Operations: Head Movement and the Extension Requirement." *Linguistic Inquiry* 28 (2): 345–356.

Bobaljik, Jonathan David, and Susi Wurmbrand. 2012. "Word Order and Scope: Transparent Interfaces and the ¾ Signature." *Linguistic Inquiry* 43 (3): 371–421.

Boeckx, Cedric, and Sandra Stjepanović. 2001. "Head-ing toward PF." *Linguistic Inquiry* 32:345–355.

Borsley, Robert D., Maria-Luisa Rivero, and Janig Stephens. 1996. "Long head movement in Breton." In *The Syntax of the Celtic Languages: A Comparative Perspective*, edited by Robert D. Borsley and Ian Roberts, 53–74. Cambridge: Cambridge University Press.

Bošković, Željko. 2007. "On the Locality and Motivation of Move and Agree: An Even More Minimal Theory." *Linguistic Inquiry* 38 (4): 589–644.

Bošković, Željko. 2014. "Now I'm a Phase, Now I'm Not a Phase: On the Variability of Phases with Extraction and Ellipsis." *Linguistic Inquiry* 45 (1): 27–89.

Bošković, Željko, and Jairo Nunes. 2007. "The Copy Theory of Movement: A view from PF." In *The Copy Theory of Movement*, edited by Jairo Nunes and Norbert Hornstein, 13–74. Oxford: Blackwell Publishers.

Branan, Kenyon, and Michael Yoshitaka Erlewine. 2020. *Anti-pied-piping*. Ms., National University of Singapore.

Brattico, Pauli. 2021. "Predicate clefting and long head movement in Finnish." *Linguistic Inquiry*: 1–57.

Brody, Michael. 2000. "Mirror Theory: syntactic representation in perfect syntax." *Linguistic Inquiry* 31 (1): 29–56.

Büring, Daniel. 1997. *The Meaning of Topic and Focus: The 59th Street Bridge Accent Routledge Studies in German Linguistics*. London and New York: Routledge.

Bury, Dirk. 2003. "Phrase Structure and Derived Heads." PhD diss., University College London.

Cable, Seth. 2004. *Predicate Clefts and Base-Generation: Evidence From Yiddish and Brazilian Portuguese.* Ms., MIT, Cambridge, MA.

Cable, Seth. 2007. "The Grammar of Q: Q-Particles and the Nature of Wh-Fronting, as Revealed by the Wh-Questions of Tlingit." PhD diss., Massachusetts Institute of Technology.

Cable, Seth. 2010. *The Grammar of Q: Q-Particles, Wh-Movement and Pied-Piping.* Oxford: Oxford University Press.

Caink, Andrew. 1999. "Against 'Long Head Movement': lexical insertion and the Bulgarian auxiliary 'BE'." In *Topics in south Slavic syntax and semantics*, edited by Mila Dimitrova-Vulchanova and Lars Hellan, 91–124. Amsterdam: John Benjamins.

Chan, Brian Hok-Shing. 2013. "Sentence-final particles, complementizers, antisymmetry, and the Final-over-Final Constraint." In *Theoretical Approaches to Disharmonic Word Order*, edited by Theresa Biberauer and Michelle Sheehan, 445–468. Oxford: Oxford University Press.

Chan, Kwun Kin. 2016. *A study of sentence-final phrasal reduplication in Cantonese.* MA thesis, The Chinese University of Hong Kong.

Chao, Yuen Ren. 1968. *A Grammar of Spoken Chinese.* Berkeley: University of California Press.

Cheng, Lisa Lai-Shen. 1991. "On the Typology of WH-Questions." PhD diss., Massachusetts Institute of Technology.

Cheng, Lisa Lai Shen. 2008. "Deconstructing the shì … De construction." *Linguistic Review* 25:235–266.

Cheng, Lisa Lai-Shen, and Luis Vicente. 2013. "Verb doubling in Mandarin Chinese." *Journal of East Asian Linguistics* 22 (1): 1–37.

Cheng, Siu Pong. 2015. "The Relationship of Syntactic and Semantic Aspects of Postverbal Particles and Their Preverbal Counterparts in Hong Kong Cantonese." PhD diss., The Chinese University of Hong Kong.

Cheung, Candice Chi-Hang. 2008. "Wh-fronting in Chinese." PhD diss., University of Southern California.

Cheung, Candice Chi-Hang. 2015. "On the Fine Structure of the Left Periphery." In *The Cartography of Chinese Syntax*, edited by Wei-Tien Dylan Tsai, 75–130. Oxford: Oxford University Press.

Cheung, Lawrence Yam-Leung. 1997. *A study of right dislocation in Cantonese.* MA thesis, The Chinese University of Hong Kong.

Cheung, Lawrence Yam-Leung. 2005. *Syntax and semantics of dislocation focus construction in Cantonese.* MA thesis, University of California, Los Angeles.

Cheung, Lawrence Yam-Leung. 2009. "Dislocation focus construction in Chinese." *Journal of East Asian Linguistics* 18 (3): 197–232.

Cheung, Lawrence Yam-Leung. 2015. "Bi-clausal sluicing approach to dislocation copying in Cantonese." *International Journal of Chinese Linguistics* 2 (2): 227–272.

Chomsky, Noam. 1957. *Syntactic structures.* Mouton.

Chomsky, Noam. 1973. "Conditions on Transformations." In *A Festschrift for Morris Halle*, edited by Stephen Anderson and Paul Kiparsky, 232–286. New York: Holt Rinehart / Winston.

Chomsky, Noam. 1977. "Conditions on transformations." In *Essays on form and interpretation*, 81–162. New York, New York: Elsevier North-Holland, Inc.

Chomsky, Noam. 1981. *Lectures on government and binding*. Dordrecht, The Netherlands: Foris Publications.

Chomsky, Noam. 1986. *Barriers*. Cambridge, Massachusetts: MIT Press.

Chomsky, Noam. 1994. *Bare phrase structure*. Cambridge, MA: MITWPL.

Chomsky, Noam. 1995a. "Bare phrase structure." In *Government binding theory and the minimalist program*, edited by Gert Webelhuth, 383–439. Oxford: Oxford University Press.

Chomsky, Noam. 1995b. *The Minimalist Program*. Cambridge, Massachusetts: MIT Press.

Chomsky, Noam. 2000. "Minimalist inquiries: the framework." In *Step by step: Essays on minimalist syntax in honor of Howard Lasnik*, edited by Roger Martin, David Michaels, and Juan Uriagereka, 89–156. Cambridge, MA: MIT Press.

Chomsky, Noam. 2001. "Derivation by phase." In *Ken Hale: a life in language*, edited by Michael Kenstowicz, 1–52. Cambridge, MA: MIT Press.

Chomsky, Noam. 2008. "On Phases." In *Foundational Issues in Linguistic Theory: Essays in Honor of Jean-Roger Vergnaud*, edited by Robert Freidin, Carlos Otero, and Maria Luisa Zubizarreta, 133–166. Cambridge: MIT Press.

Chomsky, Noam. 2015. "Problems of projection: Extensions." In *Structures, Strategies and Beyond*, edited by Elisa Di Domenico, Cornelia Hamann, and Simona Matteini, 3–16. Amsterdam and Philadelphia: John Benjamins Publishing Company.

Chomsky, Noam. 2019. *The UCLA Lectures (April 29 – May 2, 2019)*. http://lingbuzz.net/lingbuzz/005485.

Chomsky, Noam. 2021. "Minimalism: Where Are We Now, and Where Can We Hope to Go." *Gengo Kenkyu* 160:1–41.

Chou, Chao-ting Tim. 2013. "Unvalued interpretable features and topic A-movement in Chinese raising modal constructions." *Lingua* 123:118–147.

Cinque, Guglielmo. 1999. *Adverbs and functional heads: a cross-linguistic perspective*. New York: Oxford University Press.

Collins, Chris. 1997. *Local economy*. Cambridge, MA: MIT Press.

Constant, Noah, and Chloe Gu. 2010. "Mandarin 'even', 'all' and the Trigger of Focus Movement." *University of Pennsylvania Working Papers in Linguistics* 16(1): 4.

Corver, Norbert, and Jairo Nunes. 2007. *The Copy Theory of Movement*. Amsterdam/Philadelphia: John Benjamins Publishing Company.

Davis, Colin. 2020. "Crossing and stranding at edges: On intermediate stranding and phase theory." *Glossa: a journal of general linguistics* 5 (1): 1–32.

Dékány, Éva. 2018. "Approaches to head movement: A critical assessment." *Glossa: a journal of general linguistics* 3 (1): 1–43.

den Besten, Hans. 1983. "On the Interaction of Root Transformations and Lexical Deletive Rules." In *On the Formal Syntax of the Westgermania*, edited by W. Abraham. Amsterdam, The Netherlands: John Benjamins Publishing Company.

den Besten, Hans, and Gert Webelhuth. 1990. "Stranding." In *Scrambling and Barriers*, edited by Günther Grewendorf and Wolfgang Sternefeld, 77–92. Amsterdam: John Benjamins Publishing Company.

den Dikken, Marcel. 2006. *Relators and Linkers*. Cambridge, MA: MIT Press.

Donati, Caterina. 2006. "On *Wh*-head movement." In *Wh-movement: Moving On*, edited by Lisa Lai-Shen Cheng and Norbert Corver, 21–46. Cambridge, MA: MIT Press.

Drummond, Alex, Norbert Hornstein, and Howard Lasnik. 2010. "A Puzzle about P-Stranding and a Possible Solution." *Linguistic Inquiry* 41 (4): 689–692.

Embick, David, and Roumyana Izvorski. 1997. "Participle-Auxiliary Word Orders in Slavic." In *Formal Approaches to Slavic Linguistics (FASL): The Cornell Meeting 1995*, edited by Natasha Kondrashova, Wayles Browne, Ewa Dornisch, and Draga Zec, 4:210–239. Ann Arbor: Michigan Slavic Publications.

Embick, David, and Rolf Noyer. 2001. "Movement operations after syntax." *Linguistic Inquiry* 32 (4): 555–595.

Emonds, Joseph E. 1970. "Root and Structure-Preserving Transformations." PhD diss., Massachusetts Institute of Technology.

Emonds, Joseph E. 1976. *A Transformational Approach to English Syntax*. New York, New York: Academic Press.

Emonds, Joseph E. 1978. "The Verbal Complex V′-V in French." *Linguistic Inquiry* 9:151–175.

Erlewine, Michael Yoshitaka. 2015. *In defense of Closeness: focus-sensitive adverb placement*. Ms., McGill University. https://mitcho.com/research/closeness.html.

Erlewine, Michael Yoshitaka. 2017. "Why the null complementizer is special in complementizer-trace effects." In *A pesky set: Papers for David Pesetsky*, edited by Claire Halpert, Hadas Kotek, and Coppe van Urk, 371–380. MIT Working Papers in Linguistics.

Erlewine, Michael Yoshitaka. 2020a. "Anti-locality and subject extraction." *Glossa* 5 (1): 1–38.

Erlewine, Michael Yoshitaka. 2020b. *Mandarin shì clefts and the syntax of discourse congruence*. Ms., National University of Singapore. https://ling.auf.net/lingbuzz/005176.

Ernst, Thomas, and Chengchi Wang. 1995. "Object preposing in Mandarin Chinese." *Journal of East Asian Linguistics* 4 (3): 235–260.

Fanselow, Gisbert. 2002. "Against remnant VP-movement." In *Dimensions of movement: From features to remnants*, edited by Artemis Alexiadou, Elena Anagnostopoulou, Sjef Barbiers, and Hans-Martin Gärtner, 91–125. 1. Amsterdam: John Benjamins.

Fanselow, Gisbert. 2003. "Münchhausen-style head movement and the analysis of Verb-Second." In *Syntax at sunset 3: Head movement and syntactic theory*, edited by Anoop K Mahajan, 40–76. Los Angeles and Postdam: UCLA / Universität Potsdam Working Papers in Linguistics.

Fanselow, Gisbert, and Damir Cavar. 2002. "Distributed Deletion." In *Theoretical Approaches to Universals*, edited by Artemis Alexiadou, 65–107. John Benjamins Publishing Company.

Fiengo, Robert. 1977. "On Trace Theory." *Linguistic Inquiry* 8:35–61.

Fox, Danny. 2000. *Economy and semantic interpretation*. Cambridge, MA: MIT Press.

Fox, Danny, and David Pesetsky. 2005. "Cyclic Linearization of syntactic structure." *Theoretical Linguistics* 31 (1–2): 1–46.

Fukui, Naoki, and Yuji Takano. 1998. "Symmetry in Syntax: Merge and Demerge." *Journal of East Asian Linguistics* 7 (1): 27–86.

Funakoshi, Kenshi. 2012. "On Headless XP-Movement / Ellipsis On Headless XP-Movement / Ellipsis." 43 (4): 519–562.

Funakoshi, Kenshi. 2014. "Syntactic head movement and its consequences." PhD diss., University of Maryland, College Park.

Funakoshi, Kenshi. 2019. "Verb-raising and VP-fronting in Japanese." *The Linguistic Review* 37 (1): 117–146.

Fung, Roxana Suk-Yee. 2000. "Final particles in Standard Cantonese: semantic extension and pragmatic inference." PhD diss., The Ohio State University.

Gallego, Ángel. 2010. *Phase Theory*. Amsterdam: John Benjamins.

Georgi, Doreen, and Gereon Müller. 2010. "Noun-Phrase Structure by Reprojection." *Syntax* 13 (1): 1–36.

Gergel, Remus. 2009. *Modality and Ellipsis. Diachronic and synchronic evidence*. Berlin: Mouton.

Giannakidou, Anastasia, and Lisa Lai Shen Cheng. 2006. "(In)definiteness, polarity, and the role of wh-morphology in free choice." *Journal of Semantics* 23 (2): 135–183.

Giorgi, Alessandra, and Giuseppe Longobardi. 1991. *The Syntax of Noun Phrases*. Cambridge: Cambridge University Press.

Gribanova, Vera. 2017. "Head movement and ellipsis in the expression of Russian polarity focus." *Natural Language and Linguistic Theory* 35 (4): 1079–1121.

Groat, Erich, and John O'Neil. 1996. "Spell-Out at the LF Interface." In *Minimal Ideas*, edited by Werner Abraham, Samuel David Epstein, Hóskuldur Thráinsson, and C Jan-Wouter Zwart, 113–139. Amsterdam: John Benjamins Publishing Company.

Grohmann, Kleanthes K. 2003. "Successive Cyclicity Under (Anti-)Local Considerations." *Syntax* 6 (3): 260–312.

Hale, Ken, and Samuel Jay Keyser. 2002. *Prolegomenon to a theory of argument structure*. Cambridge, Massachusetts: MIT Press.

Hall, David. 2015. "Spelling Out the Noun Phrase: Interpretation, Word Order, and the Problem of Meaningless Movement." PhD diss., Queen Mary, University of London.

Han, Chung-hye, Jeffrey Lidz, and Julien Musolino. 2007. "V-Raising and Grammar Competition in Korean: Evidence from Negation and Quantifier Scope." *Linguistic Inquiry* 38 (1): 1–47.

Harbour, Daniel. 2008. "Discontinuous Agreement and the Syntax-Morphology Interface." In *Phi Theory*, edited by Daniel Harbour, David Adger, and Susana Béjar, 185–220. Oxford: Oxford University Press.

Harizanov, Boris. 2019. "Head movement to specifier positions." *Glossa: a journal of general linguistics* 4 (1): 140. 1–36.

Harizanov, Boris, and Vera Gribanova. 2019. "Whither head movement?" *Natural Language and Linguistic Theory* 37 (2): 461–522.

Harley, Heidi. 2004. "Wanting, Having, and Getting: A Note on Fodor and Lepore 1998." *Linguistic Inquiry* 35 (2): 255–267.

Harley, Heidi. 2013. "Diagnosing Head Movement." In *Diagnosing Syntax*, edited by Lisa Lai-Shen Cheng and Norbert Corver, 112–120. Oxford: Oxford University Press.

Hartman, Jeremy. 2011. "The Semantic Uniformity of Traces: Evidence from Ellipsis Parallelism." *Linguistic Inquiry* 42 (3): 367–388.

Heim, Irene. 1982. "The Semantics of Definite and Indefinite Noun Phrases." PhD diss., University of Massachusetts, Amherst.

Heim, Irene, and Angelika Kratzer. 1998. *Semantics in Generative Grammar*. Oxford: Blackwell.

Hein, Johannes. 2018. "Verbal Fronting: Typology and theory." PhD diss., Universität Leipzig.

Hinterhölzl, Roland. 2002. "Remnant movement and partial deletion." In *Dimensions of Movement: From Features to Remnants*, edited by Artemis Alexiadou, Elena Anagnostopoulou, Sjef Barbiers, and Hans-Martin Gaertner, 127–150. John Benjamins.

Hiraiwa, Ken. 2002. "Predicate clefts in Bùlì: categories and phases." *Linguistic Analysis* 32(3–4): 544–583.

Holmberg, Anders. 2000. "Scandinavian Stylistic Fronting: how any category can become an expletive." *Linguistic Inquiry* 31 (3): 445–483.

Holmberg, Anders. 2015. *The syntax of yes and no*. Cambridge: Cambridge University Press.

Homer, Vincent. 2015. "Neg-raising and positive polarity: The view from modals." *Semantics and Pragmatics* 8 (4): 1–88.

Horvath, Julia. 1986. *FOCUS in the Theory of Grammar and the Syntax of Hungarian*. Dordrecht, Holland: Foris Publilcations.

Hsieh, Feng-fan, and Rint Sybesma. 2011. "On the Linearization of Chinese Sentence." In *Korean Journal of Chinese Language and Literature*, 53–90. 1.

Hsu, Brian. 2021. "Coalescence: a unification of bundling operations in syntax." *Linguistic Inquiry* 52 (1): 39–87.

Hsu, Yu-yin. 2016. "Sentence-Initial Modals as Focus Operators at CP in Chinese." In *Proceedings of CLS 51*, 257–268. Chicago Linguistic Society.

Hsu, Yu-yin. 2019. "Marking Propositional Focus: A Function of Pre-Subject Modals." In *Indian University Linguistics Club Working Papers*, edited by Kaitlyn Lee-Legg and Wamsley James, 20–42. 2.

Huang, C.-T. James. 1982. "Logical relations in Chinese and the theory of grammar." PhD diss., Massachusetts Institute of Technology.

Huang, C.-T. James. 1987. "Existential Sentences in Chinese and (In)definiteness." In *The Representation of (In)definiteness(14)*, edited by Eric J Reuland and Alice G B ter Meulen, 226–253. Cambridge, Massachusetts: MIT Press.

Huang, C.-T. James. 1993. "Reconstruction and the structure of VP: some theoretical consequences." *Linguistic Inquiry* 24 (1): 103–138.

Huang, C.-T. James. 1994. "Verb Movement and Some Syntax-Semantics Mismatches in Chinese." *Chinese Language and Linguistics* 2:587–613.

Huang, C.-T. James. 1997. "On lexical structure and syntactic projection." *Chinese Language and Linguistics* 3:45–89.

Huang, C.-T. James, Yen-Hui Audrey Li, and Yafei Li. 2009. *The syntax of Chinese*. Cambridge, MA: Cambridge University Press.

Huhmarniemi, Saara. 2012. "Finnish A'-movement: Edges and Islands." PhD diss., University of Helsinki.

Iatridou, Sabine, and Hedde Zeijlstra. 2013. "Negation, Polarity, and Deontic Modals." *Linguistic Inquiry* 44 (4): 529–568.

Iorio, David Edy. 2015. "Subject and object marking in Bembe." PhD diss., University of Newcastle upon Tyne.

Israel, M. 1996. "Polarity Sensitivity as Lexical Semantics." *Linguistics and Philosophy* 19 (6): 619–666.

Jackendoff, Ray. 1997. "Twistin' the night away." *Language* 73 (3): 534–559.

Julien, Marit. 2002. "Optional *ha* in Swedish and Norwegian." *The Journal of Comparative Germanic Linguistics* 5 (1): 67–95.

Kandybowicz, Jason. 2008. *The Grammar of Repetition: Nupe grammar at the syntax–phonology interface by*. Amsterdam/Philadelphia: John Benjamins Publishing Company.

Kato, Yasuhiko. 2000. "Interpretive asymmetries of negation." In *Negation and polarity*, edited by Laurence R. Horn and Yasuhiko Kato, 62–87. Oxford: Oxford University Press.

Kayne, Richard. 1975. *French Syntax: the Transformational Cycle*. Cambridge, Massachusetts: MIT Press.

Kayne, Richard. 1994. *The Antisymmetry of Syntax*. Cambridge, Massachusetts: MIT Press.

Keine, Stefan, and Rajesh Bhatt. 2016. "Interpreting verb clusters." *Natural Language and Linguistic Theory* 34 (4): 1445–1492.

Kim, Shin-Sook. 2002a. *Focus Matters: Two Types of Intervention Effect*. Paper presented at WCCFL 21, UC Santa Cruz.

Kim, Shin-Sook. 2002b. "Intervention Effects are Focus." In *Japanese/Korean Linguistics 10*, edited by Noriko Akatsuka and Susan Strauss, 615–628. Stanford: CSLI Publications.

Kim, Shin-Sook. 2006. "Questions, Focus, and Intervention Effects." In *Harvard Studies in Korean Linguistics XI*, edited by Susumu Kuno, 520–533. 2. Harvard-Yenching Institute.

Kim, Soowon. 1999. "Sloppy/Strict Identity, Empty Objects, and NP Ellipsis." *Journal of East Asian Linguistics* 8 (4): 255–284.

Kishimoto, Hideki. 2007. "Negative scope and head raising in Japanese." *Lingua* 117 (1): 247–288.

Kishimoto, Hideki. 2013. "Verbal complex formation and negation in Japanese." *Lingua* 135:132–154.

Ko, Heejeong. 2005. "Syntax of *Why-in-situ*: Merge into [Spec,CP] in the Overt Syntax." *Natural Language and Linguistic Theory* 23 (4): 867–916.

Ko, Heejeong. 2007. "Asymmetries in Scrambling and Cyclic Linearization." *Linguistic Inquiry* 38 (1): 49–83.

Koeneman, Olaf. 2000. *The Flexible Nature of Verb Movement*. Utrecht: LOT.

Koopman, Hilda. 1984. *The Syntax of Verbs*. Dordrecht, The Netherlands: Foris Publications.

Koopman, Hilda. 1997. "Unifying Predicate Cleft Constructions." In *Proceedings of the 23rd Annual Meeting of the Berkeley: Special Session on Syntax and Semantics in Africa*, 71–85.

Koopman, Hilda Judith, and Anna Szabolcsi. 2000. *Verbal complexes*. Cambridge, Massachusetts: MIT Press.

Kotek, Hadas. 2016. "On the semantics of wh-questions." In *Proceedings of Sinn und Bedeutung 20*, edited by Nadine Bade, Polina Berezovskaya, and Anthea Schöller, 424–447.

Kotek, Hadas. 2019. *Composing questions*. Cambridge: The MIT Press.

Krifka, Manfred. 2008. "Basic notions of information structure." *Acta Linguistica Hungarica* 55 (3–4): 243–276.

Lai, Jackie Yan-ki. 2019. "Parallel copying in dislocation copying: evidence from Cantonese." *Journal of East Asian Linguistics* 3:243–277.

Lambova, Mariana. 2004. "On Triggers of Movement and Effects at the Interfaces." In *Studies in Generative Grammar, 75: Triggers*, edited by Anne Breitbarth and Henk van Riemsdijk, 231–258. Berlin: De Gruyter.

Landau, Idan. 2006. "Chain Resolution in Hebrew V(P)-fronting." *Syntax* 9 (1): 32–66.

Landau, Idan. 2020. "A Scope Argument against T-to-C Movement in Sluicing." *Syntax* 23 (4): 375–393.

Lapointe, Stephen G. 1980. "A note on Akmajian, Steele, and Wasow's treatment of certain verb complement types." *Linguistic Inquiry* 11 (4): 770–787.

Lasnik, Howard, and Mamoru Saito. 1984. "On the Nature of Proper Government." *Linguistic Inquiry* 15 (2): 235–290.

Law, Ann. 2003. "Right disloccation in Cantonese as a focus-marking device." In *University College London working Papers in Linguistics 15*, edited by Ad Neeleman and Reiko Vermeulen, 243–275. London: UCL.

Law, Paul, and Juvénal Ndayiragije. 2017. "Syntactic Tense from a Comparative Syntax Perspective." *Linguistic Inquiry* 48 (4): 679–696.

Lechner, Winfried. 1998. "Phrasal comparatives and DP-structure." In *Proceedings of the North East Linguistic Society*, edited by Pius N Tamanji and Kiyomi Kusumoto, 237–252. University of Toronto: Graduate Linguistic Student Association.

Lechner, Winfried. 2007. *Interpretive Effects of Head Movement*. Accessed May 1, 2021. http://ling.auf.net/lingBuzz/000178.

Lechner, Winfried. 2017. *In defense of semantically active head movement*. Papers presented at Workshop for Martin Prinzhorn Technical University Vienna, November 11, 2017.

Lee, Tommy Tsz-Ming, and Ka-Fai Yip. Accepted. 'Hyperraising, evidentiality, and phase de-activation', *Natural Language and Linguistic Theory*.

Lee, Tommy Tsz-Ming Lee, and Victor Junnan Pan. To appear. "Licensing VP movement and ellipsis in Mandarin and Cantonese," P roceedings of WCCFL-40.

Lee, Tommy Tsz-Ming. 2017. "Defocalization in Cantonese right dislocation." *Gengo Kenkyu* 152:59–87.

Lee, Tommy Tsz-Ming. 2020. "Defending the Notion of Defocus in Cantonese." *Current Research in Chinese Linguistics* 99 (1): 137–152.

Lee, Tommy Tsz-Ming. 2021a. "Right dislocation of verbs in Cantonese: A case of head movement to specifier." In *Crossing-over: new insights into the dialects of Guangdong*, edited by Choi Lan Tong and Io-Kei Joaquim Kuong, 104–121. Macua: Hall de Cultura.

Lee, Tommy Tsz-Ming. 2021b. "Specific unknowns: A case study of epistemic indefinites in Cantonese." *Proceedings of the Linguistic Society of America* 6 (1): 107–117.

Lema, José, and Maria-Luisa Rivero. 1990. "Long Head Movement: ECP vs. HMC." In *North East Linguistics Society*, 20:333–347.

Li, Charles N., and Sandra A. Thompson. 1981. *Mandarin Chinese: A Functional Reference Grammar*. Berkeley: University of California Press.

Li, Haoze, and Candice Chi-Hang Cheung. 2012. "The syntactic analysis of focus intervention effects in Mandarin." *Linguistic Sciences* 11 (2): 113–125.

Li, Haoze, and Candice Chi-Hang Cheung. 2015. "Focus intervention effects in Mandarin multiple wh-questions." *Journal of East Asian Linguistics* 24 (4): 361–382.

Li, Yafei. 1990. "Xo-binding and Verb Incorporation." *Linguistic Inquiry* 21 (3): 399–426.

Li, Yen-Hui Audrey. 1990. *Order and constituency in Mandarin Chinese.* Dordrecht: Kluwer Academic Publishers.

Li, Yen-Hui Audrey. 2005. "Shenglue yu chengfen queshi [Ellipsis and missing objects]." *Language Sciences* 4 (2): 3–19.

Li, Yen-Hui Audrey. 2014. "Born empty." *Lingua* 151:43–68.

Lin, Tzong-Hong Jonah. 2010. "Structures and functional categories of Mandarin sentences." *UST Working Papers in Linguistics* 6:41–79.

Lin, Tzong-Hong Jonah. 2011. "Finiteness of Clauses and Raising of Arguments in Mandarin Chinese." *Syntax* 14 (1): 48–73.

Lin, Tzong-Hong Jonah. 2012. "Multiple-modal constructions in Mandarin Chinese and their finiteness properties." *Journal of Linguistics* 48 (1): 151–186.

Lin, Jo-Wang, and Chih-Chen Jane Tang. 1995. "Modals as verbs in Chinese: a GB perspective. Bulletin of the Institute of History and Philology, Academia Sinica 66: 53–105." *Bulltetin of the Institute of History and Philology, Academia Sinica* 66:53–105.

Linebarger, Marcia C. 1987. "Negative polarity and grammatical representation." *Linguistics and Philosophy* 10:325–387.

Liu, Danqing. 2004. "Identical topics: a more characteristic property of topic prominent." *Journal of Chinese Linguistics* 32 (1): 20–64.

Mahajan, Anoop K. 2003. "Word Order and (Remnant) VP Movement." In *Word Order and Scrambling*, edited by Simin Karimi, 217–237. Oxford: Blackwell.

Marantz, Alec. 1997. "No Escape from Syntax: Don't Try Morphological Analysis in the Privacy of your own Lexicon." In *University of Pennsylvania Working Papers in Linguistics*, edited by Alexis Dimitriadis, Laura Siegel, Clarissa Surek-Clark, and Alexander Williams, 201–225. University of Pennsylvania.

Martins, Ana Maria. 2007. "Double realization of verbal copies in European Portuguese emphatic affirmation." In *The Copy Theory of Movement*, edited by Norbert Corver and Jairo Nunes, 77–118. Amsterdam and Philadelphia: John Benjamins.

Massam, Diane. 2000. "VSO and VOS: Aspects of Niuean Word Order." In *The Syntax of Verb Initial Languages*, edited by Andrew Carnie and Eithne Guilfoyle, 97–116. Oxford University Press.

Matthews, Stephen, and Virginia Yip. 1998. "Verb-copying Constructions in Cantonese." In *Studia Linguistica Serica: Proceedings of the 3rd International Conference on Chinese Linguistics*, edited by Benjamin T'sou, 175–189. Hong Kong: City University of Hong Kong.

Matthews, Stephen, and Virginia Yip. 2011. *Cantonese: A Comprehensive Grammar.* 2nd. London: Routledge.

Matushansky, Ora. 2006. "Head Movement in Linguistic Theory." *Linguistic Inquiry* 37 (1): 69–109.

Matyiku, Sabina Maria. 2017. "Semantic effects of head movement: Evidence from negative auxiliary inversion." PhD diss., Yale University.

May, Robert. 1977. "The Grammar of Quantification." PhD diss., Massachusetts Institute of Technology.

May, Robert. 1985. *Logical Form: Its Structure and Derivation*. Cambridge, MA: MIT Press.

McCloskey, James. 1996. "On the Scope of Verb Movement in Irish." *Natural Language and Linguistic Theory* 14 (1): 47–104.

McCloskey, James. 2016. "Interpretation and the typology of head movement: A re-assessment." *Workshop on the Status of Head Movement in Linguistic Theory Stanford*, September 15, 2016.

Miyagawa, Shigeru. 2001. "EPP, scrambling, and wh-in-situ." In *Ken Hale: A life in Language*, edited by Michael Kenstowicz, 293–338. Cambridge, MA: MIT Press.

Molnárfi, László. 2002. "Focus and antifocus in modern Afrikaans and West Germanic." *Linguistics* 40 (382): 1107–1160.

Moltmann, Friederike, and Anna Szabolcsi. 1994. "Scope interaction with pair-list quantifiers." In *Proceedings of NELS 24*, edited by Mercè Gonzàlez, 381–395. GLSA, University of Massachusetts, Amherst.

Müller, Gereon. 2004. "Verb-Second as vP-First." *The Journal of Comparative Germanic Linguistics* 7 (3): 179–234.

Nchare, Abdoulaye Laziz. 2012. "The Grammar of Shupamem." PhD diss., New York University.

Nevins, Andrew, and Pranav Anand. 2003. "Some agreement matters." In *Proceedings of WCCFL 22*, edited by G. Gardina and M. Tsujimura, 101–114. Somerville, MA: Cascadilla Press.

Nilsen, Øystein. 2003. "Eliminating Positions: Syntax and semantics of sentence modification." PhD diss., Utrecht University.

Nishiyama, Kunio, and Eun Cho. 1998. "Predicate Cleft Constructions in Japanese and Korean: The Role of Dummy Verbs in TP/VP Preposing." *Japanese/Korean Linguistics* 7: 463–479.

Nunes, Jairo. 1995. "The copy theory of movement and linearization of chains in the Minimalist Program." PhD diss., University of Maryland.

Nunes, Jairo. 1998. "Bare X-bar theory and structures formed by movement." *Linguistic Inquiry* 29 (1): 160–168.

Nunes, Jairo. 2004. *Linearization of Chains and Sideward Movement*. Linguistic Inquiry Monographs. Cambridge, Massachusetts: MIT Press.

Nunes, Jairo. 2011. "The Copy Theory." In *The Oxford Handbooks in Linguistics Minimalism*, edited by Cedric Boeckx, 143–172. Oxford: Oxford University Press.

Nunes, Jairo, and Ronice Muller de Quadros. 2006. "Duplication of *wh*-elements in Brazilian Sign Language." In *Proceedings of NELS 35*, edited by L. Bateman and C. Ussery, 466–477. Amherst: GLSA.

Oku, Satoshi. 1998. "A Theory of Selection and Reconstruction in the Minimalist Perspective." PhD diss., University of Connecticut.

Pan, Victor Junnan. 2011. "ATB-topicalization in Mandarin Chinese: an Intersective Operator Analysis." *Linguistic Analysis* 37 (1–2): 231–272.

Pan, Victor Junnan. 2014. "Wh-ex-situ in Mandarin Chinese: Mapping Between Information Structure and Split CP." *Linguistic Analysis* 39 (3–4): 371–414.

Pan, Victor Junnan. 2017. "Optional projections in the left-periphery in Mandarin Chinese." In *Studies in Syntactic Cartography*, edited by Fuzhen Si, 216–248. Beijing: China Social Sciences Press.

Pan, Victor Junnan. 2019. *Architecture of the periphery in Chinese*. New York: Routledge.

Pan, Victor Junnan. 2020. "Deriving Head-Final Order in the Peripheral Domain of Chinese." *Linguistic Inquiry*: 1–34.

Paris, Marie-Claude. 1979. "Some aspects of the syntax and semantics of the "lian. Ye/DOU" construction in mandarin." *Cahiers de Linguistique d'Asie Orientale* 5:47–70.

Paris, Marie-Claude. 1998. "Focus operators and types of predication in Mandarin." *Cahiers de linguistique – Asie orientale* 27 (2): 139–159.

Paul, Waltraud. 2021. "Nobody there? On the non-existence of nobody in Mandarin Chinese and related issues." *Canadian Journal of Linguistics*: 1–38.

Pesetsky, David. 1998. "Some Optimality Principles of Sentence Pronunciation." In *Is the Best Good Enough?*, edited by Pilar Barbosa, Danny Fox, Paul Hagstrom, Martha McGinnis, and David Pesetsky, 337–384. Cambridge, Massachusetts: MIT Press.

Pesetsky, David. 2013. *Russian case morphology and the syntactic categories*. Cambridge, MA: The MIT Press.

Pesetsky, David. 2020. "The unity of movement." Lectures given at The St. Petersburg Institute of Linguistics, Cognition / Culture (NYI), July 20–31, 2020.

Pesetsky, David, and Esther Torrego. 2007. "The syntax of valuation and the interpretability of features." In *Phrasal and Clausal Architecture: Syntactic Derivation and Interpretation*, edited by Simin Karimi, Vida Samiian, and Wendy K Wilkins, 262–294. Amsterdam: John Benjamins Publishing Company.

Platzack, Christer. 2013. "Head Movement as a Phonological Operation." In *Diagnosing Syntax*, edited by Lisa Lai-Shen Cheng and Norbert Corver, 21–43. Oxford: Oxford University Press.

Pollock, Jean-Yves. 1989. "Verb Movement, UG and the Structure of IP." *Linguistic Inquiry* 20 (3): 365–424.

Preminger, Omer. 2019. "What the PCC tells us about "abstract" agreement, head movement, and locality." *Glossa: a journal of general linguistics* 4 (1): 1–42.

Rackowski, Andrea, and Lisa Travis. 2000. "V-initial Languages: X or XP Movement and Adverbial Placement." In *The Syntax of Verb Initial Languages*, edited by Andrew Carnie and Eithne Guilfoyle, 117–142.

Ramchand, Gillian, and Peter Svenonius. 2014. "Deriving the functional hierarchy." *Language Sciences* 46:152–174.

Richards, Marc. 2009. "Internal pair-merge: The missing mode of movement." *Catalan Journal of Linguistics* 8:55–73.

Richards, Norvin. 1997. "Competition and disjoint reference." *Linguistic Inquiry* 28 (1): 178–187.

Richards, Norvin. 1998. "The principle of minimal compliance." *Linguistic Inquiry* 29 (4): 599–629.

Richards, Norvin. 2001. *Movement in language: interactions and architectures*. Oxford: Oxford University Press.

Rivero, Maria-Luisa. 1991. "Clitic and NP Climbing in Old Spanish." In *Current Studies in Spanish Linguistics*, edited by Hector Campos and Fernando Martínez-Gil, 241–282. Washington, D.C.: Georgetown University Press.

Rivero, Maria-Luisa. 1993. "Long head movement vs. V2, and null subjects in old Romance." *Lingua* 89 (2–3): 217–245.

Rivero, Maria-Luisa. 1994. "Clause Structure and V-Movement in the Languages of the Balkans." *Natural Language and Linguistic Theory* 12 (1): 63–120.

Rizzi, Luigi. 1990. *Relativized minimality*. Cambridge, Massachusetts: MIT Press.

Rizzi, Luigi. 1997. "The fine structure of the left periphery." In *Elements of grammar*, edited by Liliane Haegeman, 281–337. Dordrecht: Kluwer Academic Publishers.

Rizzi, Luigi. 2001. "Relativized Minimality Effects." In *The handbook of contemporary syntactic theory*, edited by Mark Baltin and Chris Collins, 89–110. Malden, MA: Blackwell.

Rizzi, Luigi. 2004. "On the Cartography of Syntactic Structures." In *The Structure of CP and IP*, edited by Luigi Rizzi, 3–15. Oxford: Oxford University Press.

Rizzi, Luigi. 2011. "Minimality." In *The Oxford Handbook of Linguistic Minimalism*, edited by Cedric Boeckx, 220–238. Oxford: Oxford University Press.

Rizzi, Luigi, and Ian Roberts. 1989. "Complex inversion in French." *Probus* 1 (1): 1–30.

Roberts, Ian. 1991. "NP-Movement, Crossover and Chain-Formation." In *Representation and Derivation in the Theory of Grammar (22)*, edited by Hubert Haider and Klaus Netter, 17–52. Dordrecht: Kluwer Academic Publishers.

Roberts, Ian. 1994. "Two Types of Head Movement in Romance." In *Verb Movement*, edited by David Lightfoot and Norbert Hornstein, 207–242. Cambridge: Cambridge University Press.

Roberts, Ian. 2001. "Head Movement." In *The Handbook of Contemporary Syntactic Theory*, 2nd, edited by Mark Baltin and Chris Collins, 113–147. Oxford: Blackwell.

Roberts, Ian. 2010. *Agreement and head movement: clitics, incorporation, and defective goals*. Cambridge: The MIT Press.

Roberts, Ian. 2011. "Head Movement and the Minimalist Program." In *The Oxford Handbook of Linguistic Minimalism*, edited by Cedric Boeckx, 195–219. Oxford: Oxford University Press.

Rochemont, Michael. 1986. *Focus in generative grammar*. Amsterdam, The Netherlands: John Benjamins Publishing Company.

Rooth, Mats. 1985. "Association with Focus." PhD diss., University of Massachusetts, Amherst.

Rooth, Mats. 1992. "A theory of focus interpretation." *Natural Language Semantics* 1 (1): 117–121.

Ross, John. 1967. "Constraints on variables in syntax." Ph.D. dissertation, Massachusetts Institute of Technology.

Sag, Ivan. 1976. "Deletion and logical form." PhD diss., Massachusetts Institute of Technology.

Saito, Mamoru. 2003. "A derivational approach to the interpretation of scrambling chains." *Lingua* 113 (4–6): 481–518.

208   The Unity of Movement

Sato, Yosuke, and Masako Maeda. 2021. "Syntactic Head Movement in Japanese: Evidence from Verb-Echo Answers and Negative Scope Reversal." *Linguistic Inquiry*, no. early access: 1–18.

Schoorlemmer, Erik, and Tanja Temmerman. 2012. "Head movement as a PF-phenomenon: Evidence from identity under ellipsis." In *Proceedings of the 29th West Coast Conference on Formal Linguistics*, 232–240. Somerville, Massachusetts: Cascadilla Press.

Shi, Dingxu. 1994. "The Nature of Chinese Wh-Questions." *Natural Language and Linguistic Theory* 12 (2): 301–334.

Shi, Dingxu, Canlong Wang, and Zhiyu Zhu. 2002. "Xianggang shumian hanyu jufa bianyi: yueyu de iyou, wenyan de bao liu ji qita [Syntactic change on Hong Kong written Chinese: the change, formal style and others in Canonese]." *Applied Linguistics* 3:23–32.

Shibata, Yoshiyuki. 2015. "Exploring Syntax from the Interfaces." PhD diss., University of Connecticut.

Shimoyama, Junko. 2006. "Indeterminate Phrase Quantification in Japanese." *Natural Language Semantics* 139–173 (14): 2.

Shyu, Shu-ing. 1995. "The Syntax of Focus and Topic in Mandarin Chinese." PhD diss., University of Southern California.

Shyu, Shu-ing. 2004. "(A)symmetries between Mandarin Chinese lian...dou and shenzhi." *Journal of Chinese Linguistics* 32 (1): 81–128.

Shyu, Shu-ing. 2016. "Minimizers and even." *Linguistics* 54 (6): 1355–1395.

Simpson, Andrew. 2014. "Sentence-Final Particles." In *The Handbook of Chinese Linguistics*, edited by C.-T. James Huang, Yen-hui Audrey Li, and Andrew Simpson, 156–179. Oxford: John Wiley / Sons.

Simpson, Andrew, and Soyoung Park. 2019. "Strict vs. Free word order patterns in Korean nominal phrases and Cyclic Linearization." *Studia Linguistica* 73 (1): 139–174.

Simpson, Andrew, and Zoe Wu. 2002. "Understanding cyclic Spell-Out." In *Proceedings of North East Linguistic Society 32*, edited by Masako Hirotani, 2:499–518.

Soh, Hooi Ling. 1998. "Object scrambling in Chinese." PhD diss., Massachusetts Institute of Technology.

Soh, Hooi Ling. 2005. "Wh-in-Situ in Mandarin Chinese." *Linguistic Inquiry* 36 (1): 143–155.

Stepanov, Arthur. 2012. "Voiding island effects via head movement." *Linguistic Inquiry* 43 (4): 680–693.

Surányi, Balázs. 2005. "Head movement and reprojection." *Annales Universitatis Scientiarum Budapestinensis de Rolando Eötvös Nominatae. Sectio Linguistica* 26:313–342.

Surányi, Balázs. 2008. "The theory of head movement and cyclic spell out." In *Sound of silence: Empty elements in syntax and phonology*, edited by Jutta Hartmann, Veronika Hegudus, and Henk van Riemsdijk, 293–337. Amsterdam: Elsevier.

Svenonius, Peter. 1994. "C-selection as feature-checking." *Studia Linguistica* 48 (2): 133–155.

Svenonius, Peter. 2016. "Spans and words." In *Morphological Metatheory*, edited by Daniel Siddiqi and Heidi Harley, 201–222. Amsterdam/Philadelphia: John Benjamins Publishing Company.

Sybesma, Rint. 1999. *The Mandarin VP*. Amsterdam: Kluwer Academic Publishers.

Szabolcsi, Anna. 2010. *Quantification*. Cambridge: Cambridge University Press.

Szabolcsi, Anna. 2011. "Certain verbs are syntactically explicit quantifieers." *The Baltic International Yearbook of Cognition, Logic and Communication* 6:1–26.

Takahashi, Daiko. 1990. "Negative polarity, phrase structure, and the ECP." *English Linguistics* 7:129–146.

Takahashi, Daiko. 2002. "Determiner raising and scope shift." *Linguistic Inquiry* 33 (4): 575–615.

Takano, Yuji. 2014. "Japanese Syntax in Comparative Persp." In *Japanese Syntax in Comparative Perspective*, edited by Mamoru Saito, 139–180. Oxford: Oxford University Press.

Takita, Kensuke. 2010. "Cyclic Linearization and Constraints on Movement and Ellipsis." PhD diss., Nanzan University.

Tang, Sze-Wing. 1998a. "On the Inverted Double Object Construction." In *Studies in Cantonese Linguistics*, edited by Stephen Matthews, 35–52. Hong Kong: Linguistic Society of Hong Kong.

Tang, Sze-Wing. 1998b. "Parametrization of features in syntax." PhD diss., University of California, Irvine.

Tang, Sze-Wing. 2001. "The (non-)existence of gapping in Chinese and its implicaitons for the theory of gapping." *Journal of East Asian Linguistics* 10 (3): 201–224.

Tang, Sze-Wing. 2002. "Focus and dak in Cantonese." *Journal of Chinese Linguistics* 30 (2): 266–309.

Tang, Sze-Wing. 2015. *Yueyu yufa jiangyi [Lectures on Cantonese Grammar]*. Hong Kong: The Commercial Press.

Toyoshima, Takashi. 2000. "Heading for their own places." *Proceedings of the 9th Student Conference in Linguistics (SCIL 9)*: 93–108.

Toyoshima, Takashi. 2001. "Head-to-spec movement." In *The minimalist parameter: Selected papers from the Open Linguistics Forum*, edited by Galina M. Alexandrova and Olga Arnaudova, 115–136. Amsterdam: John Benjamins.

Travis, Lisa. 1984. "Parameters and Effects of Word Order Variation." PhD diss., Massachusetts Institute of Technology.

Trinh, Tue. 2009. "A constraint on copy deletion." *Theoretical Linguistics* 35 (2–3): 183–227.

Truckenbrodt, Hubert. 2006. "On the semantic motivation of syntactic verb movement to C in German." *Theoretical Linguistics* 32 (3): 257–306.

Tsai, Wei-Tien Dylan. 1994. "On Economizing the Theory of A-Bar Dependencies." PhD diss., MIT.

Tsai, Wei-Tien Dylan. 2015. "On the Topography of Chinese Modals." In *Beyond Functional Sequence*, edited by Ur Shlonsky, 275–294. New York: Oxford University Press.

Tsai, Wei-Tien Dylan. 2021. "On applicative Why-questions in Chinese." In *Why is 'Why' Unique?*, edited by Gabriela Soare, 197–218. Berlin: De Gruyter Mouton.

Uriagereka, Juan. 1998. "A note on rigidity." In *Possessors, predicates and movement in the determiner phrase*, edited by Artemis Alexiadou and Chris Wilder, 361–382. Amsterdam: John Benjamins Publishing Company.

Ürögdi, Barbara. 2006. "Predicate fronting and dative case in Hungarian." *Acta Linguistica Hungarica* 53 (3): 291–332.

Vicente, Luis. 2007. "The Syntax of Heads and Phrases: A Study of Verb (Phrase) Fronting." PhD diss., Universiteit Leiden.

von Fintel, Kai, and Irene Heim. 2011. *Intensional semantics (Spring 2011 edition).* Unpulished lecture notes.

Wechsler, Stephen. 1991. "Verb Second and Illocutionary Force." In *Views on Phrase Structure, Studies in Natural Language and Linguistic Theory, vol 25,* edited by Katherine Leffel and Denis Bouchard, 177–191. Kluwer Academic Press.

Wei, Wei Haley, and Yen-Hui Audrey Li. 2018. "Adverbial Clauses in Mandarin Chinese." *Linguistic Analysis* 1–2:163–330.

Wiklund, Anna-Lena. 2010. "In search of the force of dependent verb second." *Nordic Journal of Linguistics* 33 (1): 81–91.

Wiland, Bartosz. 2008. "Circumstantial evidence for syntactic head movement." In *Proceedings of the 27th West Coast Conference on Formal Linguistics,* edited by Natasha Abner and Jason Bishop, 27:440–448. Somerville, MA: Cascadilla Proceedings Project.

Wilder, Chris. 1994. "Coordination, ATB, and Ellipsis." *Groninger Arbeiten zur Germanistischen Linguistik* 37 (1991): 291–331.

Williams, Edwin. 1978. "Across-the-Board Rule Application." *Linguistic Inquiry* 9 (1): 31–43.

Wu, Dazhen. 2020. "Yueyu 'shi-guo' de cihuihua ji yuji yanbian [Lexicalization and Semantic Change: Cantonese Si3 Gwo3]." *Current Research in Chinese Linguistics* 99 (2): 359–374.

Wurmbrand, Susi. 1999. "Modal verbs must be raising verbs." *Proceedings of the West Coast Conference on Formal Linguistics* 18: 599–612.

Xiang, Ming. 2008. "Plurality, maximality and scalar inferences: A case study of Mandarin *Dou.*" *Journal of East Asian Linguistics* 17 (3): 227–245.

Yang, Barry Chung-Yu. 2008. "Intervention effects and the covert component of grammar." PhD diss., National Tsing Hua University, Hsinchu.

Yang, Barry Chung-Yu. 2012. "Intervention effects and *wh*-construals." *Journal of East Asian Linguistics* 21 (1): 43–87.

Yang, Xiaolong, and Yicheng Wu. 2019. "A dynamic account of lian…dou in Chinese verb doubling cleft construction." *Lingua* 217:24–44.

Yatsushiro, Kazuko. 2009. "The distribution of quantificational suffixes in Japanese." *Natural Language Semantics* 17 (2): 141–173.

Yip, Ka-Fai. 2020. "Syntax-prosody Mapping of right-dislocation in Cantonese and Mandarin." In *Phonologiccal Externalization volume 5,* edited by Hisao Tokizaki, 73–90. Sapporo: Sapporo University.

Yip, Ka-Fai, and Tommy Tsz-Ming Lee. 2022. 'Modal movement licensed by focus', in New Explorations in Chinese Theoretical Syntax: Studies in honor of Yen-Hui Audrey Li, ed. *Andrew Simpson,* p.165–192. Amsterdam: JohnBenjamins.

Yip, Ka-Fai, and Tommy Tsz-Ming Lee. 2020. "Generalized Scope Economy." In *Proceedings of the 32nd North American Conference on Chinese Linguistics (NACCL-32),* edited by Kaidi Chen, 345–360. Storrs: University of Connecticut.

Yip, Ka-Fai, and Tommy Tsz-Ming Lee. 2022. "Modal movement licensed by focus Ka-Fai." In *New Explorations in Chinese Theoretical Syntax. Studies in honor of Yen-Hui Audrey Li.* Edited by Andrew Simpson, 165–192. Amsterdam and Philadelphia: John Benjamins.

Yip, Moira. 1988. "Template morphology and the direction of association." *Natural Language and Linguistic Theory* 6 (4): 551–577.

Yip, Ka-Fai, and Comfort Ahenkorah. To appear. "Non-agreeing resumptive pronouns and partial Copy Deletion," *UPenn Working Papers in Linguistics* 29.1.

Yuan, Michelle. 2017. "More on Undermerge: phrasal and head movement interaction in Kikuyu." In *A Pesky Set: Papers for David Pesetsky*, edited by Claire Halpert, Hadas Kotek, and Coppe van Urk, 543–552. Cambridge, MA: MIT Working Papers in Linguisitcs.

Zeijlstra, Hedde. 2017. "Two varieties of Korean." Presentation at Sinn und Bedeutung 22 (Microvariation in Semantics) on Sept 6, 2017.

Zubizarreta, María Luisa, and Jean-Roger Vergnaud. 2017. "Phrasal Stress and Syntax." In *The Wiley Blackwell Companion to Syntax (Second Edition)*, edited by Martin Everaert and Henk C. van Riemsdijk. John Wiley / Sons.

Zwart, C Jan-Wouter. 2001. "Object shift with raising verbs." *Linguistic Inquiry* 32 (3): 547–554.

Index

A
Across-the-Board Movement 147–148
Agree 73, 80–82, 94
Anti-locality constraint 171
Argument ellipsis 89
Aspectual verbs 2, 98, 112, 115–116

B
Ban on Excorporation 14
Ban on Head Extraction 14
Bare Phrase Structure 15
Base generation (of verbs) 36, 83–86, 150–152

C
C-command 13–14
Categorial feature 103, 158–161
Categorial selection 90, 92
Chain Uniformity Condition 9, 15, 22
Conflation 21
Copy Deletion 164, 168
Copy Deletion Suspension 169
Copy theory of movement 58, 79, 163
Cyclic Linearization 164, 167–169

D
Defocus feature 73–78, 80–82, 91, 94
Derived nominals 42
Discourse effects 34, 41, 48–54, 103
Discourse topics 49, 50–51, 52, 54, 78–79
Displaced VP 92–93

E
EPP 74, 76
Economy condition on identical copies 182

Empty Category Principle 10, 13
Existential constructions 42
Extension Condition 12–13

F
Focus alternatives 131–134
Focus constructions with *dak* 42, 65–67, 98
Focus feature 73–78, 80–82, 91, 94
Focused elements 112–113
Focused elements 65–70

G
Generalized Head Movement 21
Genus-species effects 56

H
Head Movement Constraint 9, 17, 23, 28, 30–35, 64, 90, 126
Head movement 3, 8
Head movement to the specifier position 22–23, 72–78
Head-to-head adjunction 8, 29

I
Idiomatic expressions 62–63
Interpretive effects 23
Intervention effects 29
Island effects 59–61, 79–80, 148–150

L
Last resort 174, 183
Left periphery 79
Lexical Integrity Hypothesis 14
Long Head Movement 16, 33

M
Modal verbs 2, 41, 71, 98, 110–111, 116–118
Morphological fusion 18, 184
Move α 8

N
Negative Polarity Items 106–107
Negative auxiliary inversion 108

O
Object movement 178–179, 180
Overt head movement 99

P
Phrasal movement 3
Post-syntactic movement 19
Predicate cleft 16–17, 34
Pro 95
Proper Binding Principle 13, 189

Q
Quantificational elements 70–72, 118–124, 127
Quantificational scope 105, 129–131

R
Relativized Minimality 11, 31, 64
Remnant (phrasal) movement 20, 36, 87–88, 153–154, 188–190
Reprojective movement 21
Right dislocation 47, 135, 164, 166–167

S
Scope Economy 105, 127–129, 135, 157–158
Scope effects 18
Scope-shifting head movement 99, 124–127
Scrambling 188
Semantic identity 57, 171
Semantic types 103, 131, 134
Sentence-final particles 42–47, 76–78
Sentential negation 136–137
Shortest Move 143–147
Sideward movement 21

Spell-Out Domain Parameter 187
Strict Cycle Condition 12
Structural types 15, 29, 32
Structure Preservation 9

V
VP ellipsis 154–155
Verb doubling constructions 1, 27

Verb fronting constructions 16–17, 34, 163

W
Wh-expressions 67–69, 105